CHRISTIAN MYSTICISM IN THE ELIZABETHAN AGE WITH ITS BACKGROUND IN MYSTICAL METHODOLOGY

LONDON: HUMPHREY MILFORD
OXFORD UNIVERSITY PRESS

CHRISTIAN MYSTICISM IN THE ELIZABETHAN AGE

WITH ITS BACKGROUND IN MYSTICAL METHODOLOGY

By

JOSEPH B. COLLINS, S. S., D. D., Ph. D.

BALTIMORE

THE JOHNS HOPKINS PRESS

1940

Imprimatur:

FRANCIS M. KELLY, S. T. D.
Bishop of Winona

Nihil Obstat:

LOUIS A. ARAND, S. S., D. D.
Censor deputatus

PRINTED IN THE UNITED STATES OF AMERICA
BY J. H. FURST COMPANY, BALTIMORE, MARYLAND

Dedicated

TO THE MEMORY OF

DR. EDWIN GREENLAW

AND

IN TESTIMONY OF GRATITUDE AND AFFECTION

TO

DR. CHARLES G. OSGOOD

PREFACE

The field covered by this study of Christian mysticism in the Elizabethan Age is practically uncharted and uncultivated. This period has been looked upon as contributing little to the development of mystical literature, notwithstanding the reasonable inference that mystical writing could not have ended suddenly with the death of Rolle's followers in the fourteenth century, or have begun abruptly later with Crashaw in the Jacobean period. Religious writing in the Elizabethan era was not wholly given over to theological polemic and mere pious hymnology. That the tradition of Christian mysticism is reflected in this period with perhaps as clear force and emphasis as in any other will appear in the following pages.

To obviate the danger of constructing merely subjective standards for analysis and evaluation of individual works of mystical writers, I have strictly adhered to the traditional methodology of the mystics themselves—those who were considered as such by contemporaries and subsequent writers of mystical tracts and treatises. Although Christian mysticism especially of late has many well-informed critics and authorities, it has few historians. Accordingly Part I of this work brings together for the first time in brief compass, an historical analysis of the specific method of Christian mysticism from its beginnings in Plato to its golden age in the late medieval period. This is the necessary background for Elizabethan mysticism and, indeed, for the mysticism of any period.

Because it is the modern way to analyze mysticism chiefly in its so-called higher stages, it was necessary to point out the no less important preliminary ways or stages of the mystical life as they are reflected in mystical literature. Modern Christian mysticism owes much to the psychological acuteness of two sixteenth century Spanish mystics, St. Teresa of Avila and St. John of the Cross, in expressing the higher and more complex intimacies of the divine union. Their terminology has now become classical. Yet mystics had for centuries exemplified the same basic principles and had experienced the same inner de-

velopment of soul, without, however, the keen analysis and the
success of Teresa and John of the Cross in naming the various
higher stages of the mystical union. In keeping with a present-
day tendency among writers on mysticism, this work applies
mysticism equally to all the stages or ways of growth in the
spiritual life, even to the lower stages or ways commonly called
" ascetic." For they too contribute to the wholeness of the
spiritual life and to the unity of religious perfection. Mystical
theology included the lower rungs as well as the higher reaches
of the ladder of perfection. Mysticism, however, in the following pages is not vague or diffuse in meaning, but is strictly
limited to its traditional usage in expressing the varied and
progressive steps which lead to the " vision splendid." The
methodology of Christian mysticism arises from many possible
sources. It is a methodology which is limited at best. There is
not a wide range of subjects nor a broad scope allotted by the
mystics for their progress along the mystic way, and much repetition is to be expected in all their writings. The wonder with
the Christian mystics is, not that they report so much, but that
they find so many ways of presenting the same ideas with fresh-
ness and vigor within the traditional bounds. This is the
mysticism which is found in Elizabethan literature, and in
the treatises of the medieval period which in turn reflect the
mysticism of the patristic era. And for a fuller view of the
method which mysticism in the west developed it was thought
fit to begin with Plato and Neoplatonism before attempting an
historical sketch of the methodology of Christian mysticism.

It is hoped that students of literature will have less difficulty
than heretofore in recognizing the specific elements of Christian
mysticism in literature, in distinguishing what is purely philosophical from what is purely devotional, and in appreciating
the unbroken stream of mysticism which has never been alien
or apart from English letters.

This study grew out of a paper read before the Journal Club
of The Johns Hopkins University on March 19, 1931, entitled
" Mystical Elements in Spenser's *Fowre Hymnes*." At the
suggestion of the late Dr. Edwin Greenlaw, research was begun
on the literature of medieval mysticism for further elucidation

of Spenser's hymns. This aim and purpose has at no time been
lost sight of. Under the kindly direction of Dr. Charles G.
Osgood, of Princeton University, the entire plan of this work
was reorganized and enlarged to its present proportions. Without his patient and painstaking interest, his valuable and fruitful suggestions, and his scholarly supervision, this work on
Elizabethan mysticism would not have been written. The writer
of this study is very grateful to Rev. Carlton Sage, M. A.,
S. T. L. for his deep interest in reading the manuscript and
for his valuable suggestions, and also to Rev. Dr. L. A. Arand
for his careful reading of the manuscript. The author especially thanks Professor Osgood for his kindness and scholarly
interest in preparing the book for publication.

JOSEPH B. COLLINS.

The Catholic University of America,
    Washington, D. C.

CONTENTS

xi

PART II

MYSTICAL LITERATURE OF FOREIGN ORIGIN IN THE ELIZABETHAN AGE

CHAPTER

PART III

CHRISTIAN MYSTICISM IN NATIVE ENGLISH WRITERS

PART I

THE METHOD OF MYSTICISM

CHAPTER I

THE METHOD OF MYSTICISM IN GENERAL, PLATONIC MYSTICISM IN PARTICULAR

A study of mysticism by way of its method tends to preclude the notorious difficulties of constructing for it an adequate definition. The writings of the mystics, irrespective of time or country, show forth a number of common features. They reveal an attempt on the part of the individual soul to arrive at a self-proposed Object, conceived as apart from itself in terms of the Absolute and final Reality. They also indicate an enjoyment of communion or intimate union with the Object, this Reality, this Divine Being, a union commonly transient, even momentary in character, which brings the soul to further longing, to greater purification, and to a deeper contemplation. " At all times and in many ways," writes Dom Cuthbert Butler, " the idea of communion with divinity, and the effort to achieve it, and the conviction of the individual that he has achieved it, are common features in religions of all kinds, and are amongst the most universal expressions of the religious consciousness." [1] This authority points out that " the expressions of all the mystics, non-Christian as well as Christian, are couched in the same language; all make, in one way or another, the same claim of entering into immediate relation and contact with the Divinity or with Ultimate Reality." [2] Miss Evelyn Underhill speaks of the common features of all mystical contemplation where consciousness passes through much the same stages, follows the same general laws, and obeys the same psychological inspirations, in the course attending it.[3]

The religious nature, moreover, of all mysticism is determined by the philosophical attitude of the mystic toward the final and ultimate Object in whom the contemplative soul pro-

---

[1] *Western Mysticism* (London, 1927), p. 196.
[2] *Ibid.*, p. 349.
[3] *Mysticism* (London, 1910-1930), pp. 90-94; cf. also T. M. Watt, *The Intuition of God* (London, 1929), p. iii.

1

poses to find Unity and rest apart from the multiplicity and longing of its own inner life. Contemplation, love-inspired and knowledge-seeking, is the basis and essential condition of mysticism regardless of the nature of the ultimate Object or Reality. Thus, to prepare for fruitful contemplation, the Buddhist, the Hindoo, the Neoplatonist, and the Christian take up ascetic exercises of purification; and during the course of contemplation, experience the inexplicable and indescribable joys of the mystics. The method of mysticism in general consists of purification of the soul, and by means of contemplation, its ascent to God. So far, chiefly as regards method, the mysticisms of West and East meet on common ground. Upon closer analysis, the methodology of Western mysticism presents the developments which are recorded in the ensuing pages.

The mystics have recorded for us the means which they used to accomplish the mystic quest. In the elements that make up their writings, one discerns the outlines and the outer shell which contain the inner kernel of the ineffable mystic experience itself. The literature of the mystics is the literature of their methodology. They speak for themselves, not indeed so much about union with the Absolute, as of the necessary preludes to this union; not in analysis of the psychological or ontological aspects of spiritual communion, so much as in an arrangement of veritable rungs of the spiritual ladder by which the soul ascends to perfection. This is the essence of the method of mysticism as mystical literature comprises it.

PLATO'S MYSTICAL METHOD

Plato was the first formulator of a mystical method. Taking mysticism in that simplest of general descriptions, as *a journey of the soul to God on the wings of contemplation,*[3a] one finds in Plato many of the basic principles and undeveloped implications which go to make up all forms of mysticism in the

---

[3a] Suggested by the long list of definitions of mysticism gathered by Dean Inge in his *Christian Mysticism* (London, 1899), Appendix. Cf. also Introduction to *Lyra Mystica,* ed. by Charles C. Albertson (New York, 1932), pp. xxv-xxix.

West.[4] The Neoplatonists derive from him their intellectual ascent to the One by a simple yet profound identification of the Platonic Ideas with the essence of God. From Plato and the Neoplatonists, the Christian mystics received ready-made a more or less definite concept of the progress of the immortal soul to a personal God by an ascent from " the things that are made "[5] to Him who is the Source and End of all things. Platonic philosophy enunciated principles and beliefs in which men are always interested—the immortality of the soul, the existence of God, the basic differences between the world of sense and the world of reality, and the perpetual warfare going on in the heart of man between his higher and his lower nature. This is Plato's contribution not only to religion, but also to mysticism.[6] One can discern three outstanding points of movement or centers of mystical development in Plato's doctrines: Purification, Contemplation, and Ascent.

Purification

The necessity of purification enters into the very essence of Plato's philosophy.[7] The starting point of his thought concerns the inquiry about the good and the beautiful, the knowledge, contemplation, and enjoyment of which is the exalted objective of the soul. But to achieve this end the soul must remove the hindrances which proceed from the bodily senses. Hence, the perfect deliverance from all the evils which beset the soul consists in a virtual separation of the soul from the body—that philosophic dying by which the soul even before the body's death is fitted for incorporeal existence.[8] Plato taught the propriety of such pleasures as are genuine and free from passion, for after all, the chief constituents of happiness are

[4] Cf. Friedrich von Hügel, *The Mystical Element of Religion* (London and New York, 1909), I, 18-19.

[5] Rom. i. 20.

[6] Paul Elmer More, *The Religion of Plato* (Princeton University Press, 1928), p. vii.

[7] *Phaedo*, 67, 64, 69; *Theaetetus*, 168; *Symposium*, 201-212.

[8] Eduard Zeller, *Plato and the Older Academy* (London, 1876), p. 441. See also A. E. Taylor, *Plato: The Man and His Work* (New York, 1936), p. 182.

virtue and wisdom. The following words of Plato have so
many echoes in the spiritual writings of the Christian mystics
that they warrant a quotation in full.

In this present life, I reckon that we make the nearest approach
to knowledge when we have the least possible concern or interest
in the body, and are not saturated with the bodily nature, but remain pure until the hour when God himself is pleased to release us.
And then the foolishness of the body will be cleared away and we
shall be pure and hold converse with other pure souls, and know of
ourselves the clear light everywhere; and this is surely the light of
truth.   For no impure thing is allowed to approach the pure.[9]

The central doctrine of the *Phaedo* is in brief, as Professor
Taylor points out, the Hellenic counterpart of the mystical way
of Christianity.   Plato presents the Socratic teaching of the
need of a purification of the soul which consists both in freeing
it from sense and in freeing it from the clinging business of
this life.   All this is a necessary prelude to the enjoyment of
spiritual good both here and hereafter.[10]

The striking figure of the good and bad horses and the
charioteer is a composite picture of the soul which has within
itself the conflicting principles of good and evil, of reason and
passion.[11]   To bring about a peaceful calm to these evil inclina-
tions is a long and arduous task, and the well-known doctrine
of moderation or self-control is but part of the purification
which prepares the soul for ascent to the world of true reality,
of perfect Goodness and Beauty.   "Hence the first duty of the
soul, when it hears the call," says Dr. More speaking of this
phase of Plato's thought, "is to arouse itself from its lethal
state of indolence, and to gird itself as for a journey.[12]

Ascent and Contemplation

The journey which Plato conceived as necessary for the
soul was one of mystical ascent.   He called it a "heavenward
pilgrimage"[13] accomplished on the wings of contemplation.[14]

[9] *Phaedo*, 67 (Jowett's translation).
[10] *Phaedo*, 66-68; Taylor, p. 181.
[11] *Phaedrus*, 253, 254.
[12] *The Religion of Plato*, p. 323.
[13] *Phaedrus*, 256.
[14] *Symposium*, 211 *et seq.*

The truly mystical character of Platonic contemplation is admirably shown by Professor Taylor. Of the famous speech of Diotima in the *Symposium* he writes: " We can best describe the purpose of the speech in the language of religion by saying that it is the narrative of the pilgrimage of the soul on the way of salvation, from the initial moment at which it feels the need of salvation to its final ' consummation.' In spite of all differences of precise outlook, the best comment on the whole narrative is furnished by the great writers who, in verse and prose, have described the stages of the ' mystic way ' by which the ' soul goes out of herself,' to find herself again in finding God. In substance, what Socrates is describing is the same spiritual voyage which St. John of the Cross describes, for example, in the well-known *En una noche oscura* which opens his treatise on the *Dark Night,* and Crashaw hints at more obscurely all through his lines in *The Flaming Heart,* and Bonaventura charts for us with precision in the *Itinerarium Mentis in Deum.* The Christian writers see by a clearer light and they have an intensity which is all their own, but the journey they describe is recognizably the same—the travel of the soul from temporality to eternity." [15] The primary impulse of this flight of the soul, as was the case with its purification, is the desire and longing of the soul for the beautiful and the good.[16] Since love is a desire for beauty,[17] then love and contemplation of the beautiful constitute the keystone in Plato's mystic arch. The philosopher is the perfect lover; and to him alone are given the wings which permit him to soar into the realm of true and absolute Beauty.[18] The notion of Ascent in Plato's doctrine is inseparable from his concept of contemplation. Indeed, the entire progress of the soul is an intellectual ascent above created things through contemplation of them, and a recognition (based on the doctrine of pre-existence) of that beauty and truth which once it knew, but which now lie hidden in their earthly images.[19]

[15] *Op. cit.,* p. 225. See also pp. 230-231.
[16] *Symposium,* 201, 204-5; *Phaedrus,* 237.
[17] *Phaedrus,* 237; *Symposium,* 201.
[18] *Phaedrus,* 249.
[19] *Phaedrus,* 247. " Love in the *Phaedrus* and *Symposium*," writes Dr. Jowett, " is not merely feeling usually so called, but the mystic contemplation

There is little of the emotional in Plato; even his theory of love, i.e., his " noble " love, not lust, is preeminently a force which proceeds from the world of Ideas, and in turn causes the mind of the true lover to reascend to his true home in the " interior of heaven." [20] Plato is chiefly concerned with an intellectual realization of Beauty; it is his passion for knowledge that gives motivation for his mystical methodology. From his essential " other-worldliness " arises the spirit of mysticism.

The life of the gods, Plato says, is one of peaceful contemplation of the Ideas, not in their earthly shadows, but in their true and formless essences.[21] The life of the flesh-laden soul, however, once it is inflamed with desire for true knowledge, like a bird, restless in its cage, perpetually aspires for the upper world.[22] Not once, but thrice, Plato endeavors to describe the nature of the soul's ascent with the employment of a wealth of myth and imagery.[23] The holy woman, Diotima, revealed to Plato that " the true order of going or being led by another to the things of love, is to use the beauties of earth as steps along which one mounts upwards for the sake of that other beauty, going from one to two, and from two to all fair forms, and from fair forms to fair actions, and from fair actions to fair notions, until from fair notions one arrives at the notion of Absolute Beauty, and at last knows what the essence of beauty is." " This," she concludes, " is that life above all others which men should live, in the contemplation of beauty absolute." [24]

Plato's conception of contemplation is one which is common to all later systems of mysticism. First, it is an *active* method whereby the eye of the soul is fixed upon the beauty of earthly objects, then by an inner ascent, it gradually perceives the beauties of institutions, laws and sciences, until in the " vast

of the beautiful and the good" (Introd. to Trans. of *Plato's Dialogues*, 3rd Edition, 1895, I, 525).

[20] *Symposium*, 203. The Platonic philosophy of love which is Plato's *amor mysticus* is found in all its essential forms in *Phaedrus*, 237-256 and *Symposium*, 201-212.

[21] *Phaedrus*, 247.   [22] *Phaedo*, 67-68.

[23] *Phaedrus*, 250-252 and *Symposium*, 210, 211.

[24] *Symposium*, 211 (Jowett's Translation).

sea of beauty " the substantial unity of universal beauty dawns upon the observing soul. The contemplating soul will create for itself, virtually, as steps of its own elevation, " fair and noble thoughts and notions in a boundless love of wisdom." These are the holy sentiments and the high resolves which are the necessary concomitants and the fruit of all mystical contemplations. Secondly, the *passive* aspect of Platonic contemplation consists in sharply defined intellectual notions—the distinction felt by the soul, as never before, between earthly and heavenly knowledge; between the perishing beauties of all visible things and the Ideas, chief of which is Beauty, absolute, separate, simple, and unchanging. This philosophic conception of contemplation as the last stage in Plato's mystical journey is, for the purified soul, one of tranquil communion while still in this life with the Highest Good.[25]

Platonic Union

The quiet and intimate association with the highest of the Ideas constitutes the intellectual union of the mind of the philosopher with the Source of all knowledge. Plato describes it as a sort of friendship with God,[26] and a state of unclouded vision; [27] " a clinging in recollection to those things in which God abides, and in beholding which He is what He is." [28] Furthermore, in this blissful condition of mind, the lover of truth becomes truly perfect, he forgets earthly interests, and is rapt in the divine. The vulgar deem him mad and they rebuke him, not knowing that he is inspired.[29] This is as far as Plato goes. If we consider the *separate* subsistence of the Ideas, and especially of the Idea of the Good in relation to God, then Plato would bring the contemplating mind only as far as the Ideas; and not into proximate union with God who is apart from and above them. Or, taking the Idea of the Good as identical with God, and highest in the hierarchical Ideas as they exist in the mind of God, then there is still wanting that explicit

---

[25] *Symposium,* 210, 212; *Phaedrus,* 256.
[26] *Symposium,* 212.   [28] *Ibid.,* 249.
[27] *Ibid.,* 211.   [29] *Ibid.,* 249.

notion of the personality of God to bring Plato into full harmony with the contemplative union of the later mystics.[30]

NEOPLATONISM

The pure stream of Greek philosophy of which Plato was the font does not cease to flow at the death of Aristotle, but is rather diverted by incoming currents. The philosophy of the East, marked by a singularly theological spirit, gave a new turn to the thought of Greece and Rome. The syncretic movement in Greek philosophy accompanied the shift of the seat of philosophy from Athens to Alexandria. It was here, the meeting-place of Eastern and Western civilizations, where numerous schools of thought flourished in the shadow of the famous Library, that Neoplatonism arose and the second phase in the development of the method of mysticism took place.

Plato systematically developed a basis for the mystic experience in his emphasis upon purification and contemplation as prerequisites for the inner ascent of the soul to God; but he did not make the daring metaphysical leap to an intimate union with the Absolute which is characteristic of the Neoplatonist mysticism. Our knowledge of the Ideas in this life, according to Plato, is not by immediate vision or contact, but by inference, as Dr. More observes. The Ideas considered as entities in themselves and apart from the knowing mind, preclude a theory of knowledge which demands a union of subject and object or a coalescence of knower and known, which is fundamental in the Unitive stage of Neoplatonic mysticism.[31]

It is precisely here in the unique character of the last or Unitive stage that a new movement, and a second phase in the mystic method must be noted. The elements which made pos-

---

[30] Concerning the problem of the unity of the Ideas, see Zeller, *Plato and the Older Academy* (London, 1876), pp. 280 ff.; 160; 495; also Turner, *History of Philosophy* (Boston, 1903), pp. 99 ff. Plato, in common with the ancient philosophers, did not develop a clear notion of divine personality; this was the work of the Christian thinkers. Plato speaks of God as a personal Being in the *Timaeus, 37*, wherein says Taylor, "we see that the 'efficient cause' of the world is thought of definitely as a 'personal' God" (*op. cit.*, p. 441).

[31] *The Catholic Faith* (Princeton, 1931), p. 222.

sible a conception of close and intimate union with the Absolute extended back into the various roots, both Greek and Oriental, of Neoplatonism itself. The first impulse given by the followers of Plato and Aristotle to a solution of the problem of knowledge was a metaphysical one, in that God and the Ideas were melted together in the conception of one supreme Unity. God was reduced to an abstraction by the Pythagorizing Platonists and placed far from the approach of men. The Gnostics, however, invented a series of mediators between man and the Deity, and a ladder was let down, as it were, whereby divine influences could descend upon the soul, and draw it up toward the Source of Existence.[32] Finally, although the Oriental *Mysteries* regarded the ultimate union of human and divine as wholly inexplicable, yet by an esoteric process of initiation and expiation, they considered it possible that the soul which had gone astray in matter could by an occult process return to God.[33] Neoplatonism, as it was developed by Ammonius Saccas, and perfected by the great Plotinus, drew from these focal issues its own characteristic doctrines. The century preceding the Christian era, and the following three centuries mark both the development of Neoplatonism, and its arrival at the full stature of a complete philosophico-theological system. This theosophy, for such essentially is Neoplatonism, was evolved from many disparate elements, but chiefly from the perennial stream of Plato's speculation and mystical methodology.

Neoplatonism, then, in its purely mystical elements furnishes a necessary prelude to a study of Christian mysticism. A strong current of Neoplatonism flows uninterruptedly through the great period of medieval mysticism. This is due mainly to the enormous influence of St. Augustine and the Pseudo-Dionysius, whose writings bear the undoubted influence of Plotinus and Proclus respectively.[34]

[32] Edward Caird, *The Evolution of Theology in Greek Philosophies* (Glasgow, 1904), II, 81.

[33] A. Wautier D'Aygalliers, *Ruysbroeck the Admirable* (London, 1925), p. 248.

[34] For a brief summary of the wide influence of Plotinus on speculative mysticism, see Joseph Mareschal, *Studies in the Psychology of the Mystics* (London, 1927), p. 297.

Plotinus (205-270) is the greatest of the Neoplatonists. The integrity of his system was preserved until well into the fifth century, largely because of its hostility to Christianity. An Egyptian by birth, Plotinus taught at Alexandria and at Rome, where he endeavored to unite in one complete spiritualistic philosophy the doctrines of Plato and the highest speculations of the Oriental theologies. Plotinus is a figure of great importance in the history of mysticism, chiefly because of his unexcelled expression of the mystic union, and its accompanying ecstasy. He was an avowed disciple of Plato, and his greatest contribution to the method of mysticism, viz., the unitive experience, is based upon and is a culmination of the purificatory and contemplative doctrines of the *Phaedrus* and *Symposium*. The general direction of the *Enneads* of Plotinus and these dialogues of Plato is along parallel lines. We shall discover that Plotinus does not improve upon Plato's first stages of the mystic way; but he goes far beyond Plato, and at least apparently further than any subsequent mystic in the daring penetration of his soul into the depths of the Absolute. Porphyry tells us that he was " pure of soul and ever tending toward the Divine which he loved with all his heart. He strove strenuously to set free his soul and to ascend above the bitter waves of this sanguinary existence. And thus by a divine illumination and by meditation and the methods described by Plato in the *Symposium*, he would lift himself up to the First and All-transcendent God." [35]

The Preparatory Stage—Purification

The structure of Plotinus' mystical method rests upon his metaphysical " chain of becoming," which reaches from matter up to the abstract Being or One. The *cosmic* trinity of Plotinus is the Supreme *Nous* or Intellect; [36] the World-Soul, and the Plastic Forces (λόγοι σπερματικοί) or entities flowing out from the World-Soul in graded degrees of purity, among which are individual human souls; while Matter is last in the descending

---

[35] *Life,* 23 (from Greek text of E. Brehier [Paris, 1924], which is used for the following quotations from Plotinus).

[36] Also variously translated *Word* or *Spirit*.

scale of excellence.[37] Plotinus goes further still, and back of
all this Becoming stands the pure, ineffable, indescribable Existence which he called the One, Pure Being.[38] It is to arrive
at this abstract and transcendent Being that Plotinus draws up
his philosophy of the mystic ascent. The successive gradations
of the ascent to the One represent in an inverted order, the steps
of creative energy by which all things are evolved from this
One. This is the basis for the doctrine of the Neoplatonic
cosmic circle of love, which, by way of Proclus and the Pseudo-
Dionysius,[39] became a popular concept of religious love in
Christian mysticism. In a lesser degree the descent and ascent
of the individual soul to God correspond directly to the process
of purification through which every soul must pass in returning
from her exile in Matter to an identification with God.[40] This
purification is of elemental importance in Plotinus' system, as
it is in Plato's. Attacking the impractical morality of the
Gnostics, Plotinus says:

They neither know what virtue is nor what are the methods of
moral training, nor how the soul is to be cared for and purified.
They say to us: " Look to God." But it is useless merely to affirm
this unless they can tell us how we are to look to Him. And it
might be asked, what is to prevent us from looking to God, while
at the same time freely satisfying our sensual appetites and not
restraining our angry passions. Virtue perfected, enlightened, and
deeply rooted in the soul will reveal God to us, but without it He
will be but an empty name.[41]

The moral discipline which Plotinus here enjoins is aimed at
a liberation of the soul from the trammels of the senses which
weaken that love for God which is the motivating force in the
ascent to the One. Love is fully as important in the teaching
of Plotinus as it is in Plato.

[37] *Enneads,* vi. 7, 22; vi. 7, 42; vi. 9, 3; vi. 9, 9.
[38] *Enneads,* vi. 9, 3. Plotinus tells us that in the One man breathes and
has his being; and for the loving soul, the One is conceived in relation of a
father to his loving daughter. (*Enn.,* vi. 9, 9.)
[39] *De Divinis Nominibus,* cap. iv, J. P. Migne, *Patrologiae Graecae Cursus
Completus* (Paris, 1857-59), III, 702 ff. This is the Greek and Latin text.
[40] *Enn.,* 1. i. 12.
[41] *Enn.,* ii. 9, 15 (condensed). Cf. also *Enn.,* iv. 6, 3; vi. 9, 8.

Contemplation and Ascent

Plato and Plotinus shared the belief that all existence is an overflow of the divine Goodness,[42] which, in turn, is identified with the highest Beauty.[43] Thus Plotinus accounts for the inner yearning of the soul for a union with the One, who is at once both the Good and the Beautiful. For, since love is a desire for beauty,[44] then the individual soul initiates its mystic flight by contemplating, first, the external beauties which are but reflections of the Divine Beauty; [45] secondly, by ascending to that universal Beauty of the Absolute One, and then virtually spring away from the ladder upon which it has ascended.

They who would love mould themselves in likeness to their beloved. In the same way the soul loves [God], being stirred by Him to love from the beginning. The soul which has the loved One before it waits for no reminder from the beauties of our world. But having the loved One in its possession, it will recognize whom it has. It is ever seeking and yearning to be borne toward the loved One, it has no regard for things of this world; and beholding the beauties of this universe, it has no care for them.[46]

It is noteworthy that Plotinus adds a non-Platonic element which the purified soul requires for its contemplation, that is, a special gift to the soul, a " grace " or as Plotinus puts it, " God is arrived at not by experimental knowledge ($\epsilon\pi\iota\sigma\tau\acute{\eta}\mu\eta$) nor by intellectual perception ($\nu\acute{o}\eta\sigma\iota\varsigma$) as other things are knowable, but by a presence better than knowledge." [47]

The Plotinic Union

The preparatory stage of Plotinus' mysticism, one of ascetic purification, has elements in common with the initial steps of purely Christian mystical methodology. The contemplation of Plotinus, however, which leads to divine union, is ego-centric and negative in character. It involves a gradual elimination of sense phenomena, a stripping of the soul of its participation in the *Nous* which implies a " becoming "; then, it goes still higher

---

[42] *Enn.*, vi. 7, 23.
[43] *Enn.*, i. 6; vi. 7, 21-28.   [44] *Enn.*, vi. 5, 10; vi. 7, 22.
[45] *Enn.*, vi. 7, 31; vi. 7, 33 which is directly in the manner of the *Phaedrus* and *Symposium*. See also *Enn.*, ii. 9, 4; iii. 2, 4.
[46] *Enn.*, vi. 7, 31.   [47] *Enn.*, vi. 9, 4.

and farther, beyond the limits of existence itself for a still purer unity, and finds in the awful solitude of that supreme elevation that the central source of all things does not lie without, but *within;* and thus by introspection does the soul unite with the One. All positive attributes of the One are withdrawn, for " the One whose nature is to bring all things into being cannot be any of those things itself."[48] At the end of the *via negativa* the soul conceives the abstract negative Being of God not by a working of reason, but in the supreme essay of the soul, by a special intuition. So intimate is this union, that the subject is somehow fused with the Object, and the soul finds itself in God and God in itself.[49] Let us hear Plotinus himself speak of the vision.

Unless the soul attains the vision, it has no knowledge of the splendor there. It has never felt and grasped to itself such an expression of love as in the vision of the lover come to rest in whom he loves. . . . From none is it [i. e. the vision of God] absent and yet it is absent from all. And being present it is perceived only by those who are able to receive it—they who are disciplined so that they are of one accord, they who are able to touch It by a likeness and by a kindred power in them which comes from Him; that power which remains as it was when it came from Him. Thus they are now able to see as God by nature is given to be seen.[50]

The mystical ecstasy which Plotinus describes is but part of that " deification "[51] which he considered as the end of the mystic quest, and the crowning experience of this Odyssey of the soul to a final haven in the Absolute.

He who has seen It, knows whereof I speak: that the soul has another life as it nears to God, and is now come to Him, and has a share in Him so that, restored, it knows that the Dispenser of true life is here present, it needs naught else; and on the other hand we must put aside everything else and abide in This alone, and become This alone—detached from all temporal things. The soul is anxious to be free, so that we may attach ourselves to It by the whole of our being; no part of it *not touching God.* Then it will be possible for the soul to see both God and herself divinely,

---

[48] *Enn.,* vi. 9, 3.
[49] *Enn.,* vi. 9, 11.
[50] *Enn.,* vi. 9, 4.
[51] See below, p. 33.

and she will see herself illumined, full of intelligible light; or rather she will be light itself—pure, unfettered, agile, *become a God* or rather *being a God,* and wholly aflame. But this would be quenched should the soul again take up its weary burden.[52]

One agrees with the testimony of Porphyry that Plotinus knew by personal experience whereof he spoke. This biographer says that Plotinus enjoyed the vision of God, " for to be in union with Him was the sole aim of his life; and during the time that I was with him on four occasions he, in one ineffable Act, attained to this End." [53] To such experiences of the divine union in Plotinus, countless mystics beginning with St. Augustine are directly or indirectly indebted for voicing their moments of blissful union.[54] Plotinus evolves a definite method of expressing the mystical experience which is the " high-water mark " of transcendental mysticism. Others will approach his expressions, but none will go beyond them. He is a safe preceptor, for on the one hand he halts his ascent before the substantial identity of the individual soul is lost in the One; [55] and on the other hand he avoids the actuality, if not the possibility of pantheism. He is a true representative of the mystical method which has been seen in Plato and will appear again and again in greater or less degree in the Christian mystics. " We find in Plotinus," says Father Sharpe, " the most advanced conceptions of the great Christian mystics." [56] In the closing sentences of the *Enneads,* Plotinus, as if conscious of a need of repeating his method *in nuce* tells us,

Such is the life of the gods, such is also that of divine and happy men; detachment from all things here below, scorn of all earthly pleasures, and flight of the alone to the Alone.

[52] *Enn.,* vi. 9, 9.   [53] *Life,* 23.

[54] St. Augustine shows acquaintance with each of the six *Enneads* of Plotinus, and refers to him by name five times. Indeed, the famous passage in the *Confessions* (see below) which describes the rapturous conversation between St. Augustine and Monica at Ostia (*Conf.* IX, 10) is a close imitation of the ecstatic passages of Plotinus. (*Enn.,* v. 1, 1-3; vi. 9, 9-11.)

[55] The soul becomes established in the union, " not at all deviating from its own essence " τῇ αυτοῦ ουσία ουδαμοῦ αποκλινῶν (*Enn.,* vi. 9, 11).

[56] A. B. Sharpe, *Mysticism: Its True Nature and Value* (London, 1910), p. 151.

Chapter II

CHRISTIAN MYSTICISM IN GENERAL

Christian mysticism both in its spirit and its method is *sui generis*. A number of new and basic factors inherent in the Christian religion sets its mysticism quite apart, and renders it readily distinguishable from that which is purely Platonic or Oriental.[1] The life which the Christian mystic embraces, and reflects in his literature, is one which goes beyond the requirements of the ordinary rules of Christian conduct, and it perfectly fulfills the greater obligations enjoined by the evangelical counsels.[2]

The Christian mystic, then, is one who holds a philosophy of life which aims to elevate the soul to a higher plane than that of his fellow-followers of Christ; he is convinced that personal perfection is an Ideal worthy of attainment, and that the Person and teachings of Christ make for him an ever-present Model toward which he directs his spiritual aspirations and ambitions. The Christian mystic uses for the accomplishment of the Life-ideal a system and a method which are partly instinctive and psychological, and partly the heritage of the mystics who preceded him. This method, for practical purposes of study and analysis, may be said to embrace the three stages of the mystical way which we have noted among non-Christian mystics: Purgation, Contemplation, and Union with God.

Contemplation is here used in a more comprehensive sense than is customary among modern writers of mystical theology. They, following the usage determined by St. Teresa and St. John of the Cross, restrict the meaning of contemplation to the higher mystical states, and, furthermore, they recognize two essential and radically different kinds of contemplation, viz., " acquired " and " infused." Many authorities would limit the term to only what is understood as " infused " contemplation,

---

[1] Cf. von Hügel, *op. cit.*, I, 25-28.
[2] Cf. *Dictionnaire de Spiritualité ascétique et mystique* (Paris, 1933), II, 434-470.

which is a higher form than either meditation or " acquired "
contemplation, and is notably due to extraordinary grace of God
poured into a fully purified and passively receptive soul.[3] This
differs fundamentally from "acquired " contemplation, which
in the words of Scaramelli, " is that contemplation which, with
the aid of grace, we can acquire by our own endeavor, and particularly by a long practice of meditation." [4] Thus the view
that contemplation is a higher form of prayer than ordinary
discursive meditation, and that it is accompanied by a spiritual
uplifting of the mind, together with loving gaze upon its object,
be it God or Christ or the heavenly joys, etc., is abundantly
present in the patristic and medieval mystics.[5] This broad
sense of the word contemplation is in keeping with this study
of Christian mysticism from a literary rather than from a
theological standpoint.   Thus Abbé Vernet points out that,
" the word ' contemplation ' in the middle ages has more than
one meaning. It is synonymous not only with ' contemplation
properly so called ' (that is, *infused* contemplation), but also
sometimes with petition or meditation, and with prayer in all
its forms." [6] Garrigou-Lagrange shows that the Christian
mystic exemplifies in his life these three main stages or steps:
Purification, Contemplation, and Union which, following the
usage of the Pseudo-Dionysius, became the three " ways " of
Christian mysticism: Purgative, Illuminative, and Unitive in
the more fully developed terminology of the medieval period.[7]
This very important three-fold " way " will be considered in its
proper place.

The Christian mystic takes the principles and the three modes
of inner action and development already seen in non-Christian
mysticism, and applies to them his own theology. And in so

[3] " Passive or mystic unitive way is characterized by *infused* contemplation,
or contemplation *properly so called* " (A. Tanqueray, *The Spiritual Life*
[Tournai, 1930], p. 607). Cf. also Poulain, *The Graces of Interior Prayer*
(London and St. Louis, 1904), p. 60; Garrigou-Lagrange, *Christian Perfection and Contemplation* (London and St. Louis, 1937), p. 223.

[4] Cited by Poulain, *op. cit.,* p. 61.

[5] Cf. P. Pourrat, *Christian Spirituality* (London, 1924-1928), II, 121-128;
III, 4-8.

[6] Felix Vernet, *Medieval Spirituality* (London and St. Louis, 1930), p. 160.

[7] *Op. cit.,* p. 171.

doing he revitalizes them and expands them according to Christian teachings and the personal bond which exists between his soul and Christ, the Mediator between God and Man.[8] One may speak of the science which treats of this journey of the soul to God by way of Christ as Christian mysticism. It rests definitely upon this all-embracing doctrine of the Mediatorship of Christ. It is no longer simply the Platonic formula: Man-God; but it is the Christian formula: Man-Christ-God. "We here touch on a point of the utmost significance," writes Dr. Paul Elmer More. "There is no profounder mark of the originality of Christianity than its conception of the Logos as becoming a Mediator between two natures instead of existing as an intermediary between two natures."[9] The Divine Word or Logos assuming human nature and becoming man gives to Christian mysticism that practical basis for its contemplations which is poles asunder from the abstract, intellectual ascent of the Neoplatonists. "All types of mysticism have the same psychological antecedents in the human soul. They all seek the Ultimate Life of God, and rejoice in an immediate sense of His Presence. But the Christian mystic approaches that Ultimate Life through an historic Life in whom it finds God. Its intuition of God is qualified by its faith in Jesus Christ."[10]

Hence one must avoid at the outset the error of supposing that all mystics regardless of creed or philosophy, whether Christian, Buddhist, or Neoplatonist, hold to one truth wholly identical and differ only in terminology. Granted that the essential experience of non-Christian mystics is a true experience of God, whatever its cause by the Divine dispensation may be, nevertheless the Christian revelation interprets the experience of the mystics more fully than any other, and gives them far greater scope and power for the exercise of their peculiar gifts. And this is due chiefly to the essential fact that the Christian mystic possesses a personal love of a personal God, often lacking in other mystics, and moreover he derives inspiration and

[8] Cf. Evelyn Underhill, *The Mystic Way* (London, 1913), pp. 278-296.
[9] *Christ the Word* (Princeton, 1927), p. 76.
[10] T. M. Watt, *The Intuition of God* (London, 1929), p. iii.

3

direction from a personal love for the Incarnate Son of God which for him is full of meaning and power.[11] In the following chapter these elements will be seen in four outstanding mystics of the patristic period.

Clement of Alexandria, justly termed the " Saint of Disinterested Love," [12] weaves round the figure of Christ his rich store of Platonic learning, and in his great work of Christian apologetic makes Christ " the true Instructor." " Having now accomplished those things, it were a fitting sequel," says Clement, " that our Instructor Jesus should draw for us the model of the true life, and train humanity in Christ." [13] St. Augustine had chided the Neoplatonists for their rejection of Christ, " because of His humble birth and shameful cross." [14] He found in the Platonist writings much concerning the divine nature of the Logos, but nothing of the humility of the Incarnation.[15] For both Clement and St. Augustine the true knowledge of the Christian Gnostic was a participation in the " Word made Flesh," whose truths are to be contemplated so that the Christian may attain to union with the Father. Thus, the spiritual light of the soul which is brought to focus on the life of the Divine Mediator is a true norm of Christian mysticism.[16]

The Christian doctrine of sin, as it motivates the purificatory processes of Christian mysticism, occupies a characteristically large part of mystical treatises. The corruption of the human race, a commonplace of Jewish theology, did not fail to impress even the pagans. The teaching, however, regarding Original Sin which followed the tradition of Genesis and the expositions of sin in the New Testament, emphasized that *personal malice* of disobedience to moral mandates which became a primary motive in the asceticism and purgation of Christian mysticism. The Christian feeling towards sin, as applied to

[11] E. I. Watkin, *The Philosophy of Mysticism* (London, 1920), p. 29.

[12] Charles Bigg, *Christian Neoplatonists of Alexandria* (New York, 1886), p. 272.

[13] *Paedagogus*, I, xii.

[14] *De Civitate Dei*, X, 28. " Porphyry, because of pride, refused to recognize that Christ is the Principle by which all things were made, and by whose incarnation we are purified" (*ibid.*, X, 25).

[15] Cf. *Confessions*, VII, 9.   [16] Underhill, *Mysticism*, p. 120.

the first or Purgative way of Christian mysticism, sharply differentiates Christian [17] and non-Christian [18] purification. Platonist asceticism is rarely more than a freedom from the senses to ensure that virtue and wisdom necessary for intellectual contemplation and ascent to the simple purity of the Absolute.[19] Sin was, moreover, the determining factor in the Incarnation and Redemption which engendered the mixed sentiments of sorrow and love which abound in the ascetic parts of Christian mystical treatises. Whereas the Neoplatonists were content to leave the work of purification to man's moral idealism, the Christian mystics took a different part. For them purification was essential for salvation. Since man necessarily falls frequently,[20] the moral ideal must be *visibly* brought before him in the person of the Incarnate God, who summons every man to imitation and to participation in the divine life.[21]

St. Augustine, prince of Christian mystics, distinguished the Christian from the Neoplatonists, when he said that the Christian directs his gaze, not upon himself, but upon the Incarnate Son of God, from whose lowliness he learns to know his own pride and to put it away.[22] Important is the testimony of a late medieval writer, until recently thought to be Albertus Magnus. " We should notice here," he says, " the difference which exists between the contemplation of Christians and that

[17] Cf. Clement of Alexandria, *Paedagogus,* I, 13 for exposition of the doctrine of original sin, and an analysis of the nature and malice of sin in general.

[18] " The Neoplatonists taught that the divine stood in essential union with spirit and in essential opposition to non-spirit. That being their theory, morality necessarily meant the mortification of the body and its senses. The aim of Neoplatonic ethics was not the transformation of sense, but its destruction " (Karl Adam, *Saint Augustine* [New York, 1923], p. 22. Cf. also p. 33).

[19] Plotinus is, perhaps, the sole exception. " This remarkable figure stands out as the sole instance in which all the conditions of true mysticism (with the necessary exception of faith) seem to have been fulfilled " (A. B. Sharpe, *Mysticism, Its True Nature and Value* [London, 1910], p. 147). Even in Plotinus there is no evidence of that personal sense of sin as an offense against the divine majesty which is the impelling *motif* of Christian mystical discourses.

[20] Proverbs, xxiv. 16.

[21] St. Augustine, *Contra Academicos,* III, 19.

[22] Adam, *Saint Augustine,* p. 36.

of pagan philosophers. The latter sought only their own perfection, and hence their contemplation affected only their intellect; they desired only to enrich their minds with knowledge. But the contemplation of the saints, which is that of Christians, seeks as its end the love of God whom they contemplate. Hence it is not content to find fruit for the intelligence, but penetrates beyond to the will, that it may there enkindle love." [23] Hence the love of the Christian mystic is not ego-centric and abstract but rather Christocentric and no less affective than intellectual.

The remainder of this study of the methodology of Christian mysticism comprises two chief sections corresponding to the two main phases or periods in the history of Christian mysticism. The first, or patristic, period is that of beginnings, and we shall treat it in relation to the three stages already observed in our analysis of Plato and Plotinus. It extends roughly to the end of the sixth century. The second period includes the entire medieval period and ends before the diffusion of the complex methodology and expert analysis of the mystical states by St. Teresa of Avila and St. John of the Cross in the late sixteenth century.

---

[23] *On Union with God,* attrib. to Albertus Magnus, trans. in *Angelus Series* (St. Louis, 1913), p. 60.

CHAPTER III

THE METHOD OF PATRISTIC MYSTICISM

The *fons et origo* of all Christian mysticism is found in the Johannine writings and in the Epistles of St. Paul. The teaching of the Fourth Gospel on the " great Commandment " [24] and the fervent declarations of charity embodied in the Epistles of St. John [25] gave substance to that treatment of divine love which is essential in Christian mysticism. St. Paul presented Christ as the Ideal and Model for Christian perfection even to mystical identity with Him.[26] In what became the *locus classicus* as evidence for the mystic experience, St. Paul related how he " was caught up into paradise and heard secret words which it is not granted to man to utter." [27] The Pauline contemplation was not a mere intellectual process, but an emergent knowledge of God arrived at from the visible creation,[28] which was conditioned by ascetic pains [29] and vitalized by conscious imitation of Christ suffering.[30] From such sharply defined New Testament patterns the mystics of the patristic age gradually wove the fabric of Christian spirituality.

The Church Fathers and the monastic founders do not present a synthesis of spirituality; that was a contribution of the Middle Ages. Nevertheless, as Abbé Pourrat observes,

[24] "As the Father has loved me, I also have loved you. Abide in my love" (John xv. 9). Cf. also John viii. 42; xiv. 15, 21, 23; xv. 9-10; xvi. 27; xvii. 26.

[25] " God is love; and he that dwelleth in love dwelleth in God and God in him" (I John iv. 16). Cf. also I John iv. 7-21; II John 5-6.

[26] " And I live, now not I: but Christ liveth in me " (Gal. ii. 20). Cf. also Rom. vi. 11; xiii. 14; II Cor. iii. 18; iv. 10; I Cor. xi. 1; Gal. iii. 27; Eph. iv. 5.

[27] II Cor. xii. 4.

[28] "For the invisible things of him from the creation of the world are clearly seen, being understood by the things that are made, His eternal power also and divinity " (Rom. i. 20).

[29] " But I chastise my body and bring it into subjection" (I Cor. ix. 27). Cf. also Gal. v. 24; Col. i. 24.

[30] Cf. Gal. vi. 14, 17; II Cor. iv. 10-11. See especially Fernand Prat, *The Theology of St. Paul,* trans. by John L. Stoddard (London, 1927), II, 189.

21

" under a variety of forms of religious life, the same spiritual doctrine is to be found." [31] The ascetic element is predominant in patristic mysticism; just as it is never apart from any mystical philosophy.[32] From a study of four chief figures in this period, the marks of patristic mystical method may be discerned, and the way laid for an understanding of the fully perfected expositions to be found in medieval mysticism. Clement of Alexandria, St. Augustine, St. Gregory, and the Pseudo-Dionysius, out of many worthy representatives of mysticism among the Greek and Latin Fathers, present not so much essential changes in methodology, as a growth toward maturity and an emphasis upon certain details of their respective systems.

Clement of Alexandria (150-217) represents the doctrines of the Christian Neoplatonists of Alexandria; St. Augustine (354-430) is by many considered the real founder of Christian mysticism [33] and the teaching of St. Gregory (540-604), similar to that of St. Augustine, is a culmination of monastic spirituality. The first *ex professo* mystical treatise is the *Mystica Theologia* by that unknown writer of the fifth century who is generally referred to as the Pseudo-Dionysius.[34]

Purification and Asceticism

Clement of Alexandria held up to the Christian Gnostic a lofty and sincere asceticism as prerequisite to the contemplation of divine things which is the aim and purpose of the " higher life."[35] In the manner of Saint Paul,[36] Clement compares this ascetic training with the discipline of the Greek athlete preparing for the Olympic games.[37] " He who holds con-

---

[31] *Christian Spirituality*, I, 304.   [32] Cf. Von Hügel, II, 342.

[33] See Cuthbert Butler, *Western Mysticism*, p. 24. Cf. also *Dictionnaire de Théologie Catholique*, ed. by Vacant and Mangenot (Paris, 1903), art. S. Augustine.

[34] A good account of this most important figure in the history of Christian mysticism is given in Hastings, *Encyclopedia of Religion and Ethics* (New York, 1908), art. Dionysius the Areopagite.

[35] " For what else do we say is incumbent on the rational creature, I mean man, than the contemplation of the Divine" (*Paedagogus*, I, 12). See also *Stromata*, VII, 10 for brief exposition of Clement's " scale of perfection."

[36] Phil. iii. 12-14.   [37] *Stromata*, VII, 7.

verse with God," enjoins Clement, " must have his soul immaculate and stainlessly pure," and then, " he will advance on the road to perfection by learning, training, well-doing, and pleasing God." [38] Clement uses the technical terms of the surgeon who applies sharp remedies for the disease of sin.[39] He says that as there is one mode of training for philosophers, another for orators, and another for athletes, " so there is a generous disposition, suitable to the choice that is set upon moral loveliness resulting from the training of Christ." [40]

St. Augustine's teaching on purification is a repetition with even greater emphasis of that of Clement. " For Augustine, as for all true mystics, the indispensable condition of contemplation is such a purification of soul as will render it fit for the ascent to the contemplation of God: a purification which is the result of a long process of self-denial and self-conquest, of mortification and the practice of virtue—in short, asceticism in the broad and full meaning of the word, viz., ' training.' " [41] " In vain," says St. Augustine, " does one strive for the vision of God who does not shun the stains of sin." [42] That he felt throughout the years of his spiritual travail the imperative need of purification of body and soul, his own *Confessions* bear ample testimony.[43] He praised the purgative doctrines of Socrates as set forth by Plato, which affirm that God could be apprehended only by a purified mind; and then with true mystical insight he continues, " all diligence ought to be given to the purification of the life by good morals, in order that the mind, delivered from the depressing weight of lusts, might raise itself by its native vigor to eternal things, and with purified understanding, contemplate that Nature which is incorporeal and unchangeable light, where live the causes of all created natures." [44] But St. Augustine the Christian adds what

---

[38] *Ibid.*

[39] *Paed.*, I, 12. Compare St. Augustine's "cleansing and healing" of the soul in *De Quantitate Animae,* 73, 74, 75.

[40] *Paed.*, I, 12. For other references to Clementine purgation, see *Exhortation*, XI; *Strom.*, VI, 9; VII, 10-11; and especially VII, 12.

[41] Butler, *Western Mysticism,* p. 36.

[42] *Collatio*, XIV, 1, 2 (cited by Butler, *ibid.*).

[43] Cf. Adam, *op. cit.,* pp. 23-25.   [44] *De Civit. Dei,* VIII, 3.

Plato omitted; and in the *De Quantitate Animae,* he gives the credit to God and His grace for bringing about this necessary purification.[45]   For that is true religion by which the soul through reconciliation again makes herself fast or " religate " to the one God, from whom she had cast herself away by her own sin.[46]

Nowhere can we see more clearly the typical Christian concept of the Purgative way of the mystics than in St. Augustine's commentary on Psalm xli: " Like as a hart desireth the water-brooks, so longeth my soul after Thee, O God." The tenor of freedom from personal sin is clear. " God knows that I am no longer covetous, that I no longer set my heart on the property of any man; that I am not inflamed with the passion of unlawful love; that I do not pine away with hatred or ill-will against any man,—I am free of them." [47]

Equally decisive are the injunctions given by St. Gregory to purify the eyes of the soul before they are fit to behold the divine vision. " The sweetness of contemplation shows that things earthly are to be despised; it reveals things spiritual to the eyes of the mind, and hides things bodily." [48]   And again he writes, " Nor can the eyes of the mind be fixed upon that which it has seen within itself when rapt in contemplation, because it is compelled by its evil customs to sink downwards." [49] Dom Cuthbert Butler observes that, " there is no need to labor the point that Gregory's view of the Purgative way is the same as that of St. Augustine." [50]   St. Gregory, true to his monastic conception of the value of the active as well as the contemplative life, saw a purgative element in labor and works of charity.   " Whoever has already subdued the promptings of the flesh, has this work yet to accomplish, to discipline his soul by holy exercises; and if he has achieved this, then he has over

[45] *De Quant. Animae,* 73, 74, 75.
[46] " Est enim religio vera, qua se uni Deo anima, unde se peccato velut abruperat, reconciliatione religat " (*ibid.,* 80).
[47] Cited by Butler, p. 27.   [48] *Hom. on Ezechiel, lib.* II, *Hom.* ii, 3.
[49] *Morals on Job,* XXIII, 43. This chapter is strongly reminiscent of Plato, wherein Gregory describes the alternate pantings, risings, sinkings, and struggles of the soul to adhere to the object of its gaze.
[50] *Op. cit.,* p. 95.

and above to extend his mind to the secret pursuits of inward contemplation." [51] The soul must learn to empty itself completely of images and sense-perceptions which detract its inward gaze and prevent a clear perception of spiritual truths.[52] But even more, there must be a surcease of all temporal strivings— no earthly glory, no carnal pleasure, and a stern discipline through virtuous living.[53]

As one would expect in the *Mystica Theologia* of the Pseudo-Dionysius, there is much of Neoplatonism and less of pure Christianity in his treatment of the Purgative way. There is an odd blending of the leaven of Judaism, too, in the reference to the mystical experience of Moses which is frequently found in writings of the later mystics. " It was not without a deeper meaning that the divine Moses was commanded first to be himself purified, and then to separate himself from the impure; and after all this purification he heard many voices of trumpets, and saw many lights shedding manifold beams—and he came to the height of the divine ascent." [54] We miss the distinctly high moral tone of St. Augustine and St. Gregory; and we hear instead a rather formal lesson in Neoplatonic abstraction. He states the importance of the natural faculties in mystical contemplation as a first principle of mystical theology. " Giving thyself diligently to contemplation, leave the senses and the operations of the intellect, and all things sensible and intelligible, and things that are and things that are not, that thou mayest rise as may be lawful for thee, by ways above knowledge to Him who is above all knowledge and all being." [55]

Contemplation

The " higher life " which Clement of Alexandria proposed for the Christian was in the main an intimate contemplation of God on the part of the " Earth-liberated soul." [56] There are no definite limits to the objects of contemplation; it embraced " the

[51] *Mor. on Job*, VI, 56. Cf. V. 54, 55.
[52] *Hom. on Ezech.*, II, 9.   [53] *Mor. on Job*, VI, 56-61.
[54] *De Mystica Theologia*, cap. 1, Migne, *P. G.*, III, 999.
[55] *Ibid.* Translated by Sharpe, *op. cit.*, p. 208.
[56] *Stromata*, VII, 10; VII, 13.

Divine," the teachings of the Logos-Instructor, and the nature of man.[57] Clement hoped that the true Gnostic who reached the summit of " the mystic stages of Christian perfection " would " pray that such contemplation grow and remain in him." [58] Rarely did Clement enter upon those subtle searchings of the heart and mind to account for the presence of the Deity which are the burden of countless passages in later mystic writers since St. Augustine. He felt that there is a transcendent, clear, and absolutely pure vision which is the privilege of intensely loving souls.[59] Once he speaks of the soul in the act of contemplative prayer rising aloft, " winged with longing for the better things," and thus is it " advanced into the region of holiness, haughtily despising the chain of the flesh." [60]

It is to St. Augustine we look for the first definite constructive system of contemplation and ascent to God. Despite his apparently cold metaphysical analysis, St. Augustine's contemplation glows with the true mystic's fire. His mysticism is not confined to the oft-quoted scene with his mother Monica at Ostia,[61] but is frequently repeated with never-varying precision. Stated briefly and substantially, St. Augustine employed the following method.

1.   The consciousness of an intense, yet ill-defined longing for God.[62]

2.   A search for the changeless Truth,[63] and immutable Light.[64]

3.   He contemplates the visible objects of nature, but they are only to assist him in his quest. He finds them without exception subject to change and decay. God is not there.[65]

---

[57] *Paed.,* I, 12.
[58] *Strom.,* VII, 7.
[59] *Ibid.,* VII, 3.
[60] *Ibid.,* VII, 7.
[61] *Confessions,* IX, 10.
[62] " Thou hast made us for Thyself, and our heart is restless till it rest in Thee " (*Conf.,* I, 1).
[63] " This mind of ours seeks to find something that is God. It seeks to find a Truth not subject to change; a substance not capable of failing " (*Enarratio in Ps.* XLI, 7).
[64] *Conf.,* VII, 16; *Sermo,* LII, 16.
[65] " What shall I do, that I may find my God? ' The invisible things of God being understood by the things made ' (Rom. i. 20). I will consider

4. Turning then by introspection, he analyses the faculties of his own soul.[66]

5. He finds God at last, both *in* and *above* his own soul.[67]

The following powerful passage presents the details of the entire progress of the contemplative soul to God.

Step by step was I led upward, from bodies to the soul which perceives by means of the bodily sense; and thence to the soul's inward faculty to which the bodily senses report external things, which is the limit of the intelligence of animals; and thence again to the reasoning faculty, to whose judgment is referred the knowledge received by the bodily senses. And when this power also within me found itself changeable, it lifted itself up to its own intelligence, and withdrew its thoughts from experience, abstracting itself from the contradictory throng of sense images, that it might find what that light was wherein it was bathed when it cried out that beyond all doubt the unchangeable is to be preferred to the changeable; whence also it knew That Unchangeable: and thus with the flash of one trembling glance it arrived at THAT WHICH IS. And then at last I saw Thy ' invisible things understood by the things that are made.' [68]

the earth, and its great beauty; I marvel at the greatness of the sea; I look up and behold the heavens, and gaze upon the beauty of the stars; I wonder at the splendor of the sun and the moon. Yet, although I praise these things— for Him who made them, I thirst" (*Enarr. in Ps.* XLI, 7. Text here condensed.) Also, *Conf.,* X, 6, 3: " I asked the Earth, and it said, 'tis not I. And all things therein confirmed the same. I asked the Sea and the waters and the living things thereof; and they answered, we are not thy God, seek higher above us. I asked the moving air above, and the whole region of it with its inhabitants cried out, *Anaximines is mistaken, I am not God.* I asked the Heavens, the Sun, the Moon, and the Stars; neither are we, said they, the God whom thou seekest.—My asking was my considering them, and their answering was the beauty I discovered in them." (Translation with slight Variation from Pusy). Cf. also *Conf.,* IX, 10 (scene with Monica at Ostia) given in full below.

[66] "And I turned my eyes upon myself, and I said to myself, and what art thou? And I answered, a man. And behold in this man are presented to my consideration the body and the soul. Now which of these is it that gives to me my God? . . . But that is better which is the more interior " (*Conf.,* X, 6, 3). Cf. also *Enarr. in Ps.* XLI, 8 and *Conf.,* IX, 10 below.

[67] " Thou wert more inward to me than my most inward part, and higher than my highest " (*Conf.,* III, 11). This is a brief but splendid description of the *immanence* and the *transcendence* of God. Cf. also *Enarr. in Ps.* XLI, 10.

[68] *Conf.,* VII, 23. I owe this exquisite translation to Dom Butler, pp. 42-43.

St. Augustine repeats the scheme of contemplation with no essential variation in the beautiful discourse with his mother prior to her death at Ostia. This sublime passage will repay study, not so much because it is strikingly reminiscent of Plotinus, but for its vital bearing on the type of contemplation characteristic of the medieval mystics. Nothing attests more the ever-present Augustinian influence in the golden age of Christian mysticism than the tenacity with which the spirit and general method of his contemplation were repeated. Although I have given, for purposes of clarity, five points in St. Augustine's method of contemplation, it is evident that they can be reduced to two.

The first three points include the contemplation of physical creation. This is implicitly based upon the Platonic conception of the ascent of the soul *via* physical beauties to the Beauty Absolute. And it is explicitly due to St. Augustine's favorite Pauline doctrine: The invisible things of God are understood by the things that are made.[69] Later mystics will make much of this transcendent or " extra-spective " mode of contemplation. They will in meditative contemplation add the heavenly court—angels and saints,—and the divine attributes from the Pseudo-Dionysius and St. Gregory, and in so doing a complete *Theocentric* method of contemplation will be constructed. These lines from the Ostia discourse of St. Augustine will serve as an illustration.

We were speaking then together, alone, very sweetly; and we were enquiring between ourselves in the presence of the Truth, which Thou art, what would be the eternal life of the saints. But as yet we gasped with the mouth of our heart after those celestial streams of Thy fount, so that being even so much as sprinkled with its drops, we might according to our capacity in some way think upon so high a mystery.

And our converse had come to that point wherein we knew that the very highest delight of the bodily sense in the brightest possible earthly sunshine was not to be compared nor even mentioned in respect to the sweetness of that life. And then raising up ourselves with a more burning fervor toward the Self-same (the unchanging God), we did by degrees pass through all bodily things,

[69] Rom., i. 20.

even the very heavens whence sun and moon and stars shine upon the earth. And yet higher still we ascended by inward musing, and discourse, and the admiring of Thy works; and soaring up we came to our own minds and went beyond them that we might arrive at last at the region of unfailing plenty, where Thou dost feed Israel forever with the food of truth, where life is Wisdom by whom all things were made. And while we were discoursing and panting after it, with one full beat of the heart we touched upon it—and we sighed, and we left there bound, the first fruits of the Spirit.[70]

The final points (the fourth and fifth as I have noted them in St. Augustine's scheme) make up *one* step, that of introversion, which is the analysis of his own faculties, which finally brings him, in a deep interior silence, to that supernal Light which he recognizes " in one trembling glance." [71] This is that Light which to later mystics, following the Dionysian teaching and that of St. Gregory, became a " divine Darkness."

In the *Mystica Theologia* of the Pseudo-Dionysius, contemplation and ascent are considered under two leading ideas which are of great significance in the later history of Christian mysticism. First, the ascent to God by way of abstracting His attributes. Second, the End of the ascent is a " divine Darkness." Hence this unknown disciple of Proclus is true to the negative and abstract mysticism which is marked in Plotinus; and in the five short chapters of his *Mystica Theologia* he gave to countless generations of mystics a mode of expressing their own rapturous intercourse with God.

The ascent to God by way of abstracting His attributes consists in a consideration of those qualities which we predicate of God, and a gradual elimination of them even " from the last to the first, abstracting all, so as to unveil and to know that which is beyond knowledge, and which in all things is hidden from our eyes by that which can be known. And so to behold that supernatural darkness which is hidden by all such light as is in created things." [72] We are referred to his work on the divine attributes,[73] and he mentions *passim* a number

---

[70] *Conf.*, IX, 10.
[71] " Pervenit ad Id quod est in actu trepidantis aspectus " (*Conf.*, VII, 17).
[72] *De Mystica Theologia*, cap. II, Migne, *P. G.*, III, 1026.
[73] *De Divinis Nominibus*, *P. G.*, III, 586 ff.

of them.[74] Then he demonstrates how no quality can be properly attributed to God.[75]

The end of the ascent, according to the Pseudo-Dionysius, is a " divine darkness." That the process of abstracting from God those human qualities with which we are forced to endow Him does not leave God a mere lifeless and unintelligible abstraction, is the teaching of the fourth chapter of the *Mystica Theologia*.[76] For God completely transcends our knowledge and leaves us in a state of comparative ignorance,[77] and *from our viewpoint* looking up from below, He is enveloped in a complete though " luminous darkness," [78] which is a *darkness* because of the absence of created light, *luminous* because of the divine presence there mysteriously made known. Thus, the contemplative steadily withdraws all things visible from his gaze, and fixes his inward eye upon the transcendent qualities of God (the attributes), and then one by one abstracts these also, leaving only the essence of God, so that in a deep silence, in ignorance and darkness, the supercelestial Light will illumine him. Such is the gist of the Dionysian teaching. Its philosophical implications, favorable or otherwise to subsequent mysticism, are not in the province of this study of mystical method to discuss.[79]

The chief importance of the Pseudo-Dionysius does not lie in the originality of his thought. The mystical ascent to God in the Dionysian sense is implicit in Plotinus and Proclus, although both imply a positive increase of light and knowledge in the soul's divine ascent. The conception of the " divine darkness " is mentioned by Clement in words which identify this " darkness " with " ignorance " in its Dionysian sense. " And when the Scripture says, ' Moses entered into the thick

[74] *Ibid.* "In libro autem de divinis nominibus, (celebravimus) quomodo *Bonus* nominetur, quomodo *Ens*, quomodo *Vita*, et *Sapientia*, et *Virtus*, et quaecumque alia spiritualem Dei concernunt appellationem" (*De Mystica Theologia, P. G.*, III, 1034). (Italics pointing out the attributes are mine.)
[75] *P. G.*, III, 1039.   [76] *P. G.*, III, 1039.
[77] " They enter into the true mystical darkness of ignorance," *ibid.*, cap. I, *P. G.*, 1002. Cf. also *De Div. Nom.*, VII, 3, *P. G.*, 870 ff.
[78] *Ibid.*, cap. II.
[79] See P. E. More, *The Catholic Faith*, pp. 244 ff ; for a favorable criticism, see von Hügel, *The Mystical Element in Religion*, II, 366.

darkness where God was,' this shows that God is invisible and beyond expression by words." [80] Another possible source for the " divine darkness " is verse 10 of Psalm xvii, " Caligo sub pedibus ejus " (Darkness is under his feet), which is thus commented upon by St. Gregory: " By those beneath He is not seen in that brightness wherewith He exercises dominion among those above." [81] The concept of God existing either in super-essential Light or in a luminous cloudlike darkness is a most popular one in mystical literature from Dante (*Paradiso*, XXXIII) to the English author of *The Cloud of Unknowing*, and *The Dark Night of the Soul* of St. John of the Cross.

The chief importance of the Pseudo-Dionysius is in his construction of a formal system of mystical theology. It was brief; it enjoyed for over a thousand years the prestige which comes from its supposed authorship by a saint and disciple of St. Paul. The Pseudo-Dionysius was the chief medium in the medieval period for the theology of the angelic hierarchy,[82] of the divine attributes,[83] and of the " divine darkness "; and by way of the translation of John Scotus Erigena in the ninth century, and the numerous commentaries in the Middle Ages and Renaissance, the Pseudo-Dionysius exerted a powerful influence upon the mystics of those periods.

St. Gregory's contemplation, in contrast to that of the Pseudo-Dionysius, is devoid of technicalities of Neoplatonist philosophy, but is strongly reminiscent of St. Augustine [84] with whose writings St. Gregory was thoroughly conversant.[85] Here is a brief exposition of Gregorian contemplation, with the interesting addition of the scale of celestial beings.

Whoever is so rapt in contemplation, as, being raised up by divine grace, already to engage his thought on the choirs of angels, and fixed on things sublime, and ceasing every inward act—such a

[80] *Strom.*, V, 12.   [81] *Mor. on Job*, XVII, 39.
[82] *De Caelesti Hierarchia, P. G.,* III, 119 ff.
[83] *De Div. Nom., P. G.,* III, 586 ff.
[84] The introspection and turning of the soul in upon itself before it sees the Spirit is marked in St. Gregory. Cf. *Mor. on Job*, VI, 56.
[85] Butler, p. 106. Mr. F. H. Dudden shows that St. Gregory's theology is little more than a popularization of St. Augustine. (*Gregory the Great* [London, 1905] pp. 293, 468.)

one is not contented with beholding the glory of angelic brightness, unless he is able also to behold Him who is above the angels. . . . Hence, from these choirs of angels he directs the eye of his mind to contemplate the glory of the Majesty on high.[86]

St. Gregory is intent upon ascending by the ladder of created things to the divine Essence.[87]   But, as did St. Augustine, he pauses to contemplate a few of the divine attributes, of which Wisdom is especially prominent—" Wisdom which is God." [88]

When we are brought at last to the contemplation of Wisdom, the mere immensity thereof, which by itself lifts man up to himself, denies the human mind full knowledge, so that it should by touching love this Wisdom, and yet never passing through, penetrate it.[89]

The Union with God

The mystics of this period, as, indeed, in all periods of mysticism, arrive at the End of the road, but are quite helpless to describe their arrival. It is a wholly unique experience which they have longed for, which they have seen and felt in terms of light and sweetness, and is recalled with deep gratitude mingled with regret that the experience defies description. St. Augustine, soaring upward in rapture, perceived " That which Is " in the flash of one trembling glance, " But," he adds, " I could not fix my gaze thereon; and, brought back to my weak and usual self, I had as it were but perceived the odor of that which I could not feed upon." [90]   So also St. Gregory tells us, " After the mind of him that loves is filled with so great a gift of contemplation, it has power to see what it has not the power to explain." [91]   And furthermore he says, " Because after the stress of labors, after the storms of temptations, the soul is oft suspended on high in its operations, so that it contemplates the divine Essence which indeed it can feel but it cannot express." [92]

[86] *Mor. on Job*, XXXI, 99-100.
[87] *Hom. on Ezech.*, II, ii, 8, 12, 13; *ibid.*, XXIV, 6.
[88] *Mor. on Job*, XVIII, 88.
[89] *Ibid.*, XXII, 50. Cf. St. Augustine's " We touched upon that eternal Wisdom " (*Conf.*, IX, 10).
[90] *Conf.*, VII, 17.   [91] *Mor. on Job*, XV, 20.   [92] *Mor. on Job*, XXIV, 12.

Clement of Alexandria speaks of this transforming union with God as an " assimilation " [93] and he goes no further. Perhaps " Deification " better expresses it, a word which the Pseudo-Dionysius employed.[94] The contemplative in this highest degree of the spiritual life is ever more and more lifted up into the similitude of that which he adores and loves until he has in a manner become God. This is to be taken in the sense of which St. John of the Cross speaks as follows: " My understanding went forth out of itself, and from human and natural became divine; for united to God in that purgation (of the Night of the Spirit), it understands no more by its natural force, but by the Divine Wisdom to which it is united." [95]

Neither St. Augustine nor St. Gregory does more than give the name of "rapture" or "ecstasy" to these supreme moments when " os ad os loquitur " in the deep silence of the mystic fusion. St. Paul's text, " caught up into the third heaven," not knowing " whether he was in the body or out of the body," [96] is a favorite one with the mystics in relating the unique nature of the divine communion. " When the attention of the mind is wholly turned away and withdrawn from the bodily sense," says St. Augustine, " it is called an ecstasy." [97] The eyes do not see, nor are sounds heard, and it is a state midway between sleep and death.[98] In its intellectual aspect, he describes the ecstatic union as a quick and transient vision of the brightness of the Lord brought through a special intellectual intuition, which is accomplished by the grace of God who takes hold of the soul, " so that God speaks mouth to mouth (os ad os loquitur), not with the mouth of the body, but with the mouth of the mind." [99] St. Gregory habitually speaks of the soul being " rapt " [100] and borne above the world and outside

---

[93] *Strom.*, V, 3; VI, 9; V, 11; VII, 10.
[94] *Epistola II Caio Monacho, P. G.*, III, 1067.
[95] Translated by Watkin, *The Philosophy of Mysticism* (London, 1920), p. 268. Cf. also p. 314, and especially Butler, pp. 158-160.
[96] II Cor., xii. 2. St. Augustine, in a superb illustration of his mysticism, comments on this passage in *Liber de Diligendo Deo*, Epistle CXLVII; also in *De Genesi ad Litt.*, XII.
[97] *De Genesi ad Litt.*, XII, 25.
[98] *Ibid.*, XXVI, 53.
[99] *Ibid.*, XII, 26, 54.
[100] *Hom. on Ezech.*, II, ii, 13.

4

the world,[101] and entirely caught up to God.[102] There is seen the "eternal brightness of God"[103] yet only dimly to the blinking eyes of the mind.[104]

The divine union is an experience of highest emotional content. For St. Augustine it was a "holy inebriation"[105] that thrilled him with love and awe.[106] Sometimes he rejoiced in a certain inward sweetness[107] which was a foretaste of the joys of heaven. The soul of St. Gregory was set on fire when he tasted of the inward sweetness of divine union;[108] he felt, too, a fullness of knowledge[109] during those blissful moments of vision of the divine light.[110] And in full harmony with these expressions of the supreme mystical experience follows the exalted Dionysian teaching. "Now we rise from below to that which is highest, and accordingly our speech is restrained in proportion to the height of our ascent—but when our ascent is achieved, then will words altogether fail, and we shall be absorbed in the Ineffable."[111]

An important work of somewhat different nature which must receive notice in an account of mysticism in the patristic period is the *Consolation of Philosophy* by Boethius.[112] It enjoys a place in the history of Christian mysticism only

---

[101] *Epist.,* i. 5.
[102] *Mor. on Job,* XXIII, 12.
[103] *Ibid.,* XVIII, 89.
[104] *Ibid.,* IV, 45.
[105] *Contra Faustum,* XII, 42.
[106] *Conf.,* VII, 16.
[107] *Enarr. in Ps.* XLIV, 10.
[108] *Mor. on Job,* V, 58; *Hom. on Ezech.,* II, v, 4.
[109] *Mor. on Job,* V, 66.
[110] *Mor. on Job,* XXIII, 43. Also *Hom. on Ezech.,* II, v, 4.
[111] *De Myst. Theol., P. G.,* III, 1046.
[112] Anicius Manlius Severinus Boethius, a noted Roman statesman and philosopher, was born at Rome in 480. After long enjoying the favor of King Theodoric, he was accused by enemies of disloyalty, was imprisoned, and finally by the King's orders executed in 524 or 525. The early Middle Ages depended chiefly upon the celebrated *De Consolatione Philosophiae* and upon the works of St. Augustine and the Pseudo-Dionysius for their knowledge of Plato and the Neoplatonists. This work of Boethius consists of a dialogue between himself and Philosophy or Wisdom, Queen of the Sciences. It is not a mere patchwork of Platonic and Aristotelian passages, but an original discourse, prompted by exile, loss of friends, and "a memory well stocked with poetry and thought of former days" (H. F. Stewart, Introd. to *Boethius: Tractates and Consolation* [London, 1926], p. x). The complete works of Boethius are in *P. L.,* LXIII, LXIV.

second in importance to the Dionysian writings. Both authors drew largely from Platonic sources, especially from Proclus and the late Neoplatonists. For over a thousand years these writings received a universal and sympathetic attention. The works of the Pseudo-Dionysius were venerated as semi-inspired products of a disciple of St. Paul; Boethius was considered a saint and a Christian martyr.[113] In our only complete history of Christian mysticism, Boethius is placed with St. Gregory among the famous expositors of ascetic doctrine at the close of the patristic age.[114] The *Consolation of Philosophy* is credited with having exerted a profound influence on the mystical writers of the medieval period.[115] However, aside from the strong transcendental Platonism which characterizes the work, it brings no new elements to bear upon mystical methodology.[116]

---

[113] Cf. " Testimonium variorum de Boetio et ejus Scriptis," *P. L.*, LXIII, 562-574.

[114] Pourrat, *Christian Spirituality*, I, 266.

[115] *Ibid.*, and see especially Howard R. Patch, *The Tradition of Boethius* (New York, 1935), pp. 20-45.

[116] See below, George Colville's Translation of Boethius, p. 88.

CHAPTER IV

THE METHOD OF CHRISTIAN MYSTICISM

The second period of Christian mysticism opens, after a lapse of approximately five centuries,[1] with the writings of three contemporaries in the twelfth century: St. Bernard, Abbot of Clairvaux, (1091-1153), Hugh of St. Victor (1097-1141), prefect of the monastic school near Paris, and the equally famous Richard of St. Victor who died in 1171. The works of these three great figures in the mystical movement of the medieval period mark a distinct progress in the direction of both a speculative and a devotional treatment of the spiritual life. We may place the limits of this long and flourishing era in the history of Christian mysticism between the year 1135, when St. Bernard began his *Sermons on the Canticle of Canticles,* and the year 1560, which dates the composition of another commentary on the *Canticles* by St. Teresa of Avila.[2] Although this extends beyond the usual limits of the medieval period, yet the main characteristics of medieval mysticism continue up to the time of St. Teresa and St. John of the Cross.

The methodology of the medieval period may be conveniently studied under the following headings:

The Three Ways or Stages of Medieval Mysticism.
Christocentric Contemplation.
Theocentric Contemplation.
The Union of Christocentric and Theocentric Contemplation.
The Mystical Pilgrimage of Life.

THE SCIENCE OF MYSTICAL THEOLOGY

Although the principles of orthodox mysticism are contained in the ascetical and exegetical treatises of the Fathers, Christian

---

[1] St. Gregory died in 604.
[2] Translated by David Lewis (London, 1912). Pourrat dates her *Thoughts on the Canticle of Canticles* in the year 1574 (*op. cit.,* III, 130).

mysticism, as a science, does not appear until the twelfth century.[3] The *Mystica Theologia* of the Pseudo-Dionysius in the Latin translation of John Scotus Erigena was the only treatise exclusively confined to the principles of mysticism before the appearance of the works of St. Bernard and the Victorines. St. Bernard and the Victorines make up a trio whose combined influence on mysticism and its method cannot be overestimated. In a word, Christian mysticism came of age in the twelfth and thirteenth centuries. It was a new and highly important branch of theology which itself was impenetrated with the principles of scholastic philosophy.[4] It was a science which treated of the principles of the higher life and of personal perfection. It was as if theology were transferred by the mystic from the field of speculation and applied to the problems of everyday life viewed " sub specie aeternitatis." The treatises of medieval mysticism reveal the same synthetic spirit, as well as the passion for distinction and sub-division which characterizes the prevailing theology. It derives from theology such strictly theological subjects as the creation and fall of man, the Incarnation and Passion of Christ, the heavenly spirits, and the attributes and the essence of God. To all these the mystic added his own practical and affective considerations.

THE THREE WAYS OR STAGES IN MEDIEVAL MYSTICISM

Medieval mysticism continues in its methodology the essentials of the three ways or stages which we have seen in the writings of the patristic period. These three stages or ways are widened out and further systematized in medieval treatises, so that they become topographical boundaries of a complete and balanced spiritual life. The simple formula, Purgation, Contemplation, Union, now becomes, in the authoritative treatises of St. Bernard, the Victorines,[5] St. Bonaventure, and

[3] Cf. Turner, *History of Philosophy*, p. 303.

[4] Pourrat, II, 133-134. W. R. Inge, *Christian Mysticism* (London, 1899), p. 140.

[5] *Sermons on the Canticle of Canticles,* trans. by a Priest of Mt. Melleray (Dublin, 1919), I, *Serm.* IV, *" On the Three Stages of the Soul's Progress."* Cf. also *Sermon, " On the Three Stages of the Spiritual Life,"* III, 426-437. For Richard of St. Victor, see *Benjamin Minor,* cc. V-VI, *P. L.,* CXCVI,

other great medieval mystics, Purification, Illumination, Perfection, or the Purgative, the Illuminative, and the Unitive ways. The following statement of the Pseudo-Dionysius was repeated verbatim by Hugh of St. Victor, and is the first definite pronouncement on the three ways or stages of the spiritual life. " The progress of the soul to God is brought about by an illuminative grace which makes for perfection; and thus the soul ascends to God guided by a more mysterious and more impelling power so that the soul is thereby *purified,* and *illuminated,* and *perfected."* [6] The first systematic treatment of the three ways or stages of the spiritual life is the *De Triplici Via* of St. Bonaventure.[7] St. Thomas Aquinas solidified the tradition and made it absolute when he explained the three ways or stages as those of the beginners, the advanced, and the perfect (*incipientes, proficientes, perfecti*).[8]

The primary stage or way, that of purgation or purification remains basically the same as that developed by the patristic mystics. Two of its chief aspects are highly stressed in the medieval period. First, it is a purging of the soul from sin as well as a stripping of the mind of all sensuous images. This is accomplished by an elaborate system of mortification and other ascetic practices. There is a period of intense self-discipline, and a ceaseless warfare carried on against the vices which beset the soul and tend to deprive it of the virtues.[9] The phe-

---

64-192. Hugh of St. Victor, *Expositio in Hierarch. Coelest. S. Dionysii, P. L.,* CLXXV, 923-1154.

[6] " Dispositio animorum erga Deum, ex perfectiva illuminatione ordinata, in eam immediate ascendendo, occultior et manifestior divinitatis illuminatione *purgatur,* et *illuminatur,* et *perficitur"* (*loc. cit.,* cols. 1099-1100).

[7] *S. Bonaventurae Opera Omnia* (ed. A. C. Peltier, 15 vols. Paris, 1864-1891), XII, 22-37. " Per *viam purgativam* mens ad *illuminationem* immediate erigitur (VIII, p. 8) . . . per istam *viam illuminativam* ascenditur ad *unitivam"* (p. 19). The Paris edition is used throughout this work since it contains the Pseudo-Bonaventure treatises. Occasional references are made to the definitive Quaracchi edition.

[8] *Summa Theologica,* II-II, *Q.* 24, *a.* 9.

[9] Cf. Hugh of St. Victor, *P. L.,* CLXXV, 405; CLXXVI, 999 ff. Also *P. L.,* CLXXVII, 174, 502, 513 ff. St. Bernard, *P. L.,* CLXXXII, 941-972; CLXXXIII, 524, 1085 ff. Also the popular tracts attributed to St. Bonaventure, *De Pugna Spirituali contra septem Vitia Capitalia.* (XII, 158-164) ; *Formula Aurea de Gradibus Virtutum* (pp. 187-201).

nomenon of pain and physical suffering sought and patiently endured is a striking characteristic of this discipline.[10] Secondly, the positive side of the *via purgativa* sharply differentiates the Christian mystic from his Oriental brother. The necessity of good works is insisted upon, especially in doing the seven works of mercy and in an active life which is clearly in accord with the ideals of spiritual perfection.[11]

The second stage or Illuminative way marks the soul in its first growth and fervor under the influence of *gratia illuminativa.*[12] There is a joyous consciousness of ascent, and a new and profound apprehension of the aims and ideals of spiritual perfection. In the typical methodology of this period, the Illuminative way is closely associated with contemplation upon the Humanity of Christ, which marks this stage as one of preparation for the more exalted contemplation of the Deity. Thus, Richard Rolle of Hampole considers this second stage of the mystical life as one of increased love, of sweetness, of detachment from worldly interests in which the soul is given to a devout consideration of Christ.[13]

The third and final way or stage, that of Union or Perfection, as considered in medieval treatises does not mark any significant advance over that of St. Augustine and the earlier period of Christian mysticism. We gain no new knowledge of the nature of the exalted experience of union with the Deity. " Non potest exprimi " is the final verdict of St. Bernard, and others have tried in vain to alter the truth of his assertion. We find beautiful passages on the subjects peculiar to the Unitive way—raptures, ecstasies, visions, and revelations; but we must be content with vague phrases as to those higher states, of quiet, of the " dark night of the soul," of imageless and blissful union, which St. Teresa analyzed

---

[10] St. Teresa's phrase, ' aut pati aut mori ' has many echoes in mystical writings. See, for example, *The Life of Blessed Henry Suso by Himself*, trans. by Thomas Knox (London, 1865), pp. 50 ff.

[11] Cf. *Stimulus Amoris*, by James of Milan (*S. Bonav. Opera Omnia*, XII, 657 ff.); Walter Hilton, "Mixed Life" in *Minor Works of Walter Hilton*, D. Jones, ed. (New York, 1929), p. 6.

[12] See St. Bonaventure on this in *Soliloquium*, XII, 85 ff.

[13] *Incendium Amoris*, ed. by M. Deanesly, *Prologue*. Cf. also p. 219.

for the first time.[14] The Unitive way or stage is generally the concomitant of the consideration of the Deity arrived at by gradual ascent from creatures to God in a Theocentric type of contemplation; although the bliss of ecstasy and even vision of Christ has been the reward of purely Christocentric contemplation.

It must be observed that " contemplation " usually retains its wide and general meaning in medieval writings, as it does in later literature which receives its inspiration from medieval mysticism. Hugh of St. Victor, for instance, thus speaks of contemplation in general and also of the three ways: " The mind that would contemplate God must first be purified, then illumined, and finally perfected; and the higher these means cause the soul to ascend, the closer does it come to God and the more truly does it contemplate Him." [15] Contemplation is applied both to the Humanity of Christ and to the Deity; it is exercised both in the Illuminative way, and in the Unitive way in the two types of contemplation: Christocentric and Theocentric, which now demand special attention.

CHRISTOCENTRIC CONTEMPLATION

A new and vital element in medieval mysticism is the part given to meditation upon the Humanity of Christ. It is, of course, a fundamental tenet of Christianity that in the two-fold Nature of Christ rests the sole foundation of the Christian spiritual life. In view of this, it will be seen that medieval mysticism rests upon the thesis that, although mystical attainment is ultimately a union with the Triune God, yet this is accomplished only by way of the concrete fact of the Incarnation.[16] This concept of Christ as " the Door " opening into the mysteries of the divine Nature and the secrets of mystic union is the very core of medieval mysticism. Upon this clearcut distinction between the Humanity of Christ and the Trinity

---

[14] Cf. St. Teresa of Avila, *The Interior Castle,* Fourth, Fifth, Sixth, and Seventh Mansions.

[15] *P. L.,* CLXXV, 1080 ff. See words of the Pseudo-Dionysius cited above, p. 25.

[16] Cf. Karl Adam, *Christ Our Brother* (New York, 1931), p. 64.

of three divine Persons rest what I have termed the Christo-centric and the Theocentric types of contemplation.

The Christocentric type of contemplation concerns the historic life of Christ as recounted in the Gospel narratives and the Pauline Epistles. This includes the entire story from the Annunciation and Nativity to the Passion and Resurrection. xThe motives, the specific moral teachings, and the sufferings of Christ, all are held up as necessary subjects for contemplation and imitation. Over and over again one meets what is actually an unconditional rule in medieval mysticism: By the Humanity to the Divinity.[17] The enjoyment of mystic knowledge and love of God is vouchsafed only to such as are made like to the Word Incarnate. The Nativity of Christ, His Manhood, Life, and Death are presented not only as subjects for deep and loving contemplation, but also with an eagerness to draw forth from such consideration moral fruit and spiritual direction. The Christ-pattern, then, is the supreme model for those intent on inner spiritual perfection; and this striving for perfection and arrival thereat by means of ascetical practices and contemplation is of the essence of Christian mysticism. The ineffable union with God is the sole aim and the consequence of all soul activity of the mystics; and the concomitant ecstasies and the occasional visions are, after all, the transient experiences which add a mysterious zest to the weary pilgrim as he carries on to the end of the mystic road.

It is noteworthy that the specific contemplation upon the Humanity of Christ is not found except in its basic outline in the writings of the patristic mystics.[18] The all-important conception of the Mediatorship of Christ is fundamental in the writings of the Fathers; but they insist not so much upon the recognition of the Man-Christ as upon the divine Logos, the Word made flesh who was God. This was the rallying point of the Christian when Neoplatonism was not to be combatted but to be assimilated. Origen pointed out the reason why the Christian must know Christ.[19] He, like Clement of Alexan-

---

[17] Cf. F. Vernet, *Medieval Spirituality*, pp. 89-98.
[18] Cf. Dunstan Dobbins, *Franciscan Mysticism* (New York, 1927), p. 84.
[19] *Contra Celsum, P. G.,* VIII, 455-460.

dria, pushed the distinction to its extreme limit of those who know Christ according to the flesh, and the higher class, the "Gnostics," who, on the basis of this knowledge could rise to the spiritual essence of the Word.[20]

St. Augustine saw in Christ, Man-God, the path to the land of peace which he once beheld from the wooded height of Neoplatonism, but could find no path thereto.[21] He recognized that Christ's works, written in the Gospels, are fit subjects for man's practical edification.[22] Cassian's *Institutes and Conferences,* written for monks, amply testifies to the value of consideration of Christ's human life as an example of all virtues.[23] St. Gregory, similarly, based much of this teaching upon the example given by Christ " Humano modo." [24]

There is lacking, however, that typical devotional warmth which glows throughout the pages of medieval writings. It is as though the Fathers were all too conscious of the doctrinal struggles of their time concerning the human and the divine natures in Christ; and they exhibit the Humanity of Christ in their writings rather from the intellectual than the affective aspect. And lastly, there remains the important fact that in patristic times, no systematic treatise had appeared which gave equal value to the consideration of Christ's human life and to the contemplation upon the Deity.[25]

St. Bernard's writings contain the first comprehensive treatment of the life of Christ as recorded in the Gospels. One can discern the Christocentric type of contemplation in his *Sermons.* "His great achievement," writes Dean Inge, " was to recall devout and loving contemplation to the image of the crucified Christ, and to found that worship of our Saviour as the ' Bridegroom of the Soul,' which in the next centuries inspired so

[20] Cf. R. B. Tollington, *Clement of Alexandria* (London, 1914), II, 1-34.
[21] *Conf.,* VIII, 20.
[22] *De Consensu Evangelii, Lib.* I, cap. IV, 7. *P. L.,* XXXIV, 1045.
[23] In *P. L.,* XLIX and *L.* See especially *Collatio* x, *P. L.,* XLIX, 826-827.
[24] *Mor. on Job,* VI, *P. L.,* LXXV, 760.
[25] The Pseudo-Dionysius in Erigena's Latin version teaches that one must fix his eyes upon Christ in the flesh, if he is to aspire to divine communion. (*Epistola* VIII, *P. L.,* CXXII, 1181 ff., and with it compare the original, *De Mystica Theologia, P. G.,* III, 997 ff.)

much fervent devotion and lyrical sacred poetry." [26] With this Abbé Pourrat is in complete accord. "Ever since the 12th century, the writings of St. Bernard turned hearts towards the mysteries of the earthly life of Jesus, particularly towards His birth and passion." [27] St. Bernard is careful to justify this newly conceived concentration on Christ, for he says, " Although it is true that we place our whole hope in the Man-God, we do so not because He is Man, but because He is God. . . . The lowliness of a contrite heart well accords with the humility of Christ's human nature." [28]

The medieval period presents the fullest development of this type of contemplation in treatises which range from the speculative contemplations of Hugh of St. Victor to the fervent meditative visions of Angela of Foligno and the famous *Life of Christ* by Ludolph of Saxony.[29] The well-known *Imitation of Christ* is the out-flowering of the same spirit that inspired the Christocentric *Lignum Vitae* of St. Bonaventure,[30] and the numerous mystical *Lives* of Christ which present for contemplation the entire drama of Christian salvation from the Creation to the Last Judgment. Such are, for instance, the *Meditationes Vitae Christi*, which was until recently attributed to St. Bonaventure, and the equally influential *Life of Christ* of Ludolph of Saxony.[31]

[26] *Christian Mysticism,* p. 140.

[27] II, 319.

[28] *Sermons on the Canticle of Canticles, Sermon,* X, I, 87. See especially Etienne Gilson, *The Mystical Theology of Saint Bernard,* trans. by A. H. C. Downes (New York, 1940), pp. 79-84.

[29] Hugh of St. Victor, *De Sacramentis Christianae Fidei, P. L.,* CLXXVI, *lib.* 1, *pars* VIII, cap. VI-VII. Angela of Foligno, *Book of Divine Consolation,* trans. F. Steegmann (London, 1922). Ludolph of Saxony, *Hours of the Passion,* trans. (London, 1887).

[30] *Opera Omnia* (Paris ed.), XII, 67.

[31] The Pseudo-Bonaventure *Meditationes Vitae Christi* contains the following preface to the reader. "The soul is led to a very eminent state by meditating on the life of the Savior. Yet this is but, as it were, a foundation upon which the soul rises to more sublime degrees of contemplation" (*Opera Omnia* [Paris ed.], XII, 510 ff.).

Ludolph of Saxony's *Life of Christ* has this title, which explains its nature: " Vita D. N. Jesu Christi e sacris quattuor evangeliorum Sanctorumque Patrum fontibus pie simul ac amplie derivata in christianae pietatis educationem et oblectamentum."

The Humanity of Christ was considered as an object of particular devotion and a necessary condition to higher contemplation by the mystics of the middle ages irrespective of particular " schools " of spirituality which we associate with the various religious orders.   Thus, the Dominican, Henry Suso, first directed one of his spiritual pupils " in the imitation of the mirror-like life of Christ, which is the surest way," before advising one " to soar upwards on well-worn pinions to the heights of that noble contemplation which belongs to a blissful and perfect life." [32] Father Gemelli points out that St. Bonaventure and Duns Scotus elaborated the Christocentric piety of St. Francis of Assisi into a doctrine.[33] The influence of St. Francis exerted an intensely personal and simple devotion to Christ, and his influence upon his followers and upon other mystics was enormous.   He composed little if anything beyond the superb *Canticle of the Sun*, but his life was a perfect exemplification of the true mystic.   The Benedictine, Abbot Blosius, speaks for his Order when he praises this type of contemplation. " The spiritual servant of God," he writes, " should always have the lovely life and passion of the Lord Jesus concealed as the most precious pearls in the casket of his heart. But as before said, he must not in his contemplation be without God. Whenever he finds it difficult to occupy himself with higher meditation, he should willingly go back to the lowly Manhood of our Lord, exercising himself in the remembrance of those things which he did and endured for us." [34] So also Ruysbroeck summarizes the Christocentric contemplation when he says, " We shall through the personality of Christ transcend the created being of Christ and rest in the Divine Being in eternity." [35]

It is of greatest importance to distinguish in medieval mystical methodology works which are strictly *Christocentric* from those which are *Theocentric*, that is, the contemplation of crea-

[32] *Life of Blessed Henry Suso by Himself,* trans. by T. Knox (London, 1865), p. 252.

[33] A. Gemelli, *The Franciscan Message to the World* (London, 1934), p. 281.

[34] *A Book of Spiritual Direction,* trans. by B. Wilberforce (London, 1925), p. 54.

[35] Cited by Watkin, *op. cit.,* p. 77.

tures as a means of ascent to the Deity. The *Lignum Vitae* of St. Bonaventure and likewise the *Vitis Mystica* and *De Triplici Via* exemplify the Christocentric type of contemplation. The last-named treatises coordinate the three Ways, viz., Purgation, Illumination, and Perfection with meditation upon the chief events in Christ's life.[36] Other outstanding examples of Christocentric contemplation are the familiar *Imitation of Christ* and the *Exercitia super Vita et Passione Christi* which was long attributed to the great German mystic, John Tauler.[37]

THEOCENTRIC CONTEMPLATION

Unlike the Christocentric, the Theocentric type of contemplation is not new to mysticism.[38] In its simplest form it is the ascent of the mind to God by means of His creatures, and the contemplation of these creatures and the divine attributes, even of the Divine Essence itself. The Theocentric type of contemplation, as it appears in medieval mysticism in its highest development, consists in contemplation of God as He is reflected in created things, and a gradual ascent from them to God through these steps: the earth, living creatures, the starry universe, spiritual heavens. Then rising higher to the Divine Essence, including the attributes of God, it ends in a note of ravishing ecstasy, or intimate communion as a result of this contemplation.

The framework of this type of contemplation is Platonic; and after its adoption by St. Anselm, it came to be called in medieval philosophy the method of "Platonic induction."[39]

---

[36] *Opera Omnia,* XII.

[37] *Meditations in the Life and Passion of Christ,* translated by A. Cruikshank (New York, 1925).

[38] In a recent work on Christian mysticism, the author points out these two great approaches of the contemplative to God; and also explains the essential place of Christocentric mysticism. "Genuine mysticism is Christocentric mysticism," he writes. "But this does not imply that there is no longer any Theocentric mysticism. Rather the latter is restored by sacramental union with Christ. Christ is merely the Mediator, the way to the Father. In mysticism, Christocentric is not opposed to Theocentric" (Anselm Stolz, *The Doctrine of Spiritual Perfection,* translated by Aidan Williams [London and St. Louis, 1938], p. 45).

[39] Turner, *History of Philosophy,* p. 274.

The minds of thoughtful men have always been attracted by the order and symmetry and beauty of the visible universe with its apparent manifestation of a Mind in which is reflected the fullness and perfection of created order and beauty. The things of earth make up a visible ladder upon which the contemplating mind ascends to God. This familiar conception received its metaphysical basis from Plato. The doctrine that the mind can rise in successive stages to God by contemplating beauty, material and spiritual, is elemental in Theocentric contemplation. According to Plato, all earthly beauty is but a reflection of its heavenly archetype, which, in turn, resided in the supreme Idea of Beauty.[40] St. Paul gave his sanction to this view in the familiar statement that from the understanding of visible things which are made, there follows a knowledge of Him who made them.[41]

To the combined weight of Platonic and Pauline authority, add the assertions of the same concept in the Psalms,[42] and one readily accounts for the popularity which this formula enjoyed in the writings of the Fathers. St. Augustine, whose influence was most marked of all the Church Fathers upon medieval thought, was fond of using creatures as a means of rising to God.[43] In the medieval period this was a favorite preparation for the enjoyment of the mystic union.

[40] Cf. above, pp. 5-7.

[41] Rom. i. 20: "For the invisible things of him (God) from the creation of the world, are clearly seen, being understood by the things that are made; his eternal power also, and divinity."

[42] Ps. ciii; xli. 1; lxxviii. 6; lxiii. 10; cl.

[43] See for example, *Conf.*, IX, 10 and above, p. 27. Athenagoras calls the existing order of the material world, its magnitude and beauty, "pledges of divine worship" and adds: "For the visible is the medium by which we perceive the invisible" (*Plea for Christians*, n. 4). Tertullian, true lover of Nature, says "magistra natura, anima discipula" (Nature is the teacher, the soul a pupil) (*De Testim. Animae*, c. 5). St. Basil looked upon the visible creation as "a school and institution of divine knowledge" (*Hexaëm.*, *Homil*. 1, *n*. 5). In general, the patristic period does not furnish a complete illustration of the Theocentric type of contemplation as we have noted particularly in St. Augustine. In St. Basil, however, this type of contemplation is exceedingly well set forth in one of his sermons. (*Homilia XV*, *De Fide*, *Opera Omnia S. Basilii* [Paris, 1839], II, 182-183.) Despite scattered evidence of this type of contemplation before the medieval period, it is actually popularized by such mystics as St. Bonaventure and his numerous followers.

Nature

The Theocentric type of contemplation in its initial stages is a form of " Nature " mysticism in the specific sense that Nature is the manifestation of the creative power of God and is the living reflection of His attributes, particularly of Beauty and Wisdom. In this sense, the medieval mystics were all Nature mystics; they saw the created world in a sacramental sense, a symbolic revelation of the Creator in forest and plain and mountain. St. Bernard expressed his love for nature in one of his letters. " Believe me," he wrote, " thou canst find more in the woods than in books. For trees and the stones will teach thee what thou wilt never learn from thy masters." [44] And in one of his sermons he pointed out that " the human mind has need of some kind of vehicle of a creature in order that it may mount up to a knowledge of the Creator." [45] St. Bernard's fondness for nature is brought out in a familiar but often poorly translated passage in the first biography we possess of him. " Even now he [Bernard] confesses that whatever he received from the Scriptures and whatever his spirit took from them—all came to him from his prayer and meditation in the woods and the fields. And among his friends he was wont to say in pleasantry that he really had no teachers except the beeches and the oaks." [46]

St. Francis of Assisi, a true lover of nature in its simplest and most familiar forms, was most vividly and most effectively attracted by its sacramental character.[47] The Victorines were also loud in their praises of the origin, magnitude, multiplicity, beauty, operation, and wondrous order of things contained in

[44] *Epist.*, CVI, 2, *P. L.*, CLXXXII, 242.
[45] *Serm. de Diversis*, IX, 1. *P. L.*, CLXXXIII, 565. Cf. also Bellarmine's *De Ascensione Mentis in Deum.*
[46] " Nam usque hodie quidquid in Scripturis valet, quidquid in eis spiritu-aliter sentit, maxime in silvis et in agris meditando et orando se confitetur accepisse; et in hoc nullos aliquando se magistros habuisse, nisi quercus et fagos, joco illo gratioso inter amicos dicere solet " (*S. Bernardi Vita Prima, lib.,* I, *cap.* IV, 23. *P. L.*, CLXXXV, 240).
[47] See Index for " Sensibility to Nature in St. Francis " in Father Cuthbert's *Life of St. Francis of Assisi* (London, 1916).

the universe.[48] St. Bonaventure wrote of the beauties of nature and regarded created things as " foot-prints " of the Creator. Nature to Bonaventure was not only a useful object of meditation; but moreover every Christian must join with nature in the universal chorus of praise to God.[49] This is a marked quality of the Theocentric type of contemplation; and it appears not only in the works of all the representative medieval mystics but also in the writings of St. Teresa. In one of the many instances where she refers to nature, she says that it was a help to her " to look on fields, water, and flowers. In them I saw traces of the Creator,—I mean that the sight of these things was a book unto me; it roused me, made me meditative, and reminded me of my ingratitude and of my sins." [50]

Spiritual Heavens—Angels

The next step in the Theocentric type of contemplation consists in the consideration of the spiritual heavens. There the mystic fixed the eyes of his soul upon the angels and the souls of the just; and in this exalted company paused to derive therefrom new energy for the remainder of the ascent to God. This step is wholly in keeping with the method common to scholastic theology wherein the cognoscibility of God, apart from revelation, was determined by the contemplation of the *material* and the *spiritual* universe.[51] Of the spiritual universe, the angelic beings have always attracted considerable attention both in non-Christian and Christian speculation.[52] They became a vital part of medieval contemplations, not only in virtue of their traditional ministerial activities between heaven and earth; but also because of the relative proximity to the divine

[48] Richard of St. Victor, *Benj. Major, P. L.,* CXCVI, *lib.* II, c. XIII; Hugh of St. Victor, *Expositio in Hierarch. Coelest. S. Dionysii, P. L.,* CLXXV, *lib.* III, 960 ff.

[49] *Itinerarium Mentis in Deum,* XII, 3-10.

[50] *The Life of St. Teresa by Herself,* cap. IX. Trans. by David Lewis (New York, 1911), p. 55.

[51] Pohle-Preuss, *God: His Knowledge, Essence, and Attributes* (St. Louis, 1911), p. 16; cf. St. Thomas Aquinas, *Summa Theol.,* I, Q. 1, a. 1.

[52] For an admirable historical survey of the world of spirits, see F. Prat, *The Theology of St. Paul.* Trans. by J. L. Stoddard (London, 1927), pp. 408 ff.

Presence, where, according to St. Bernard, " they contemplate the Word from a loftier level." [53] The honor which is due the angelic hosts and their intercessory power with God was treated exhaustively in scholastic theology.[54] The hierarchy of the angels in its " trinal triplicities " held a special attraction for the medieval mystics because of the comparison of gradual ascent of the contemplative mind with the ascending ranks of angelic spirits.[55] This arrangement of the choirs of angels in nine orders was entirely unknown to the Greek and Latin Fathers with the important exceptions of St. Ambrose, St. Gregory, and the Pseudo-Dionysius. It is to the great authority of the Pseudo-Dionysius, that the nine orders owed their prominence in medieval mystical treatises. St. Paul has no fixed order of classification of the nine choirs; and the Scriptures have no mention of them all together. The five names furnished by St. Paul (Eph. i. 21; Col. i. 16): principalities, powers, virtues, dominations, and thrones, are the nucleus upon which the list of nine choirs of angels has been made. At the head of these were put the seraphim and cherubim of the Old Testament, and at the end the archangels and angels mentioned here and there in the Bible. The nine-fold arrangement of the Pseudo-Dionysius differs from that of St. Gregory who in one list accounts for but eight, in another nine choirs.[56] Other patristic writers are not agreed as to the number of the choirs or their respective order of perfection; one finds four and five choirs mentioned by Origen [57] and eight by Gregory

[53] *Serm. on the Cant. of Canticles,* XIX.
[54] Cf. St. Thomas, I, *Q.* 108; *Q.* 112; *Q.* 113.
[55] Cf. St. Bonaventure, *Collat. in Hexaëmeron* (Quaracchi ed.), V, XXII, n. 24. In the *Soliloquium,* cap. IV, St. Bonaventure is more explicit.
[56] The Pseudo-Dionysius (*De Cael. Hierarchia, P. G.,* III, 369-583) is generally followed by medieval mystics. He adopted the scale in descending order of perfection: 1. Seraphim; 2. Cherubim; 3. Thrones; 4. Dominations; 5. Virtues; 6. Powers; 7. Principalities; 8. Archangels; 9. Angels. The Gregorian arrangement in ascending order is as follows: Angels, Archangels, Thrones, Dominations, Virtues, Principalities, Cherubim, Seraphim. (*Moralia,* XXXII, 23, No. 48, *P. L.,* LXXVI, 665.) Also Angels, Archangels, Virtues, Powers, Principalities, Dominations, Thrones, Cherubim, and Seraphim. (*In Evang. Homil.* XXXIV, *ibid.,* 1249.)
[57] *Contra Celsum,* IV, 29, *P. G.,* VIII, 624; *De Princip.,* 26, *P. G.,* VIII, 337.

5

Nazianzen.[58] The medieval writers do not always present a
definite number or arrangement of the choirs in their mystical
treatises, and they tend to perpetuate the skepticism of St.
Cyril of Jerusalem regarding the respect in which the angels
differ.[59] St. Bernard is not particular as to their order, but is
extremely resourceful in assigning definite privileges and prerogatives to the angelic choirs; and his influence upon later
mystical writers was profound.[60] Richard Rolle of Hampole
enumerates the " nine orders in three hierarchies," and explains
the increasing brilliance of each order as it approaches the Deity.
" This," he writes, " I say to kindle thy heart that it may desire
the fellowship of angels." [61]

There is a continuation of the upward flight of the mind
as it leaves the highest forms of created beings, viz., the angelic
hosts and the souls of the just, saints and martyrs, and plunges
into the depths of the increated Being of the Godhead. The
treatment of the souls of the just, who are considered in proximity to the angels and the Divine Essence, is in direct accord
with the doctrine of the communion of saints—a regular feature of medieval devotion, and treated at length in scholastic
theology.[62] The angelic beings, considered by St. Bernard as
" pure intelligences," [63] are placed in the direct way of the
contemplation of the attributes and the Essence of God. " They
are," he writes, " transported by an extraordinary but fully
conscious rapture of satisfaction, infinitely intense, and un-
speakably blissful, into the limitless ocean of Light Divine." [64]

This exalted stage, just short of the contemplation of God
Himself, is from a psychological aspect a spontaneous result
of the logical process by which the mind ascends to a *knowledge*
of God from the contemplation of creatures. The entire mystic

[58] *Oratio XXVIII,* 31, *P. G.,* XXXVI, 72.
[59] *Catechetical Lectures,* XV, 12.
[60] Cf. *Serm. on the Cant. of Canticles,* XIX; XXVII, pp. 185; 307. Also
De Consideratione, lib. V. cc. III-V. *P. L.,* CLXXXII, 789-795.
[61] " Ego dormio et cor meum vigilat," in *Richard Rolle of Hampole,* ed. by
C. Horstmann (London, 1895), I, 51.
[62] St. Thomas, *Summa Theol., Supplementum, Q.* 72.
[63] *Serm. on the Cant. of Canticles,* XXVII, p. 307. Cf. also *Itinerarium
Mentis in Deum,* cap. 11, p. 7.
[64] *Ibid.,* XIX, p. 188.

process, and, indeed, the ineffable mystic union itself, is an intellectual one; it is a conscious thirst for the fullness of knowledge—from which flows love which transports and enkindles the contemplating soul with a new and mysterious fervor.[65] The adage, 'Knowledge is power,' has a peculiar meaning for the mystic; and when it is said that mysticism is a philosophy of the heart, it is only true in the sense that the mystic *loves* in proportion as he *knows*. It is precisely here that speculative and mystical theology unite in their endeavor to form an idea of God, to arrive at a comparative knowledge of the divine Nature; and that in these questionings and strivings of the human intellect to know "That which Is," the theology of the divine attributes came into being.

The Divine Attributes

The divine attributes are qualities which the mind sees in created things, and posits as existing supereminently in the absolute perfections of the Divine Essence. Thus, God is wise, good, just, beautiful, merciful, and holy in the sense that these determinations found in creatures exist in their highest possible perfection in the Divine Nature.

This *positive* method of arrival at a comparative knowledge of the Essence of God by an ascent from the perfections perceived in created things to their supereminent existence in God is ultimately Platonic; and so also is the conception of true beatitude as consisting in a contemplation of the hypostatized Ideas of Beauty and Good, other attributes of the Absolute. The method of arriving at the Divine Essence by *negation* is a denial that any perfections conceivable by the finite mind can be appropriately predicated of God. This Neoplatonic conception was carried into medieval mysticism through the Dionysian writings. It was, in brief, an abstraction of all attribution of God, a taking away of all qualities, a stripping

[65] See *Summa Theol.*, II-II, Q. 180, a. 7 and also St. Thomas' *Expositio super Dionysium, De Divinis Nomin., Lect.* IX, *Opusculum* xiv. "The first union with God begins by the intelligence," wrote Lessius. "From that follows the union of heart by hope, charity, and religion" (*The Names of God*, trans. by T. J. Campbell [New York, 1912], p. 141).

of all created concepts from the divine Nature, " until God is beheld in that super-essential darkness which is hidden behind all such light as is in created things." [66] Thus conceived, the Divine Essence is *above* all wisdom, all beauty, all goodness, etc., in that it transcends the qualitative and quantitative elements of all created things.

The consideration of the divine attributes marks the zenith of the progress of Theocentric contemplation. This is often accompanied by the ineffable experiences of the mystic union, ecstasies, and transient moments of inexpressible bliss and rapture. The resultant knowledge is not a distinct concept, but an obscure though very vivid intuition infused into the soul. It is a veiled and indirect apprehension of the Godhead. [67] The mystics have found the contemplation of the divine attributes a source of great spiritual fruit. St. Bernard speaks of the soul as an admirer of the Deity venturing to inquire into the most awful mysteries of the Godhead, and drawn up sometimes to a spiritual ecstasy. [68] And he, furthermore, taught a special method of contemplating the attributes in his book, *Liber de Consideratione.* [69] Richard of St. Victor, under heavy obligations to the Pseudo-Dionysius, places the contemplation of the attributes of God second in importance only to that of the Trinity of Persons. [70] As one would expect, St. Bonaventure considers the contemplation of the " essentials " (*essentialia*) of God as one of the ways which the soul, like the High Priest, enters the Sanctum Sanctorum. " There are," he writes, " two approaches to the invisible and timeless things of God: the one which considers God in His essential nature, and the other which takes account of that which is proper to the Persons of God." [71] This contemplation of the divine attributes is usually considered as part of the exercises of the Unitive way. Indeed, St. Bonaventure clearly associates this contemplation with the third and final way of the spiritual life in his *De Triplici Via,*

---

[66] The Pseudo-Dionysius, *De Mystic. Theol., P. G.,* III, 557.

[67] Cf. Watkin, p. 229.

[68] *Serm. on the Cant. of Canticles,* LXII, p. 211.

[69] *Lib.,* V, cc. i et vii-xiv, *P. L.,* CLXXXII, 787; 795-808.

[70] *Benjamin Major,* IV, xvii, *P. L.,* CXCVI, 156-157.

[71] *Itinerarium Mentis in Deum,* p. 16.

and assigns to the Illuminative way the contemplation on Christ. " This has become the classic method," notes a recent authority, who points out that this contemplation on the attributes of God is found in the *Road to Perfection* of St. Teresa of Avila and in *The Living Flame,* the mystic poem of St. John of the Cross.[72] Walter Hilton represents the continental tradition in England, and he frequently refers in his mystical works to the " privities " of the " Blessed Trinity," which may not be seen but by the sharp eye of the contemplative.[73]

The utility of this form of contemplation is well summed up by Leonard Lessius, eminent theologian and mystic of the sixteenth century. His summary warrants an even fuller quotation than the following:

By the study of the Divine Perfections, the soul rises towards God, contemplates Him, admires, fears, venerates, loves and perpetually praises and blesses Him. . . . St. Denis, the Areopagite, exhorted his disciple St. Timothy to practise this kind of meditation. . . . And he [the Pseudo-Dionysius] is here speaking of that most excellent mode of contemplation by which after considering the divine perfections most attentively, the soul rises to something more sublime and limitless, and infinitely more noble; to something which embraces not merely the divine perfections as the created mind conceived them, but the Divine Being itself, and in an unknown manner unites itself to Him by contemplation and love.[74]

Another interesting observation concerns the number of the divine attributes and their relative priority which the mystics employ in enumerations. Speculative theology, the close ally of medieval mysticism, assigns no definite number to the possible qualities applicable to the Deity.[75] The priority of the attributes is recognized in a common classification, viz., the

---

[72] *Dictionnaire de Spiritualité ascétique et mystique,* M. *Viller* (Paris, 1937), *col.,* 1081.

[73] *The Scale of Perfection,* ed. by Evelyn Underhill (London, 1923), Bk. II, XLVI, 461.

[74] *The Names of God,* pp. 136-138. Note the various meanings given to the word contemplation.

[75] Cf. St. Thomas, *Summa Theol.,* I, Q. 13, a. 4 and *ibid., QQ.* 3-25. Here Aquinas analyzes twelve of the attributes: Simplicity, Goodness, Infinity, Immutability, Eternity, Unity, Wisdom, Truth, Love, Justice, Mercy, and Omnipotence. The number varies in other lists.

Primary or Incommunicable, and the Secondary or Communicable attributes. According to this arrangement, the Primary attributes are All-Wisdom, Self-Existence, and Omnipotence, as belonging to God alone. The Secondary perfections are predicated analogically both of God and creatures.[76] The representative treatises of medieval mysticism apparently reflect this classification; and Wisdom frequently occupies chief place of honor owing to a variety of reasons. Divine Wisdom is an attribute of the Deity, without distinction of Persons of the Trinity.[77] Wisdom is intrinsically the Knowledge and Intelligence of God, and, therefore, the basic and primordial foundation of all things, both possible and actual, are in Wisdom formally and objectively as in their exemplar or ideal cause.[78] So also Wisdom is considered the being, life, and light of intelligible things, and first turns towards the Divine Essence, understands it perfectly, being equal and commensurate with it.[79] Moreover, Wisdom enjoys greatest prominence over the other attributes in virtue of its three-fold determination as *Sapientia creans*,[80] or cause of all things, as *Sapientia disponans*, i. e., uniting all things in one harmonious whole;[81] and as *Sapientia gubernans*, otherwise known as Divine Providence.[82] The long tradition concerning Wisdom in the Sapiential Books of the Old Testament, and the numerous medieval commentaries and glosses upon them, served to accentuate the priority of Wisdom as a divine attribute. St. Bernard, the ablest champion of the attributes in the discussions of the Council of Rheims, allows his preference for Wisdom to manifest itself in his Sermons and didactic treatises.[83] Hugh of Palma, a

[76] They are: goodness, justice, intelligence. (See Catholic Ency., art. Attributes.)

[77] As for instance, St. Augustine: "The Father is Wisdom, the Son is Wisdom, the Holy Ghost is Wisdom, and together not three Wisdoms, but one Wisdom" (*De Trinitate, Lib.* VII, *cap.* 3).

[78] See *Summa Theol.*, I, Q. 15, *a.* 1 and *ibid.*, Q. 36, *a.* 7.

[79] Lessius, *op. cit.*, p. 165; cf. also p. 42.

[80] Wis., vii. 21; Ps. ciii. 24; John i. 3.

[81] Wis., xi. 21; cf. Job xxviii. 20; Rom. ii. 15.

[82] Wis., viii. 1; Rom. xi. 33.

[83] *Serm. on the Cant. of Canticles, Serm.* XV, p. 141; *ibid., Serm.* XIX, p. 186; vol. II, *Serm.* LXXX, p. 454. Cf. *Sermon* LXXX, for complete discussion of divine attributes, pp. 445 ff.

contemporary of St. Bonaventure, gave to the famous tract, *Theologia Mystica*, another title: *De Triplici Via ad Sapientiam*, and Henry Suso appropriately names his best-known work on mysticism, *The Little Book of Eternal Wisdom.*[84]

The sole use of the Theocentric type of contemplation, i.e., without the detailed meditation upon Christ, is likewise exemplified in the works of the mystics of the period. Albertus Magnus' *De adhaerendo Deo*; the two English pieces: *Dionysius Hid Divinity*, and *The Cloud of Unknowing*; and also Bellarmine's *De Ascensione Mentis in Deum per Scalas Rerum Creaturarum* are excellent illustrations.[85] Then, too, we may find the direct union and juxtaposition of the Christocentric and Theocentric types of contemplation in the same treatise. This will be considered in the writings of St. Bernard, the Victorines, and St. Bonaventure's authentic and supposititious works. The ensuing analysis of the united Christocentric-Theocentric method of contemplation will bring out the salient points of both these types of contemplation.

THE UNION OF CHRISTOCENTRIC AND THEOCENTRIC CONTEMPLATION

In the foregoing historical analysis of the Christocentric and Theocentric types of contemplation, their union in one complete mystical treatise has been purposely omitted. These two types together in mystical treatises constitute the basic framework of medieval mystic methodology. One is impressed by the sameness and repetition of the basic elements of mysticism in the representative works of the medieval period. This, however, does not open the medieval mystics to charges of "plagiarism" in the modern sense,[86] but rather, it indicates

[84] English trans. (London, 1910).

[85] *Alberti Magni Opera Omnia*, XXI (Lyons, 1651), English trans., *On Union with God*. This is a work of the 14th or 15th century erroneously ascribed to Albertus Magnus. The two English works are anonymous products of the fourteenth century. They are edited by E. Underhill (London, 1909), and by Justin McCann (London, 1924). Bellarmine's treatise is in *Opera Omnia Roberti Bellarmini* (Paris, 1874), VIII; English trans., *The Ascent of the Mind to God* (London, 1928).

[86] Cf. Underhill, in Introd. to her edition of *The Scale of Perfection*, p. xix.

the existence of a basic system of contemplation which is the result of a long tradition of writings dealing expressly with prayer, meditation, and union with God. In a word, mystical theology had developed definite methods, just as the scholastic method accounts for the arrangement and treatment of the subject-matter of philosophy and theology. Differences of treatment due to a variety of personal and extrinsic conditions as well as divisions and distinctions, appear in the several works of the same author, and certain varieties of the spiritual life receive greater or less stress. So, too, one finds ample justification for the various " schools " of Christian mysticism which authorities draw up as embodying divergent details of what is after all the same basic philosophy and method of the spiritual life.[87] This methodology rests largely upon the Christocentric and Theocentric types of contemplation together with the three ways or stages of spiritual development. The method forms the broad, general framework, irrespective of subtle distinctions of the " higher degrees of union " which have been laid down by St. Teresa and St. John of the Cross.

This aspect of medieval mysticism serves to account largely for the oft-noted similarities, " influences," identical expressions, and often parallel passages found in one mystical treatise when compared with works of predecessors or contemporaries. The similarity between the works of St. Bernard and the Victorines on the one hand, and those of St. Bonaventure on the other, is a remarkable instance of this conscious fusion of the elementary principles of mystical theology.[88] Another instance of this intimate relationship between the great mystics is that of Ruysbroeck, who is a direct descendant of the Victorines and St. Bonaventure.[89] These authorities, too, were the sources and inspiration of the English mystics, Rolle and Walter Hilton.[90] The great mystics of Germany are no exceptions. In a

[87] Cf. Pourrat, II, 334-336.

[88] " The practical identity of St. Bernard's and St. Bonaventure's thought is manifested in descriptions of the normal term of the spiritual life . . . Richard's [of St. Victor] is a spirit kindred in many ways to that of St. Bonaventure " (Dobbins, p. 171, 173).

[89] *Ruysbroeck the Admirable*, pp. 224 and 236.

[90] Margaret Deanesly, *Incendium Amoris of Richard Rolle of Hampole*

study of Meister Eckhart, the author concluded " that there was nothing new on the speculative side," yet the School of Eckhart includes the brightest names in the history of mysticism: Ruysbroeck, Tauler, and Suso.[91] John Gerson, one of the great forces of the medieval period, and author of a score of important mystical treatises, was admittedly guided by St. Bernard, the Victorines, and St. Bonaventure.[92] The invisible bond between these great mystics and others of less weight and importance consists mainly of the usages of the twofold contemplation and the threefold ways of the spiritual life. This will now be brought out in a number of the important treatises of the medieval period.

St. Bernard and the Victorines

The necessity of uniting in one treatise consideration of the historical life of Christ (Christocentric) with the contemplation of the Deity conceived at the end of the ascent from creatures (Theocentric) is stressed to a hitherto unknown degree in the writings of St. Bernard and the Victorines. These writers are exceedingly fond of allegory; and they explain the rich symbols of the Canticles or of the Ark of the Covenant and other Old Testament figures in these two types of contemplation. St. Bernard's *Sermons on the Canticle of Canticles* make up the great bulk of his mystical writings,[93] although two important non-allegorical works on mysticism are *Liber de Consideratione* and *De Diligendo Deo*.[94]

The great contributions of Hugh of St. Victor, among which

(London, 1915), p. 49. Underhill, Introd. to *The Scale of Perfection*, p. xviii; cf. also Horstmann, *Richard Rolle of Hampole* (London, 1897), Vol. I, Introd.

[91] Sister M. Odelia Funke, *Meister Eckhart* (Catholic University Press, 1916), p. 10.

[92] Cf. *Gersonii Opera Omnia* (Antwerp, 1706), III, 434, 545, 571, 883; and J. L. Connolly, *John Gerson, Reformer and Mystic* (Louvain, 1928), pp. 330-354.

[93] The allegorical writings which embody the two types in St. Bernard's writings are: *Serm.* LXII, "*The two kinds of Contemplation*," p. 204 ff.; *Serm.* XLVIII, p. 44; in Vol. II. Also *Serm.* XX, p. 194; *Serm.* X, p. 80; *Serm.* XXVII, p. 302, in Vol. I.

[94] In *P. L.*, CLXXXII, 727-808 and 973-1000.

are the *Soliloquium de Arrha Animae*, and the *De Amore Sponsi et Sponsae*,[95] place him among the most influential mystical theologians of the period.[96] The two important treatises of Richard of St. Victor which furnished the framework for numerous subsequent works on mysticism are the *Benjamin Minor* and the *Benjamin Major*.[97] The heavy veil of allegory, so dear to the medieval heart, and the frequent repetitions and digressions in these monumental pieces serve to obscure what is a perfect exemplification of the two types of contemplation and the three ways or stages of the spiritual life.

The *Benjamin Minor* is a comparatively brief analysis of the Purgative and Illuminative ways.[98] A vigorous discipline of the senses and imagination is insisted upon; and the images derived from the beauty and goodness of creatures initiate the upward movement of the soul.[99] The various virtues, personified under the figures of the sons and daughters of Jacob, are carefully analyzed; as are their opposite vices which obstruct and hamper the progress of the soul.[100] The Illuminative way with the meditation upon Christ is presented with a conviction not unlike that of St. Bernard.[101] The Theocentric type of contemplation is hardly more than touched upon in the concluding chapters of the *Benjamin Minor*. This important division is left expressly for a lengthy and detailed development in the five Books of the *Benjamin Major*. Hence the ascent of the soul is compared to the flight of an eagle [102] as it rises by virtue of the light of divine Sapience from a contemplation of nature,[103] up to the " cives coelestes," the saints and angels, and thence to the divine attributes [104] in the Trinity

---

[95] In *P. L.*, CLXXVI, 951-993.

[96] " Two visible signs (*simulacra*) were granted to man whereby he could see that which is invisible: one is of nature, the other is of grace. The sign of nature is the things of the world; the sign of grace is the Humanity of Christ " (*Expositio in Coelest. Hierarch., P. L.*, CLXXV. 926).

[97] In *P. L.*, CXCVI, 1-202.   [99] *Ibid.*, c. XIV.

[98] *Ibid.*, cc. V-VI.   [100] *Ibid.*, c. XLI ff.

[101] *Ibid.*, cc. LXXVII, LXXVIII, LXXVIX, LXXX.

[102] *Ibid.*, c. XIII, 91.   [103] *Ibid.*, c. XVI, 94.

[104] *Ibid.*, c. XX, 101. Note here the importance given Eternal Wisdom: " Sed divina Sapientia quid clarius? Quid lucidius? cui etiam nihil comparabile invenimus! " See also next chapter (XXI) and especially c. XVII, 157.

of three Persons.[105] The ascent, according to Richard, is accompanied by ecstasy and transport, such as that which St. Paul experienced when he left behind all data of sense, all figments of the imagination, and, high above the realm of reason itself, he heard and saw things wholly unutterable and indescribable.[106]

The Method of St. Bonaventure

Of the works of St. Bonaventure which portray the two-fold types of contemplation and the three ways of the spiritual life, the *Itinerarium Mentis in Deum* best illustrates the restrained reasoning of the scholastic theologian, together with the fervor and piety of the medieval mystic.[107] The prologue of this work sounds the regular Christocentric note and the directions for the Purgative way.[108] St. Bonaventure explains that the terrestrial " vestiges " of the Creator include the four elements and the beauty and excellence of nature.[109] Even the mind of man, with its memory, intellect, and will, is a reflection of the Trinity.[110] These faculties are illuminated by grace, " mediante Christo," and with full reception of the theological virtues, Faith, Hope, and Charity, the soul is well on the Illuminative way.[111] Then, ascending higher, the soul reaches the angelic choirs; and then it continues its flight and contemplates the divine attributes in the Essence of the Deity, who is at once the center and circumference of all things.[112] Thus,

---

[105] *Ibid.*, c. XVIII, p. 158.   [106] *Ibid.*, c. XIX, p. 192.

[107] Vol. XII (Paris ed.), English trans., *The Franciscan Vision* by Father James (London, 1937). Other important works of St. Bonaventure are: *Soliloquium, Vitis Mystica, De Perfectione Vitae, Lignum Vitae* and the *De Triplici Via*, which last two are mainly Christocentric. They are in complete editions of St. Bonaventure's works (Quaracchi, 1902), vol. VIII; also in Paris ed., vol. XII.

[108] " This road to final peace is none other than the most fervent love of the Crucified which so transformed Paul, when caught up to the third heaven. . . . No one can enter the heavenly Jerusalem who enters not through the Blood of the Lamb as through a door " (*ibid.*, 2).

[109] *Ibid.*, p. 6.

[110] A familiar concept in medieval treatises; it was stressed by Richard of St. Victor, *Benj. Minor, P. L.*, CXCVI, 55; and developed by St. Augustine, *De Trinitate.* Cf. St. Bernard, *Serm.* I, 94.

[111] *Itiner. Mentis in Deum.*, c. IV, 13-15.   [112] *Ibid.*, c. V.

the six steps of the contemplation and ascent of the soul in St. Bonaventure's plan lead to that seventh and final step, the " Sabbath of Quiet," whence the soul rests after its labor.[113]

A number of mystical treatises which were long attributed to St. Bonaventure were extremely potent factors in spreading the Christocentric-Theocentric types of contemplation throughout the continent and England.[114] A heavy indebtedness to St. Bernard, to the Victorines, and to St. Bonaventure is particularly remarkable in these writings. The authority of the Pseudo-Dionysius is also marked in those works which we now briefly analyze.

The work entitled, *De Septem Itineribus Aeternitatis,* is considered by Pourrat[115] to have been written by Rudolph of Bibrach of the Friars Minor in the fourteenth century. This work is especially important in that it is a veritable treasury of quotations from the great medieval authorities, as well as of St. Augustine and the Pseudo-Dionysius. The plan follows closely the *Itinerarium* of St. Bonaventure. The first two of the seven steps of the *Iter* are in the Christocentric type of contemplation, and give such directions as make up the Purgative way.[116] The third step of the *Iter* consists of a speculative discussion concerning the manner in which meditation ceases, and contemplation begins.[117] A number of authorities are quoted to the effect that a meditation on Christ is a prerequisite for the more abstract contemplation.[118] The fourth step is accomplished by cultivating the virtues, especially charity, through which the soul is united to God.[119] The fifth and sixth steps illustrate the Theocentric type of contemplation. Therein is traced the ascent of the soul through creatures, and through the higher spiritual creation " ad cujus aeternitatis plenam ex-

[113] *Ibid.,* c. VIII. The quiet and rest of the soul on arriving at the end of its Quest is not unusually termed its spiritual " Sabbath." St. Augustine (*De Quant. Animae,* XXXVI) thus expresses the final steps of the soul's journey: " purgat anima in quarto; reformat in quinto, introducit in sexto; pascit in septimo."

[114] Cf. Dobbins, *op. cit.,* p. 196 f. n.   [115] *Christian Spirituality,* II, 226.

[116] *De Septem Itin. Aetern., S. Bonaventurae Opera Omnia,* VIII, 394-419.

[117] *Ibid.,* p. 420.   [118] *Ibid.,* p. 435.

[119] *Ibid.,* p. 437; cf. St. Thomas, *Summa Theol.,* II-II, Q. 184, a. 1.

perientiam nos perducat aeterna sapientia." [120] The journey ends with the Sabbath, or seventh step, wherein the gradual deification of the soul is accomplished after the manner of the ascending purification of the grades of the angelic choirs.

The *Stimulus Amoris* is a work which merited the unstinted praise of Gerson, and was said by Luis de Granada to be hardly less valuable than the *Confessions* of St. Augustine.[121] The author of this lengthy treatise, which appeared in many manuscripts of the fourteenth and fifteenth centuries, is believed to be James of Milan.[122] He divided the treatise into three books which correspond roughly to the three ways of the spiritual life. The first book is eminently Christocentric, and is especially given over to reflection upon the Passion. Indeed, the usual Theocentric consideration of the saints, angels, and divine attributes is here introduced at length for their bearing on the Passion of Christ. The second book marks the Illuminative way of the soul, and is a meditation on the love of God for man as manifested in the Incarnation and Birth of Christ. This follows a typical consideration of Christ's entire life, not omitting the institution of the Eucharist which usually figures in this type. The second book is filled with the usual fervent ejaculations of love; and the customary plea for a reciprocation of love for God on the part of man. The Unitive way embraces the entire third book, and recounts the ecstasies and transports which accompany the deification of the soul. The final chapter is an exercise in the contemplation of the celestial Jerusalem.

Another work which exerted great influence in the fifteenth and sixteenth centuries, with its reproduction of the essential teaching of St. Bernard and the thirteenth century mystics, is the *Meditationes Vitae Christi*.[123] It is one of the apocryphal works of St. Bonaventure, now believed to be written by a

[120] *Ibid.*, p. 473.
[121] *S. Bonavent. Opera Omnia*, XII, Introd., xlvi.
[122] W. A. Phillipson, *The Goad of Divine Love* (London, 1906), Introd., p. vi.
[123] Cf. Pourrat, II, 184. This work is found in the *Opera* of St. Bonaventure, Quaracchi edition, VIII; and in the Paris edition, XII, 509 ff. My references are to the Paris edition.

Franciscan of the thirteenth century.[124] This work is a mystical biography of Christ, and is unexcelled in mystical literature for its dramatic presentation of the Gospel narrative colored and enlarged by events, conversations, and purely imaginary representations.[125] The author makes clear the Christocentric and the Theocentric types of contemplation. He expressly states that his work is for beginners in the spiritual life, and for those engaged, not necessarily in the contemplative, but in the active life. The chief occupation of these " imperfect " souls is contemplation on the humanity of Christ.[126] He then proceeds to explain the nature of the Theocentric contemplation, which follows upon a previous purification and a long exercise in the imitation of Christ. This contemplation, reserved for the few, is made up of the regular subjects of the Theocentric type, the " celestial fatherland," [127] and the majesty of the Deity as it is first seen in the divine attributes and finally in the incomprehensible Essence accompanied with rapturous ecstasy of the contemplating soul.[128]   Henry Suso, in the concluding chapters of his *Life*, set down in due order the three ways of the spiritual life together with the consideration of Christ and the contemplation of the divine perfections. " The first thing which a man should do is to turn away entirely and with all his might from the pleasures of the world, and from sinful practices, to God, with persevering prayer, seclusion, and virtuous discreet exercises, in order thus to bring his body into subjection to the spirit." This in accord with the Purgative way, is followed by the Illuminative way.   " The second thing

---

[124] *Meditationes Vitae Christi*, Introd.

[125] The author frankly avows the non-inspired additions to the gospel history of Christ. See cap. IX, p. 522.

[126] " Pro incipientibus et imperfectis est contemplatio humanitatis Christi, quam in hoc libello describo " (cap. L, p. 576).

[127] " Go you also, brothers, with abundance of piety and devotion to visit with your mind the realms above and the many mansions there in the abode of the Father. Salute with reverence each of the orders of angels, the full number of the patriarchs, the entire group of prophets, the company of the apostles; look upon the crowns of the martyrs and admire the choir of virgins bearing their lilies. . . . And this will suffice of contemplation of the heavenly Fatherland " (cap. LII, p. 578).

[128] *Ibid.*, cap. LIII, pp. 579-580.

is to offer himself willingly and patiently to bear the countless multitude of contradictions which may come upon him from God or creatures. The third thing is to take the sufferings of Christ crucified as the model on which to form himself, and to copy Him in His sweet teaching, gentle walk, and pure life, which He proposed to us as our example, and in this manner to press onwards through Him. The fourth thing to be done is to divest himself of exterior occupations, and to establish himself in a stillness and repose of soul by an energetic detachment from all things, as if he were dead to himself, and could not guide himself, and had no other thought but for the honor and glory of Christ and His Heavenly Father."

The Theocentric type of contemplation is given by Suso in the following directions.

The divine essence, of which it is said that it is a rational substance, of such nature that no mortal eye can see it in itself, may nevertheless be discerned in its effects, just as we trace a good craftsman in his works. For, as Paul says, creatures are like a mirror which reflect God. But let us pause awhile here, and reflect upon the high and venerable Master as mirrored in his works. Look above thee to the four quarters of the universe, and see how wide and high the beautiful heaven is in its swift course, and how nobly its Master adorned it with the seven planets, each of which, not to reckon in the moon, is much bigger than the whole earth, and how He had decked it with the countless multitude of the bright stars. . . . Ah, gentle God, if Thou art so lovely in Thy creatures, how exceedingly beautiful and ravishing Thou must be in Thyself! But look again, I pray thee, and behold the four elements—earth, water, air and fire, with all the wondrous things which they contain in manifold variety—men, beasts, birds, fishes, and sea-animals; and mark how they all cry aloud together, Praise and honor be to the unfathomable immensity that is in Thee! It is Thou who providest for all, each in its own way; for great and small, for rich and poor. It is Thou, O God, who doest this. Thou, O God, who art God indeed.

These considerations are of the Unitive way as Suso makes clear. He moreover directly refers to the ecstasy and joy which such contemplation effects in the soul.

Look upwards then with sparkling eyes and radiant face and

bounding heart, and behold Him and embrace Him with the infinite outstretched arms of thy soul and thy affections, and give thanks and praise to Him. See how by gazing on this mirror, there springs up speedily, in a soul susceptible of such impressions, an intense inward jubilee; for by jubilee is meant a joy which no tongue can tell, but which pours itself with might through the heart and soul.[129]

Summary of the Two Types of Contemplation

Of the two types of contemplation, that on the life and sufferings of Christ (Christocentric) is the more common in medieval methodology. The contemplation of nature and the gradual ascent of the mind to God from visible creation is one essential part of Theocentric contemplation; another part is the consideration of the heavenly court with its joyful inhabitants, and a third part is the reverent contemplation of the divine attributes and the Essence of God. The experienced student of mysticism will discern other subjects which occupy various positions of importance in mystical treatises, sometimes to the exclusion of either or both of the two types of contemplation which we have just treated. This is seen, for instance, in the *Dialogues* of St. Catherine of Sienna or in the *Revelations* of Juliana of Norwich. This is to be expected in a literature which aims at depicting the manifold and varied characteristics and tendencies of the Christian spiritual life. However, the contemplation of Christ (Christocentric) and the contemplation of God—either seen in nature or seen in His attributes (Theocentric)—are fundamental to a greater or less degree in all Christian mysticism.

THE MYSTICAL PILGRIMAGE OF LIFE

The conception of the Christian life as a pilgrimage with its attendant trials and ultimate victory is a familiar one in literature. The chief scriptural basis for this *genre* is found in a few Old Testament passages, and in the usage of the terms " pilgrims and strangers " as applied to the Christians by St.

---

[129] *Life of Henry Suso by Himself*, pp. 281-284.

Peter and by the author of the Epistle to the Hebrews.[130]   St. Gregory, commenting on the Parable of the Talents, could say that human nature, native to earth, was assumed into the divine nature at the Incarnation, and was taken on a sort of pilgrimage to heaven by the Redeemer, and, henceforth, man is a stranger and a pilgrim on this earth.[131]   St. Augustine gave his weighty authority to the conception of man as a pilgrim on the road to eternity.   " Our life in this pilgrimage," he wrote, " cannot be without temptation." [132]   And again, he tells us, " As long as we are in the body, we are on a pilgrimage from the Lord [133] (peregrinamur a Domino)."

The medieval mystics, however, first developed the allegory of the Pilgrimage of Life.   In constructing it they closely followed the example set by the *Psychomachia* of Prudentius who personified the virtues and vices and portrayed them in spiritual conflict for the possession of the soul of man.[134]   This strife between the personified virtues and vices begun largely by Prudentius was made a part of numerous mystical treatises in the medieval period.[135]   Writing in the ages of the Crusades, and assisted by the popular custom of making pilgrimages to

[130] " Ne sileas, quoniam *advena* ego sum apud te et *peregrinus* (stranger and a pilgrim) sicut omnes patres mei " (Ps. xxxviii, 13).   " Dearly beloved, I beseech you, as strangers and pilgrims, to refrain yourselves from carnal desires which war against the soul " (I Peter ii, 11), " And . . . saluting them and confessing that they are pilgrims and strangers on the earth. . . . But now they desire a better, that is to say, a heavenly country " (Heb. xi, 13, 16).

[131] *Homilia IX, in Evang.* (Matt. xxv, 14).

[132] *Enarr. in Ps. LX, 3.*

[133] *Enarr. in Ps. XLI, 10.*   In the *Confessions,* he speaks of the pledge which we who are in this pilgrimage received from God (XIII, 15).   The pilgrimage theme here noted differs vastly from that which Mr. Lewis notes in Seneca, and believes to be " based on a common cause with the Pilgrim's Progress " (*Allegory of Love* [London, 1936], p. 63).   The difference is fundamental : one is secular in purpose and end ; the other is religious.   It stresses the temporal character of earthly life as a preparation for eternal life.

[134] Aurelius Clemens Prudentius (348-406), Christian poet and ascetic, developed this conception of which traces are found in Tertullian's *De Spectaculis*, XXIX, likewise in Apuleius and Claudian.   See Lewis, *op. cit.*, pp. 66 ff. for discussion of Prudentius in the development of allegory.

[135] See above, p. 38, for list of medieval treatises exhibiting the virtues and vices contending for the soul of man.

6

holy places, medieval writers saw in the actual journey to an earthly Jerusalem, an allegorical pilgrimage of the Christian to the heavenly Jerusalem. The very real perils of the earthly journey were readily interpreted in relation to the spiritual trials of the soul of man on his pilgrimage to heaven.

St. Bernard saw in the story of the Prodigal Son an allegory of man leaving the Paradise of a good conscience, seeking new and untried experiences, and becoming acquainted with both good and evil. Hiding himself from the face of the Lord, man begins to wander over the mountains of pride, into the valleys of curiosity, through fields of pleasure and woods of luxury, through swamps of carnal desires, through the waves of worldly cares.[136] God, however, merciful to man, sends Fear, Hope, and the four cardinal virtues to conduct him along the way of Justice until, not without difficulties, he arrives at the Castle of Sapience with its moat of Humility and walls of Obedience. The castle is besieged by spiritual enemies, but Prayer mounted on Faith, ascends to the Father in heaven who dispatches Charity, "regina coeli," to bring the repentant sinner to heaven.[137] This, St. Bernard concluded, is the life story of all men. First, one is weak and foolish; afterward he is headstrong in prosperity, then fearful in adversity, and finally, man is rescued, instructed, and perfected in the kingdom of Charity. Treating the same subject elsewhere, St. Bernard explicitly links the Pilgrimage of Life theme with the method of Christian mysticism by illustrating from the Parable of the Prodigal Son the three ways or stages: Purgation, Illumination, and Perfection or Union.[138]

The pilgrimage theme lies back of such mystical treatises as St. Bonaventure's *Itinerarium Mentis in Deum* and the anonymous *De Septem Itineribus Aeternitatis* wherein the ascent of the mind to God through contemplation is conceived under the imagery of an allegorical *iter* or journey. "Thus the feet

[136] *Parabola I, De Pugna Spirituali, seu De Fuga et Reductione Filii Prodigi, P. L.*, CLXXXIII, 757.

[137] *Ibid.*, 758-761.

[138] *Sermons on the Canticle of Canticles*, " *On the Different Stages of the Spiritual Life*," III, 426-437.

of the spirit," wrote the Abbot of St. Victor " are the intellect and affections with which the devout mind makes its way along the road to eternity." [139]   This figure, which goes back to the Pseudo-Dionysius, is taken over by the author of *De Septem Itineribus Aeternitatis*. He would require the frequent washing and purification of the dust-stained feet of the pilgrim; and, moreover, calls special attention to the numerous obstacles which retard or impede the pilgrim's progress.[140]

John Gerson, Chancellor of the University of Paris and one of the greatest of the medieval mystics, was much impressed with the notion of life as a pilgrimage. " There was much more than an accident in the change of name from John Charlier to John Gerson," wrote Dr. Connolly. " It was not simply because he came from a town so called that Gerson took his name, but the word Gerson in Hebrew means ' exile ' or ' pilgrim ' and suggested to him constantly the pilgrimage that he was making from earth to a heavenly home." [141]   Gerson's well-known *De Monte Contemplationis* is an exposition of the journey of the Christian pilgrim up to and including the Mount of Contemplation. Gerson also wrote another treatise called *Testamentum Peregrini*, and also a work in Latin verse, similarly titled, both of which contain a pilgrim's last will and testament.[142]

The *Ancren Riwle*, an English semi-mystical treatise written for contemplative nuns, reveals the nature of the life pilgrimage in the following depictions.

The good pilgrim holds always on his way straight forward; although he see or hear idle sports and wonders by the way, he doth not stop as fools do, but holds on his route. . . . All pilgrims go ever forward, and do not become citizens in the world's city, yet they are sometimes delighted with the things they see by the way, and stand still a while, though not altogether, and many things happen to them whereby they are hindered, so that, the more is

---

[139] *Cantica*, cited by the author of *De Septem Itineribus Aeternitatis, Opera Omnia S. Bonaventurae* (Paris ed.), VIII, 397.

[140] *Ibid.*, p. 398.

[141] James L. Connolly, *John Gerson, Reformer and Mystic* (Louvain, 1928), p. 277.

[142] *Opera Omnia* (Antwerp, 1706), III, 767 ff.; I, 129 ff.

the harm, some come home late, some never. . . . A pilgrim is subject to manifold evils.[143]

Walter Hilton's *Parable of the Pilgrim,* a part of *The Scale of Perfection,* is one of the most detailed accounts of this allegory to be found in the writings of the mystics.[144]   In Hilton's version, the pilgrim sets out, accompanied by a guide for Jerusalem, which is " a sight of peace, and betokeneth contemplation in perfect love of God; for contemplation is nothing else but a sight of God, which is very peace." [145]   The pilgrim is then grounded in Faith, reformed by Penance, and warned to listen ever to Humility and Love.   The journey itself consists mainly in doing spiritual and corporal works as well as overcoming " certain temptations and lettings which souls feel from their spiritual enemies, in their spiritual knowing and going towards Jerusalem." [146]   So potent are these spiritual trials that the pilgrim is sorely beset, and even falls by the way. " And though thou be sometimes barred and letted in thy way through thy frailty," warns Hilton, " with such inconveniences as befall thy bodily life, through evil wile of man, or malice of the enemy; so soon as thou canst, come again to thyself, and go on with thy exercise." [147]   The temptations from the world, the flesh, and the devil are numerous, but a consciousness of supernatural aid and of the secret presence of divine power contributes to bring the pilgrim on the " right way to Jerusalem, that is, to the sight of peace and contemplation."   The mystic quest comes to a close with Hilton's paraphrase of the Psalm.

Thus prayed the Prophet to the Father of Heaven, saying: Send out Thy light and Thy Truth and He shall lead me to Thy holy hill and to Thy Tabernacles. That is, to the feeling of perfect love and the height of contemplation.[148]

[143] *The Nun's Rule, The Ancren Riwle,* modernized by James Morton, *The Medieval Library* (London, 1924), pp. 264-265.
[144] *The Parable of the Pilgrim* was separately reprinted several times; it is found in Book II, chapters 21-24 of *The Scale of Perfection.* My references are to the edition of J. B. Dalgairns (London, 1870).
[145] *Ibid.,* p. 160.
[146] This is the title of Chapter IV, p. 164.
[147] *Ibid.,* p. 167.   [148] *Ibid.,* p. 169.

When one recalls that this treatise of Hilton is part of his mystical work, *The Scale of Perfection*, it is indisputably clear that the principles of Christian mysticism enter vitally into the concept of the Christian as a pilgrim on the road of life, bent toward his heavenly home. Dante is, of course, the greatest exponent in the world literature of this pilgrimage in its fusion with the threefold ways or stages of the mystical life. In a sixteenth century mystic, Diego de Estella, one finds expression of the same idea. " We are pilgrims in this world," he wrote, " and we are travelling onward towards Thee, O Lord, as to our own country, and the native land of our souls. And whenever we commit sin, we are hindered in the way, and halt; and what is a great wonder and excites astonishment is that such trivial things should detain us." [149] There is also a great body of early and late medieval allegory of the pilgrimage which is influenced by and developed concomitantly with the mystical writings in the same *genre*. These pilgrimage writings derive from a common source as may be seen from a comparison of their main outlines. Scholars who have, however vainly, attempted to determine the exact sources of Bunyan's *Pilgrim's Progress*, observed the sameness of theme and similarity in essential details of the pilgrimage literature. Wharey, in his study of this literature prior to Bunyan, noted that, " Many of these parallelisms are easily accounted for as being the natural result of the treatment of a common theme. The need of a guide, the equipment of the pilgrim with armour, the passage through dangerous valleys, the wandering from the right path, the vision of the Heavenly City—these are points that would be naturally suggested to any one by the theme itself." [150] Wharey drew up an impressive list, headed by Lydgate's version of De Guileville's *Pélerinage* which, although not exhaustive, enumerates more than forty works very definitely classed as pilgrimage literature. He does not advert to the element of Christian mysticism or to the fact that most of

[149] *Meditations on the Love of God*, trans. by H. W. Periera (London, 1898), p. 47.
[150] James B. Wharey, *A Study of the Sources of Bunyan's Allegories* (Baltimore, 1904), p. 66.

these writings manifest characteristics originally seized upon and developed by the mystics.

The Morality plays, likewise, bear an intimate relation to the pilgrimage allegories.[151]   The Moralities in their basic outlines are founded upon the concept of man making his way to heaven, beset by the vices, aided by the virtues, and finally emerging, tried and tested, a victor in the struggle.   The mystical Pilgrimage of Life will be considered in Part III of this work for an interpretation of the first book of *The Faerie Queene* which is similar in many respects to the Moralities.

---

[151] " For I am commanded," says *Everyman,* " a pilgrimage to take, / And great accounts before God to make." Cf. W. Roy Mackenzie, *The English Moralities from the View of Allegory* (London, 1914), Chapters I and X.

PART II

MYSTICAL LITERATURE OF FOREIGN ORIGIN
IN THE ELIZABETHAN AGE

Chapter I

THE PLACE OF CHRISTIAN MYSTICISM IN LITERATURE

Prose treatises and sermons were the chief means but not the sole means of expressing Christian mysticism in the patristic and medieval periods. Early in the history of Christian mysticism poetry and hymnody became the favorite modes of expressing the mystical spirit and methodology. First in order of importance would be the so-called " Hymns of Hierothaeus," whose purportedly inspired lines are found in the Dionysian writings.[1] Notable too are the metrical portions of Boethius' *Consolation of Philosophy* which exerted a profound influence upon subsequent religious philosophical poetry. St. Bernard was a writer of divine songs, and numerous pieces were ascribed to him in course of time.[2] It can be said that the first great poem of the nascent Italian language was St. Francis of Assisi's *Canticle of the Sun* which sings of the creatures of the world giving praise to their Creator much in the manner of the Theocentric type of contemplation. Similarly the full fruits of Spanish mysticism are found in the poems of St. John of the Cross; and three of his greatest works were written as commentaries upon three mystical poems.[3] Adam of St. Victor, the " lesser Victorine," was the most important liturgical poet of the middle ages which produced such poets as Dante and Petrarch, whose Christian mysticism will be considered in these chapters.[4] Indeed, as Professor Baldwin

---

[1] *De Divinis Nominibus, lib.* IV, cc. XV-XVII; cf. also *lib.* III, *cap.* II, *P. G.,* III, 713 and 681.

[2] Cf. Vacandard, *Vie de S. Bernard* (Paris, 1927), I, 101, and *History of Christian Latin Poetry* by F. J. E. Raby (Oxford, 1927), pp. 326 ff. His supposititious poems are in *P. L.,* CLXXXIV, 1307-1330.

[3] The poems are: " The Dark Night," " The Spiritual Canticle," and " Living Flame of Love."

[4] Adam of St. Victor, *Sequentiae, P. L.,* CXCVI, 1421-1534. English translation, *The Liturgical Poetry of Adam of St. Victor* (London, 1881), by D. S. Wrongham, in three vols.

has pointed out, mysticism is a pervasive quality of most of the literature of the medieval period.[5]

The theme and method of Christian mysticism is exhibited in medieval poetry not only by the well-known figures of medieval mysticism, but also by other writers of the period who were touched by the mystic's inner fire, and who sought in poetry the means to express the glowing details of the great quest.   It is not the form or method that attracts the writers of mysticism, but in the traditional form and method they reveal their inspirations.   This is explained by Miss Evelyn Underhill.   " There are two distinct factors which must be present in every great work of mysticism," she writes.   " First, that fresh intuition of spiritual reality, that direct experience of God, which makes its creator a mystic.   Next, and, hardly less essential to his teaching office, is the element of tradition; all that spiritual culture which the writer has inherited from the past and hands on to the future, and which gives him the framework, the convention, within which his own direct experience can be expressed." [6]   In this manner the literature of mysticism comes into being.

Among the great literary mystics who were essentially poets are Jacopone da Todi and his followers, whose spiritual ideas spread quickly through Italy and beyond it, and raised the level of religious thoughts and feelings of medieval Europe.[7]   The poems of Jacopone are the precursors to the fervent hymns and spirited songs which Savonarola and his followers sang in the streets of Florence; they served to preserve the spirit of Christian mysticism when the enthusiasm for Plato and Plotinus was at its height in Italy.   Medieval lyric, too, in its moral and ethical reaches, not only on the continent but also in Eng-

[5] Charles S. Baldwin, *Medieval Poetry and Rhetoric* (New York, 1928), p. 242.

[6] Introd. to *The Vision of God* by Nicholas of Cusa, trans. by E. G. Salter (London, 1928), p. vii.

[7] Evelyn Underhill, " Two Franciscan Mystics : Jacopone da Todi and Angela of Foligno " in *St. Francis of Assisi, Essays in Commemoration* (London, 1926), p. 313. See Jacopone's " Ineffable Love Divine," of which part is translated in *Lyra Mystica*, ed. by Charles C. Albertson (New York, 1932), pp. 24-36.

land, distinctly echoes the impulses and the form of Christian mysticism.[8] Thus at the close of the medieval period, when secular and religious poetry under the stimulus of the new humanism widened its range, there remained a special *genre* of religious and devotional literature of which a part represents the basic method and transcendent spirit of Christian mysticism.

The late fifteenth century may be said to mark the penetration of Christian mysticism into "literature" in its widest sense;—the literature of the growing knowledge and the expanding vision which ushered in and accompanied the Renaissance. Men of letters were attracted by Christian mysticism, just as it had attracted Petrarch and Dante. Thus the Golden Age of Spanish literature is coincident with the period of her greatest mystics, when their works were actually numbered by the thousand.[9] And in Italy, the Christian Platonists, Marsilio Ficino and Pico della Mirandola, were brilliant leaders in the literary revival of the late fifteenth century. Nicholas of Cusa, scientist, humanist, and mystic, is author of *The Vision of God,* whose mystical doctrines are in the direct tradition of the Pseudo-Dionysius.[10] In the next century, Lefevre d'Etaples, Christian humanist and Neoplatonist of France, published scholia on the Dionysian writings, and incorporated mysticism in his Commentary on the Pauline epistles. Thus, mysticism and Christian humanism were brought together by these writers, by Erasmus [11] and St. Thomas More; and mysticism was no longer to be found solely in the literature of theology or philosophy. Writers, too, who were not themselves mystics in the same sense that St. Bonaventure or Richard Rolle were

[8] E. K. Chambers, "Some Aspects of Medieval Lyric" in *Early English Lyrics,* coll. by E. K. Chambers and F. Sidgwick (London, 1921), pp. 282 ff. See the three volumes of lyrics edited by Carleton Brown: *English Lyrics of the XIIIth Century* (London, 1932), *Religious Lyrics of the XIVth Century* (London, 1924), and *Religious Lyrics of the XVth Century* (London, 1939). See also *Cambridge Hist. of Eng. Lit.,* II, 432-435.

[9] E. Allison Peers, *Spanish Mysticism* (London, 1924), p. 3.

[10] *The Vision of God,* pp. viii, xi.

[11] For the mystical element in *The Manual of the Christian Knight* (*Enchiridion Militis Christiani*), and the *De Contemptu Mundi,* see Pourrat, *op. cit.,* pp. 51 ff.

mystics, produced mystical literature by following its spirit and its method.

In England, at the turn of the sixteenth century, Christian mysticism and the New Learning were fostered simultaneously by the Oxford Reformers, chiefly through their studies in the works of the Pseudo-Dionysius and the early Fathers of the Church.[12] Dean Colet and St. Thomas More found in these early Christian authorities much upon which they based their inspirations and desires for intimate union with God. The hostility of these humanists at Oxford to the subtle speculations then identified with Scholasticism was pronounced; they desired a reform but at the same time they apprehended the dangers of a purely pagan humanism when made a religious philosophy of life. Hence, Dean Colet, just returned from Italy, was fired by the religious fervor of Savonarola, himself a mystic and reformer, and by the writings of the Neoplatonists, Pico della Mirandola and Ficino. He wrote two treatises based upon the Dionysian writings, both of which are a further Christianization of the original, and they furnish the greatest single influence upon his other work.[13] This influence is shown in a little treatise of private meditations entitled, *A ryght fruit-full monicion*, which went through more than twenty editions and was somewhat of a household guide in spiritual matters in England for over two centuries.[14]

William Grocyn, the teacher of Colet and More at Oxford, was influenced enormously by the writings of the Pseudo-Dionysius, even after he realized their non-apostolic origin while delivering a course of lectures upon the *Celestial Hierarchies* in St. Paul's Cathedral.[15] St. Thomas More, likewise,

[12] At this period numerous editions of medieval mystical books appeared from the presses of W. de Worde, Pynson, and others. (See Appendix.)

[13] J. H. Lupton, *The Life of John Colet* (London, 1909), p. 86. See also Frederic Seebohm, *The Oxford Reformers* (London, 1869), p. 21.

[14] Lupton, *op. cit.*, pp. 252-256, and Appendix D. In the editions of 1534 and 1577 this little tract was printed with Bishop St. John Fisher's *Commentary on the Seven Penitential Psalms*. In the 1577 edition, were added two anonymous pieces: *A brief treatise exhorting sinners to repentance*, followed by *Sundry profitable contemplations gathered by the sayd Author* (*ibid.*, p. 253).

[15] Seebohm, *op. cit.*, p. 91.

furthered the Christian mystical element in the religious literature of early sixteenth century England through his translated
extracts from Pico's spiritual works,[16] but to a greater extent in
a number of short prose treatises and poems. These are, *A Dialogue of Comfort against Tribulation, The Four Last Things,*
the unfinished *Treatise upon the Passion,* and *Certein devout
and vertuouse Instructions, Meditations, and Prayers.*[17]

THE CONTINUITY OF ENGLISH MYSTICISM

The first quarter of the sixteenth century witnessed the
formal entry of Christian mysticism into modern English literature by way of the writings of More, Colet, and Grocyn.
Upon these Oxford Reformers the influence of the Pseudo-
Dionysius has been noted. There was, however, another stream
of mystical literature in England at this time which came directly from the late medieval English mystics. This little but
exceedingly potent group of mystics, some of them anonymous,
made an important contribution to mystical theology despite
the direct influence which they manifest of continental mysticism. It is to our purpose here merely to bring into the line
of mystical tradition the outstanding works of the early English mystics, and thus establish the virtual continuity of Christian mysticism in England from its beginnings to the reign of
Elizabeth.

Richard Rolle, the hermit of Hampole (1290 ?-1349), heads
the list of English mystics both in time and in importance.
Illustrations of his mysticism are best found in *The Fire of
Love (Incendium amoris), The Mending of Life (Emendatio
vitae), The Form of Perfect Living, Ego dormio et cor meum
vigilat,* and others.[18]

[16] *Life of Pico della Mirandola with divers Epistles and other Works*
(1505). Ed. by J. M. Rigg (London, 1890).

[17] A modernized version of *The Dialogue of Comfort against Tribulation*
from Rastell's edition of More's *English Works* (1557) is published by P.
E. Hallett (London, 1937). From the same source is a new edition of *The
Four Last Things* by D. O'Connor (London, 1935). See also a collection
of More's religious poetry, translations included, in *Lyra Martyrum* by J.
R. O'Connell (London, 1934), pp. 19-48.

[18] *The Fire of Love* and *Mending of Life,* Early English Text Society,

Walter Hilton, a generation later, was an Augustinian monk who passed most of his life at Thurgarten in Nottinghamshire, where he died in 1396. Hilton's *The Scale of Perfection* is one of the most impressive treatises in all the range of mystical literature. His *Letter to a devoute man in temporal estate,* is also a brief but solid contribution to English mysticism. *The Song of Angels* contains exceedingly lofty directions for contemplatives, and it relies chiefly upon the Pseudo-Dionysius.[19]

Next in general interest and value to Rolle and Hilton is *The Cloud of Unknowing,* an anonymous treatise which is the most original and subtle of all the English mystical productions. It was probably written during the last half of the fourteenth century, and as its title indicates, it reveals a familiar acquaintance with the Dionysian writings.[20] The author of *The Cloud* is now considered the author of six other shorter but no less remarkable treatises. *Denis Hid Divinity,* the first of these pieces, is a free translation of the famous *Theologia Mystica* of the Pseudo-Dionysius, whose influence is powerfully felt in all these works. Another work is the *Epistle of Privy Counsel,* a kind of supplement to *The Cloud of Unknowing.*[21] First of the four other productions of this unknown writer is *Benjamin,* a paraphrase or free version of Richard of St. Victor's *Benjamin Minor.* Three minor works of semi-mystical nature from the same pen are: *Epistle of Prayer, Epistle on Discretion,* and *On Discerning of Spirits.*[22] The first English mystic whose name we know with certainty is Margery Kempe, an anchoress of Lynn, of whose writings until recently only a

orig. series, 106; the same modernized by F. M. Comper (Methuen, 1913). *The Form of Perfect Living,* ed. by G. Hodgson (London, 1910). See also *The Life and Lyrics of Richard Rolle* by F. M. Comper (London, 1928).

[19] *The Scale of Perfection,* ed. by Evelyn Underhill (London, 1923), *The Song of Angels,* in *The Cell of Self-Knowledge* (London, 1910), *The Minor Works of Walter Hilton,* ed. by Dorothy Jones (London, 1929).

[20] *The Cloud of Unknowing,* ed. by Evelyn Underhill (London, 3rd Edition, 1934).

[21] *The Cloud of Unknowing, Denis Hid Divinity,* and *The Epistle of Privy Counsel* are published by Justin McCann (London, 1924).

[22] These four works are reprinted from Pepwell's 1521 edition by E. Gardner in *The Cell of Self-Knowledge* (London, 1910).

fragment survived. This piece, *A Short Treatyse of Contemplacyon,* was written abou 1290.[23] The last of the English mystics of this period is Juliana of Norwich (1343-c. 1413), whose *Revelations of Divine Love* is described by Miss Underhill as the most beautiful of all English mystical works.[24] There is also an undetermined amount of mystical poetry, especially in the late medieval period, which is anonymous. Some of this poetry such as " Lord, I long after Thee," and " A Song of Love-longing to Jesus " belong to the " School of Richard Rolle." [25] Other examples of fourteenth century mystical poetry are: " Christ's Gift to Man," and " Ihesu that hast me dere I-bought." [26]

A version of *The Cloud of Unknowing* is the only one of these early treatises which appeared in the Elizabethan period. It was printed on the continent in 1582.[27] At the turn of the sixteenth century and for a few decades thereafter, there was a certain interest in these English mystical writings which is hard to demonstrate, and apparently centers among the Catholic recusants both in England and abroad. Professor Chambers points out that Colet and More were familiar with the works of Rolle and Hilton and with Nicholas Love's translation of the Pseudo-Bonaventure's *Meditations on the Life of Christ,* and he cites numerous references to them in fifteenth and sixteenth century manuscripts.[28] The early decades of the sixteenth century also felt the influence of the anonymous *Denis Hid Divinity.*[29] Margery Kempe's little treatise, as has already been noted, was printed in 1501 and

[23] It was reprinted by W. de Worde in 1501, by Pepwell in 1521; the modern edition is in Gardner's *Cell of Self-Knowledge.* See especially *The Booke of Margery Kempe,* ed. by W. Butler-Bowdon (London, 1936).

[24] *Revelations of Divine Love,* ed. by Grace Warrack (London, 8th Edition, 1923).

[25] Carleton Brown, *Religious Lyrics of the XIVth Century,* pp. 94-108.

[26] Carleton Brown, pp. 113-119. See also " Lord I long for Thee" in *Religious Lyrics of the XVth Century,* edited by Carleton Brown, p. 68.

[27] Cf. Justin McCann, *The Cloud of Unknowing,* p. 291.

[28] R. W. Chambers, *The Continuity of English Prose* (London, 1932), pp. cxxix and cxxvi, and *The Place of St. Thomas More in English Literature and History* (London, 1937), p. 32.

[29] *Ibid.,* p. cxxvi.

1521, and in 1519 a version of the *Dialogues* of St. Catherine of Sienna appeared with the title, *The Orcharde of Syon . . . the revelacyons of seynt Kathryn of Senis.*[30]   Walter Hilton's *The Scale of Perfection* and a few of his minor works seem to be the only works of these early mystics which went into several reprintings after the turn of the sixteenth century. *The Scale of Perfection* was printed by de Worde in 1494, 1519, 1525, and 1533; also by Julian Notary in 1507 and by Pynson in 1517.[31]

These truly English exemplars of the great Christian mystical tradition set in motion a current which continues fairly unabated up to the last quarter of the sixteenth century when it bursts forth with new vigor, and indeed grows much stronger in the next century with the Little Gidding group of Nicholas Ferrar, the Christian Platonists at Cambridge, and especially in the writings of Crashaw, Vaughan, Traherne, and others.

ENGLISH MYSTICAL LITERATURE OF FOREIGN ORIGIN

The accession of Queen Elizabeth in 1558 and a quarter of a century thereafter witnessed a steady flow of Christian mystical writings into England from foreign sources. This literature consisted largely of editions and translations of medieval and post-medieval mystical works from the continent; and their number indicates that Christian mysticism was well known and widely read in Elizabethan England.[32]

The spirit and methodology of Christian mysticism made it readily acceptable to spiritually-minded writers during the Elizabethan period, when religious polemic was so bitter and widespread. Easily detached from all external ecclesiastical order, subjective in nature, Christian mysticism furnished a means of fervent and personal intercourse and union with God.[33] The subject matter was found in Old and New Testament

---

[30] Cf. Gardner, p. xviii.

[31] Cf. Introd. to *Minor Works of W. Hilton*, and see Chambers, p. xxix.

[32] See Appendix for list of mystical writings published in England in the sixteenth century.

[33] Cf. Margaret L. Bailey, *Milton and Jakob Boehme*, cap. II, " English Mysticism before Boehme" (New York, 1914), pp. 31 ff.

story; the Christocentric and Theocentric types of contemplation satisfied the partisans of the prevailing sects or creeds, and the three Ways of the spiritual life were open alike to Protestant and Catholic.

The works of foreign origin which are analyzed in the following pages make up fully as much of the mystical literature of the Elizabethan period as do the writings of similar nature in the same period from the pens of England's native sons. Of the non-English works, only those are here considered which were an undoubted part of late sixteenth century literature; their influences even go beyond the limits set by the dates of Elizabeth's reign.

7

CHAPTER II

LE MIROIR DE L'ÂME PÉCHERESSE,
AND QUEEN ELIZABETH'S TRANSLATION

The first mystical work of foreign origin considered for its bearing on Christian mysticism in the Elizabethan age is a translation made by Elizabeth herself of a poem written by Queen Margaret of Navarre. This work, entitled, *Le Miroir de l'âme pécheresse* [1] was translated by the then Princess Elizabeth, and presented in her own handwriting as a New Year's gift to her step-mother Queen Katharine Parr in 1544. It bore the title, *The Mirror of the Sinful Soul*. The manuscript of Elizabeth's translation, together with her letter to the queen were reproduced in facsimile and edited with an introduction by Mr. Percy W. Ames. [2] It was printed in 1548 by John Bale under a title of his own: "*A Godly Medytacyon of the Christen soule,* compyled in French by lady Margaret Quene of Navarre; and aptly translated into Englysh by the right vertuose lady Elyzabeth, daughter to our late soverayne Kyng Henry the VIII—Emprinted in the yeare of oure Lorde 1548, in Apryll." [3] This work was of interest during the period not only for Elizabeth's part in it, but the original poem had aroused considerable discussion in France at a time when partisan religious feeling was running high. [4] Margaret was an

[1] The full title of the poem is *Le Miroir de l'âme pécheresse, onquel elle recongoist ses faultes et péchéz. aussi ses graces et benefices a elle faite, p. Jesuchrist son espout. La Marguerite tres noble et précieuse sest prepossé a ceulx qui de bon cueur la cerchoient. A Alincon, 1531.* This work was first published with date in 1531; it was reprinted in 1533 together with three other mystical pieces: *Dialogue en forme de vision nocturne; Discord entre l'esprit et la chair*, and *L'oraison a Jésus-Christ*. Other editions: Lyons, 1538, Geneva, 1539, Paris, 1547, 1556. (Felix Frank, *Les Marguerites de La Marguerite des Princesses* [Paris, 1873], p. lxxxvi.)

[2] *The Mirror of the Sinful Soul,* a prose translation from the French of a Poem by Queen Margaret of Navarre, made in 1544 by the then Princess (afterwards Queen) Elizabeth (London, 1897).

[3] Frank, *op. cit.*, p. xc; cf. Cooper, *Athenae Cantab.* (Camb. 1858), I, 229. See Appendix for reference to two other editions.

[4] Fernand Mourret, *Histoire Gén. de L'Eglise*, trans. by N. Thompson (St. Louis, 1930), V, 453.

82

avowed champion of the Reform,[5] and her poem, the *Miroir,* was condemned by the theological faculty of the Sorbonne.[6] The work itself was innocent of cause of unbiased censure. Its theme lay wholly within the tradition of Christian mysticism as set forth in numerous " Specula " or " Mirrors " which were popular from the medieval period.[7]

Theodore Beza and John Bale were loud in their praises of Elizabeth's *Mirror of the Sinful Soul*[8] for the same reasons that the members of the new " Cénacle of Meux " saw in it an illustration of their religious ideals of a personal communion with God, motivated and enlightened by the sole authority of the Scriptures.[9] These qualities inherent in mystical treatises attracted Luther, who in 1518 published an incomplete edition of the anonymous fourteenth century *Theologica Germanica,* and frequently relied upon the works of Eckhart, Tauler, and other German mystics.[10]

The nature of the *Miroir* was summarized by Elizabeth in the letter prefixed to her translation.

It is intytled, or named ye miroir or glasse, of the synneful soule where in is conteyned, how she (beholding and contempling [contemplating] what she is) doth perceyue how, of herselfe, and of

[5] For Margaret's Protestant sympathies and the contradictions in her conduct and writings, see P. Jourda, *Marguerite d'Angoulême, Duchesse d'Alençon, Reine de Navarre* (1492-1549), (Paris, 1931), II, 1065-1066.
[6] Mourret, p. 453.
[7] See especially the *Speculum Peccatoris,* a medieval work attributed to St. Augustine, *P. L.,* XL, 991; also *Speculum Amatorum Mundi* and *Speculum Conversionis* by Denis the Carthusian, whose writings attained great popularity during the sixteenth century. His mystical writings: *Opuscula aliquot quae ad theoriam mysticam egregie instituunt,* were collected and published at Cologne in 1534. Perhaps the best known of the " Mirrors " is an anonymous French work which was translated by an unknown English contemplative with the title, *The Mirror of Simple Souls.* Both are medieval products. The *Miroir* of Queen Margaret through Elizabeth's published version made its appearance in English mystical literature after another *Miroir,* similar in style and matter, had been translated into English by Margaret of Richmond, mother of Henry VII. It was printed by Wynken de Worde in 1522, and bore the title, *The Mirroure of Golde to the Synfull Soule.*
[8] Frank, *op. cit.,* p. lxii.
[9] Mourret, p. 445 ff.
[10] For a list of German mystics quoted by Luther, see Denifle-Paquier, *Luther et le Lutheranisme* (Paris, 1910), vol. I.

her own strenght, she can do nothing that good is, or preuayleth
for her saluaccion: onles it be through the grace of god.[11]

The three ways or stages of the mystical ascent: Purification, Illumination, and Union, are readily discerned in this
work, which is also in accord with the Christocentric type
of contemplation. As part of the purgative process, one observes at the outset the brief evidence of a "conversion"
which has taken place in Margaret's soul, and her decision to
change the tenor of her life for the better.[12] Man cannot accomplish the miracle of his own conversion. "But," she writes
"it shall be the onely good grace of almighty god wich is never
slake to prevent us with hys mercy."[13] The ascetic note of the
Purgative way is sounded in a desire for renewal of baptismal
vows, of mortification of the flesh; and the passion and cross
of Christ are to be ever before her eyes.[14] Margaret begins to
confess her faults and spiritual indifference with hesitancy and
fear; but gradually she succeeds in unburdening her soul with
perfect openness and candor. She closes this section with these
favorite expressions of the mystics, taken from the Song of
Songs:

O my father, brother childe, and spowse, with hands joyned,
humbly upon my kness, i yelde the thanks, and praise, that it pleas-
eth the to turn thy face towards me, converting my hart, and
couering me with such grace, that thou dost se no more my yvels.[15]

The "New Life" in Christ now becomes a veritable death;
the death of worldly ideals, and the passions. "And by death,
i am ravished with hym, wich is alive."[16] The meditation upon
death, tinged with that tender melancholy which is marked in

---

[11] MS., page 3. Pagination refers to the pages of the manuscript in Mr.
Ames' edition.
[12] MS., pp. 10-13 (Frank, pp. 16-18). Professor La Franc saw in this
poem "the supreme evolution accomplished by this great soul in the course
of the three or four years which preceded and followed the death of Francis
I" (*Les Dernières poésies de Marguerite de Navarre* [Paris, 1896], p. 43).
[13] *Ibid.*, "la seule bonne grâce/ Du toutpuissant, qui jamais me se lasse./
Nous prévenir par se miséricorde" (Frank, p. 18). The original poem edited
by Professor Frank (*op. cit.*) is cited throughout.
[14] MS., p. 16 (Frank, p. 19).
[15] MS., p. 37 (Frank, p. 29).   [16] MS., p. 77 (Frank, p. 49).

the mystics, is followed by a plea for union in the language of the Pseudo-Dionysius. " Syth that i can not yet se my spowse: transforme me with hym both body and soule." [17]

The Purgative way merges gradually into the Illuminative way in Margaret's verse and Elizabeth's prose. There is a notable influence of the popular *De Contemptu Mundi* pieces of the mystics as the soul turns from the world, and aided by grace begins to contemplate the Deity.

Now syth that i have the i do forsake all them that be in the world. . . . Syth that i se the, i will loke upon nothing that shuld kepe me frome the beholding [contemplation] of thy diuinitie.[18]

The warm effulgence of grace which pours into the soul is characteristic of the Illuminative way. Margaret's reliance upon grace,[19] and her insistence on its utter necessity [20] to an apparent exclusion of ecclesiastical forms and rites are reasons for the unusual popularity of her poem among the sympathizers with the Reform. However, it is in chanting the praises of divine love that the *Miroir* ranks among the great religious love poems of the sixteenth century. The following lines are typical:

Hys desyre is to love me, and through hys love, he causeth my heart to be inflamed with love; and through such love, he fyndeth himselfe so well beloved: that hys own dede yeldeth hym content, and not myne owne love, or strenght. Contentinge himselfe, hys love doth increase more in me, than i can desyre of hym. O true lover, springe of all charitie, and the onely purse of the heavenly treasure.[21]

The eye cannot look at the sun because of its great brilliance; even so, the soul which feels but a " sparkle " of the divine love perceives this love so great and marvelous, so sweet and good, that it is impossible to declare what it really is.[22] That soul which has once felt this passing great fire, ever afterward lives languishing, desiring, and sighing.[23]

[17] MS., p. 80: " Mon doux espoux, par vostre grand puvoir,
    Transformez moy en luy toute vivante "
                                                (Frank, p. 49).

[18] MS., p. 85 (Frank, p. 52).   [21] MS., p. 118 (Frank, p. 64).
[19] MS., p. 21 ((Frank, p. 21).   [22] MS., p. 113 (Frank, p. 64).
[20] MS., p. 13 (Frank, p. 64).   [23] *Ibid.*

The way to the mystical union was just this. All the elements of a true personal experience are discernible in Margaret's descriptions of the Unitive part of the mystic ways. Through contemplation, she says, man arrives at heaven and a vision of the divine attributes.[24] The purgation from sin, and the meditation on death made a " ladder " for ascent " unto the goodly citee of iherusalem." [25] This union of the soul with God is variously spoken of as a " transformation," [26] a " joining," [27] a " ravishment," [28] and the marriage of the soul with her celestial spouse.[29] The mortal soul is considered in the mystic union as joined to the immortality of God; and that which is still mortal finds itself filled with the eternal.[30] The close of the poem recalls the vision and ecstasy of St. Paul which is familiar to the mystics, and it ends with a simple prayer to this Apostle, " who hast tasted of the same switte honye, beyng blinded for the space of three days, and ravished into the third heaven." [31]

The *Miroir* accurately reflects the many and various mystical influences in the personal life of its author. It is known that Queen Margaret studied the works of Nicholas of Cusa,[32] and her correspondence with the Abbot Briçonnet reveals a mutual understanding of the principles of Christian mysticism.[33] Briçonnet sent Margaret a number of German mystical works,[34] and consequently the influence of Ruysbroeck's *Spiritual Marriage* is especially noticeable in the *Miroir*.[35] The influence of the Pseudo-Dionysius, whose writings were well known in France, especially through the edition of Lefevre d'Etaples,[36]

---

[24] MS., p. 103 (Frank, p. 60).
[25] *Ibid.*
[26] MS., p. 94 (Frank, p. 55).
[27] MS., p. 109 (Frank, p. 63).
[28] MS., p. 77 (Frank, p. 48).

[29] MS., p. 101 (Frank, p. 59).
[30] MS., p. 112 (Frank, p. 64).
[31] MS., p. 117 (Frank, p. 66).
[32] Mourret, p. 446.
[33] Cf. Frank, p. lvi.

[34] Carlo Pellegrine, *La prima opera di Margarita di Navarra* (Catania, 1920), p. 23.

[35] In the frequent allusions to the Spouse of the soul, and the Spiritual marriage. This is, of course, found frequently in St. Bernard and other mystics.

[36] Lefevre also edited Ruysbroeck's *Ornement des noces spirituelles* (Mourret, p. 445).

is potent in the *Miroir*.[37] Margaret was counted among the Humanists, and in their circles the Dionysian writings were popular. Dante's *Divina Commedia* was also a source of inspiration to the Queen.[38]

This translation of Queen Elizabeth initiated a new species of English religious literature of mystical transcendence and spiritual fervor—the literature which flows in the main current of sixteenth century letters between the Platonic poetry of profane love and the writings of ordinary religious devotion.

[37] In such Dionysian expressions as " deification," " transformation," etc.
[38] Pellegrine, pp. 15-21.

CHAPTER III

GEORGE COLVILLE'S TRANSLATION OF BOETHIUS

The *Consolation of Philosophy* of Boethius,[1] translated by George Colville, marks an important contribution to the literature of Christian mysticism in the Elizabethan period. English literature was early acquainted with this work of Boethius through translations of King Alfred,[2] Chaucer,[3] and Lydgate, and through the commentaries of Asser and Grosseteste, Bishop of Lincoln. Queen Elizabeth translated the *Consolation* in 1593,[4] not, however, for any hope of literary reward since her work was not printed at the time. This somewhat free and often labored rendering of Boethius is but one of a number of translations which the learned queen undertook during her life.[5]

Of George Colville very little is known. His translation of Boethius' *Consolation* is always associated with his name and gives him his place in literature.[6] It was first published by John Cawood in 1556, and enjoyed a second printing in 1561. The work is of greatest value in that the translator definitely Christianizes what he deemed to be a Christian work.[7] Professor Patch has pointed out that among all the translators and commentators of Boethius, Colville appears to be the only one to make his author lead men to contemplation.[8]

[1] See Part I, p. 34.   [2] Ed. by W. J. Sedgefield (Oxford, 1899).
[3] Ed. by W. W. Skeat, *Complete Works of Chaucer*, vol. II (Oxford, 1894).
[4] *Queen Elizabeth's Englishings of Boethius, De Consolatione Philosophiae, A. D. 1593*. Ed. from the MS. by Caroline Pemberton, *E. E. T. S.*, orig. *series*, 113, 1899.
[5] Cf. *ibid.*, p. vii.
[6] *Boethius' Consolation of Philosophy, translated by George Colville*, ed. by Ernest Belfort Bax (London, 1897).
[7] "There was a noble man, a consul of Rome named Boecius, this man was a catholike man, and dysputed for the faith in the comon counsayle agaynste Nestoryus and Euthichen, as it appeareth by a booke that he made, wherein he proueth two natures in Chryste" (Colville, p. 5).
[8] H. R. Patch, *The Tradition of Boethius*, p. 76. Before this work of Colville there appeared a simplification of Boethius by the fifteenth century mys-

Colville succeeds in making clear the Christian character of the *Consolation* by adding words and phrases to the original; thus making at times more of a paraphrase than a literal translation. He also resorts to marginal comments or " glosses." He tempers Platonic passages to conform with orthodox Christian philosophy as in the curious explanation of Plato's doctrine of reminiscence.[9] The Platonic concept of Boethius, that happy men are gods through the desire of beatitude draws the translator's marginal comment: " The Prophet says, ye are all gods." [10] The references to the patience of Job under affliction, and to the apostles Thomas and Peter indicate the spirit and method of the translator.[11] Boethius' Platonic rhapsody wherein love is considered as the efficient cause and the unifying power in the universe is rendered sympathetically by Colville,[12] as, indeed, it is a favorite concept of St. Augustine,[13] the Pseudo-Dionysius,[14] and St. Thomas.[15] The love of God governs both the land and the sea, and the heavens, and composes the four elements which are naturally contrary to each other. So, too, divine love conserves virtuous folk, it knits man and wife together in chaste wedlock, and is the basis for enduring friendship.[16] This is the outflowing of that divine love which returns to its source and make up the well-known " circle of love." Colville gives the following simple paraphrase:

Thou sowest the soules in heven, and in the earth, that is to say, into aungels . . . and bodyes of mankind on the erth[;] whyche soules of mankynde, when they be convertyd unto the, by thy benygne or gentle love—thou causest them so to retourn, by thy turnynge fyer, of charitable loue.[17]

tic, Denis the Carthusian. It is significant that this work was printed (Cologne, 1540) in one volume which included his *Commentaries* on the Pseudo-Dionysius and the *Spiritual Ladder* of St. John Climacus.

[9] "And if the muse or wysedome of Plato soundeth truth, euery *forgetfull* man *recordeth* the thing he lerned before" (Colville, p. 82; compare with original in *P. L., LXIII, lib. III,* 177 ff.

[10] *Ibid.,* p. 75; cf. Ps. lxxxi. 6.

[11] *Ibid.,* p. 110. The *Consolation* reveals a certain spiritual affinity with the Books of Job and Ecclesiastes.

[12] *Ibid.,* p. 32.

[13] *De Quant. Animae, P. L., XXXII,* 1035.

[14] *De Div. Nom., P. G., III,* 699.

[15] *Summa Theol.,* I, *Q.* 26, *a.* 2.   [16] *Ibid.,* p. 32.

[17] *Ibid.,* p. 72; compare original text, *P. L., LXIII, lib. III, metrum IX.*

The chariots in which Plato and Boethius conceived the souls
of just men to be borne through the heavens become for Colville the " light carts " or the stars of heaven which guide the
souls of men to God.[18]

The mystical nature of the work, in brief, grows out of the
words which Boethius puts in the mouth of the Lady, Wisdom
or Philosophy. She consoles him with that divine science which
gradually frees his soul from despondency, from the trials of
exile, and the mutable ways of Fortune, and lifts him above
the vanities of life to fix his gaze upon the Immutable Being
whose Providence guides all things.[19] Boethius observed, on
the appearance of the vision, the Greek letters π and τ enwoven
on her vesture with a series of steps or degrees conjoining
them. Colville explains the significance of these letters :

> In the lower parte of the sayde vesture was read the Greke letter
> .P. wouen[,] whych signifyeth practise or actyffe (in the work of
> the body above worldly things),[20] and the hygher part of the ves-
> tures the Greke letter .T. whyche standeth for theoretica, that sig-
> nifieth speculacion or contemplation (occupying the mind in vir-
> tues and godly things, contemning the world).[21]

This division of Christian spirituality into the active and the
contemplative life is a commonplace in mystical theory. St.
Augustine first made a complete study of the distinction, and
he, not unlike Boethius, deemed the contemplative life as one
spent in the intellectual perception or intuition of truth which
was for him primarily religious in character, since his religious
experiences were primarily intellectual.[22] The active life consisted in the fulfilment of the obligations of duty and charity.
This division of the active and the contemplative life set the
standard for mysticism in the West, and it is found repeatedly
in treatises on the spiritual life.[23] It is frequently illustrated

---

[18] *Ibid.*   [19] Bk. I, cap. 2, 6; Bk. V. cap. 6.
[20] Words in parentheses are from the margin of translation.
[21] *Op. cit.,* p. 12; cf. *P. L.,* LXIII, 589.
[22] *De Civit. Dei,* cap. XIX, 19.
[23] St. Augustine, *Sermones,* CCLV and CLXXIX; *Contra Faustum,* XXII;
Julius Pomerius (c. 500), *De Vita Contemplativa, lib.* I, II. *P.L.,* LIX;
St. Bernard, *Serm.* (ed. Mabillon), I, 76; II, 1020; 1348; 1724; St. Thomas
Aquinas, *Summa Theol.* II-II, *Q.* 182, 1; *Q.* 188, 6; Ruysbroeck, *The*

by Leah [24] and Martha [25] as of the active life, while Rachel and Mary portray the life of contemplation.[26]

In prose and verse filled with classic allusion and sober reflection on the inconstancy of temporal things, Wisdom convinces Boethius that true happiness is to be found in himself alone,[27] and in a complete inward turning of the mind from the vanities of the world.[28] The theme of a purgation of the soul is taken up as a prerequisite to the contemplative ascent to God. " First," says Colville, " vice must be removed from a man before virtue can enter," [29] and he proceeds to paraphrase the homely ascetic advice of Boethius :

> He that wyll sowe a goodly felde with corne, fyrst he must ryd the same felde of shrubes and thorns, and cutte awaye the bushes and ferne with hoke or syth, that the newe corne may grow and encrease with ful eres.[30]

Sensible pleasures of whatsoever kind must be under the control of reason, " for he that follows the pleasures of the body is servant of the body," comments Colville in Pauline terms.[31] The safe haven of refuge from " the wicked chain of deceitful pleasures " is in God alone, in whom " is perfect felicity and rest from labors." [32]

The ascent of the soul in contemplation follows closely upon its detachment from the world.[33] This is exemplified by Boethius in a masterly abridgment of a part of the *Timaeus* in the third book,[34] and of the beautiful Hymn of Book Four, where

---

Spiritual Marriage, II, 65; *Meditationes Vitae Christi, S. Bonaventurae Opera Omnia*, XII, 570; *ibid.*, cc. 50, 51, 54, 55; *Walter Hilton, The Scale of Perfection*, cc. II, III.

[24] Cf. Genesis, xxix.   [25] Cf. Luke, x, 40-41.

[26] St. Gregory, *Hom. on Ezech.*, II, ii, 9, 10; I, iii, 9; *Mor. on Job*, VI, 56-61; Richard of St. Victor, *Benj. Minor, P. L.*, 196, cc. III, IV; *Medit. Vitae Christi*, p. 570; Walter Hilton, " The Mixed Life " in *Minor Works*, cap. ix, *op. cit.*, p. 32.

[27] This is the main burden of the first two books of the *Consolation*.

[28] Colville, p. 81; cf. *P. L.*, LXIII, *lib.* III, *metrum* XI.

[29] *Ibid.*, p. 54 in margin.

[30] *Ibid.*, cf. *lib.* III, *metrum* I.   [31] *Ibid.*, p. 66; cf. Rom. vi. 16.

[32] *Ibid.*, p. 77 and p. 87 not in original. Cf. *lib.* III, *metrum* X.

[33] Colville's marginal note, p. 89.

[34] Cf. Jowett's trans., III, 448-462; Colville, pp. 71-72; *lib.* III, *metrum* IX.

the soul winged, soars to the very throne of God in a manner that is reminiscent of the well-known mystic vision of Augustine at Ostia. Colville thus renders it in his own words.

Certes, I have swift feathers, that is to say, virtue and wisdom, that ascends unto the high heaven. Which feathers, when a swift mind has put on—it being disdainful, despises all earthly things and surmounts the globe, that is to say, the great body of the airy element, and sees the clouds behind his back,[35] and passes the top of the fiery element . . . until it rests in the house and place of the stars, and joins her ways with the sun. . . . The said mind being a knight of the shining star, that is to say of God, passes the circle of the stars, that is to say of the starry heaven, in all places; then it passes higher until it leaves the higher and uppermost firmament . . . obtaining might of the revered sight, that is to say, of God. There, beyond the highest firmament, the Lord of kings holds His sceptre, and tempers the rules or governments of the whole world.

O thou mind of mankind, if the way thou art now forgetful of, dost seek for, would bring thee thither, that is to say, unto the knowledge of GOD, after thou hast forsaken all worldly things, thou couldst say unto me, I do remember this is my country, here was I born, here will I fasten my step, that is to say, here will I rest.[36]

Colville's final comment is that this heavenly contemplation alone serves to convince man that his soul is of greater value than his body.[37] He concurs with the salutary conclusion of Boethius that the great problems of evil, of God's prescience, and human freedom are of secondary importance to the man who is in accord with Him who sees all things.[38]

The *Consolation* of Boethius and Colville's translation have a kinship with those expositions of Christian mysticism which emphasize an ascetic contempt of the world, its mutability, and the vanity of temporal things. To this is added the Theocentric type of contemplation wherein the earth-liberated soul rises from sensible things to the Creator. The treatises of this *De Contemptu Mundi genre* are very numerous in medieval and

[35] " Nubesque post tergum videt."
[36] Colville, pp. 89-90; cf. *lib.* IV, *metrum, I.* For sake of clarity I have modernized Colville's spelling.
[37] *Ibid.,* p. 133 in margin; cf. *lib.* V, *metrum* V.
[38] *Ibid.,* p. 138; cf. *lib.* V, *prosa* VI.

post-medieval Christian mysticism,[39] and they inspire an immense body of literature of a religious nature both on the continent and in England. The *Consolation* is one with much mystical literature in that it is a *vision* piece. The casting of religious thoughts and considerations into the form of a vision was exceedingly popular with the writers of mystical works. Suso's *Little Book of Eternal Wisdom* is a notable example. Moreover, the dialogue form which Boethius adopted was, since the *Soliloquium* of St. Augustine,[40] a favorite mode of expressing a didactic relationship between the mind of man and his soul or some supernatural entity, such as Wisdom or the Deity.[41]

[39] The following are notable examples: St. Bernard, *Sermons* (ed. Mabillon), pp. 358, 689; Hugh of St. Victor, *De Vanitate Mundi, P. L.,* CLXXVI; *Stimulus Amoris,* pars II, cap. 12; Lawrence Justinian, *De Contemptu Mundi, Opera Omnia* (Venice, 1751), Vol. II; Thomas à Kempis, *Imitation of Christ*; cf. also the important anonymous treatises which are mosaics of quotations from St. Augustine, St. Gregory, Alcuin, Boethius, etc. *P. L.,* XL; CLVIII; CLXXXIV; CLXXVII.

[40] *Soliloquiorum libri duo, P. L.,* XXXII.

[41] Cf. Hugh of St. Victor, *Soliloquium de Arrha Animae, P. L.,* CLXXVI; St. Bonaventure, *Soliloquium, Opera Omnia* (ed. Paris), XII, 85; Suso, *Little Book of Eternal Wisdom,* ed. by C. H. McKenna (London, 1910).

CHAPTER IV

MYSTICISM FROM ITALIAN SOURCES

The Italian influences upon early Tudor literature, which began with the Oxford Reformers and Wyatt and Surrey, grew in importance throughout the Elizabethan period. The influence of the Italian Neoplatonic humanists early exerted a powerful influence in England, which was first felt in the court circles but only long afterward by the people at large.[1] Dante and Petrarch, Tasso and Ariosto among the poets, Ficino and Pico della Mirandola among the Neoplatonist philosophers, Castiglione, model of the refined courtier, and Machiavelli were the leading representatives of the Italian Renaissance in England.

To what extent does Christian mysticism enter into the writings of the Italian Renaissance which were known and read in England? In general, the spirit and method of Christian mysticism is pronounced in Dante; is less so in Petrarch; and it furnishes but a part, albeit a very important part, of the basic spirit and method of the Christian Neoplatonists during the late fifteenth and early sixteenth centuries. In our consideration of the Italian group, the following order is employed:

> Dante and the *Divina Commedia*
> The mysticism of Petrarch
> Christian mysticism and the Italian Neoplatonists
> Benivieni's " Advice of Man to his Soul."

DANTE AND THE *Divina Commedia*

Dante's name comes into English literature for the first time by way of Chaucer, who mentions him no less than six times,[2] and whose *Hous of Fame* shows strongly the influence

---

[1] Lewis Einstein, *The Italian Renaissance in England* (New York, 1903), Introd. pp. VII, VIII; cf. also pp. 316 ff.

[2] Paget Toynbee, *Dante in English Literature from Chaucer to Cary* (New York, 1909), I, 1.

of the *Divina Commedia.*[3] Mr. Paget Toynbee has shown how
the interest in Dante, save for a period in the fifteenth century,
increased with the development of English literature. During
the reign of Elizabeth his name is frequently found in English
references to Italian writings, and brief translations into English from Dante occur in the works of eleven writers.[4] During
a period of less than thirty years, an Italian grammar expressly
written for a " better understanding of Boccaccio, Petrarch,
and Dante went through four editions." [5] That Sir Philip
Sidney had first-hand acquaintance with Dante is indicated in
his *Apologie for Poetrie*; and Spenser's editors have discovered
numerous parallels and resemblances with the *Divina Commedia*
in *The Faerie Queene* which, although undoubtedly close, do
not conclusively demonstrate actual imitation on the part of
Spenser.[6]

Dante's appeal to Elizabethan England was due no doubt
to a genuine interest in the *Divina Commedia* because of its
deeply religious character. But his real popularity was of
another sort. By a curious twist of fate this poet-scholar, who
incorporated in his masterpiece a veritable summary of medieval philosophy, theology, and mysticism, was accounted in England as a forerunner of the Reformation. Dante's clear distinction between erring churchmen and an unerring church was
lost sight of ; [7] and his unqualified exaltation of such doctrines
as Purgatory, communion of the saints, and prayers to Mary,
although abhorrent to the Reform leaders, was overlooked in
favor of his attacks upon popes and various ecclesiastics; and
his denunciations of prevailing ills in church and politics were
singled out from his great poem. Such stout champions of the
Reform in England as Bishop Jewell,[8] John Foxe,[9] and Law-

---

[3] Skeat, *Minor Poems of Chaucer* (Oxford, 1888, 2nd ed. 1896), p. lxx.

[4] Toynbee, *op. cit.,* p. xix, and *Dante Studies* (Oxford, 1921), pp. 176-179.

[5] *Principale rules of the Italian Grammar,* with a Dictionarie for the better
understandynge of Boccace, Petrarcha, and Dante, by William Thomas. First
published in 1550. Other editions : 1560, 1562, 1567.

[6] *Works of Edmund Spenser, Variorum Ed.* (Baltimore, 1932-), III, 401;
IV, 337; V, 352.

[7] Cf. *Purgatorio,* XX, 85-93.

[8] *A Defense of the Apologie of the Churche of Englande* (1567).

[9] *Book of Martyrs* (1570).

rence Humphrey [10] cited Dante to add color and authority to their partisan writings.[11] The *Theatre for Worldlings* of John van der Noodt names Dante among other great religious reformers past and present; and includes a number of celebrated medieval mystics, such as St. Bernard, St. Peter Damian, Gerson, and Denis the Carthusian. This recognition of a fellowship between the new reformers and the old served to emphasize the religious impulses and the noble mystical character of the *Divina Commedia*. Gabriel Harvey called Dante, " ryght inspired and enravished Poet," and " worthy to bee alleadged of Divines and Counsellours, as Homer is quoted by Philosophers and Oratours." [12] In the *Allegory* to his *Godfrey of Bulloigne: or the Recoverie of Jerusalem,* Edward Fairfax observed that the " Comedy of Dante " is a figure of " the Life of the Contemplative Man," and is a mixture of Action and Contemplation. It is a " Voyage " of " Contemplation of these Pains and Rewards which in another World are reserved for good or guilty souls." [13]

Dante's *Divina Commedia* contains an exposition of the basic principles and the inherent philosophy of medieval mysticism. Mr. Edmund Gardner has pointed out Dante's debt to the medieval mystics, notably St. Bernard, the Victorines, and St. Bonaventure. He has also shown numerous parallel passages in Dante and in mystical writings in the patristic and early medieval periods.[14] In the light of Christian mysticism many images of the great poem which we regard as so many flights of daring genius were familiar reminiscences of Dante.[15] In the famous letter to Can Grande,[16] Dante himself defended

[10] *Jesuitismi Pars Prima* (1582).

[11] " Dante the Reformer " is described at length by Alice Curtayne in *A Recall to Dante* (New York, 1932), pp. 75-98.

[12] Pierce's *Supererogation* (1593), in Grosart's *Prose Works,* II, 103.

[13] Quoted by Toynbee, *Dante in English Literature from Chaucer to Cary,* p. 102.

[14] *Dante and the Mystics* (London, 1912), pp. 342 ff.

[15] Frederick Ozanam, *Dante and Catholic Philosophy in the Thirteenth Century,* translated by Lucia Pychowska (New York, 1913), p. 313; cf. also Brother Azarias, *Phases of Thought and Criticism* (New York, 1892), pp. 125-182.

[16] *Epistle X.* This letter is now generally accepted as genuine by Dante

the actuality of the supreme vision in the *Paradiso* as a personal experience by direct reference to works of St. Bernard, Richard of St. Victor, St. Augustine, and the rapt vision of St. Paul.[17] Dante's evaluation of contemplation in the *Paradiso*,[18] and the prominence which he gives to the great medieval mystics bear out his own words that his poem " was written to lead to blessedness." [19] The Pseudo-Dionysius is he " who in the flesh saw deepest into the angelic nature and its ministry; " [20] so, too, Boethius is seen as " the sainted soul who unmasked the deceitful world." [21] St. Thomas and St. Bonaventure preside over the fourth heaven, that of contemplation, where are gathered hosts of contemplatives with Richard of St. Victor, " in contemplation, more than man." [22] The final ascent to the divine union was entrusted to St. Bernard who had himself tasted of the self-same peace whilst still on earth.[23]

The beginnings of Dante's mysticism are in the *Vita Nuova,* the *Convivio*, and the *Canzone*.[24] Therein love which is the ground and impulse of all mysticism undergoes a progressive purification and idealization, until it becomes the divine love that lifts Dante's soul through the three worlds of Hell, Purgatory, and Heaven. In the *Convivio*,[25] we observe the exaltation of intellectual and philosophical love which corresponds to the exalted mystical love of the *Paradiso*. The allegorical lady of

scholars. For a full discussion of its authenticity see Edward Moore, *Studies in Dante* (Oxford Clarendon Press, 1903), pp. 284-374.

[17] " Let them read Richard of St. Victor in his book *De Contemplatione,* let them read Bernard *De Consideratione,* let them read Augustine *De Quantitate Animae*" (*Epistle to Can Grande*, para. 28).

[18] *Par.,* XXII, 61-72; XXXI, 109-111.

[19] Epistle to Can Grande: "Not for speculation, but for practical effect was the whole work undertaken. . . . The end of the whole and of the parts is to remove those living in this life from the state of misery, and to lead them to the state of felicity" (X, 15-16).

[20] " che, giuso in carne, più addentro vide/l'angelica natura e il ministero " (*Par.,* X, 116-117).

[21] " l'anima santa, che il mondo fallace/fa manifesto " (*Par.,* X, 125-126).

[22] " che a considerar fu più che viro " (*Par.,* X, 132).

[23] " colui, che in questo mondo, contemplando, gustò di quella pace " (*Par.,* XXXI, 110-111).

[24] Gardner, *op. cit.,* p. 7 ff.

[25] *Canzone,* II, 16, 80-84. "The most perfect lyrical expression of the mysticism of the *Convivio* " (Gardner, p. 18).

8

the *Convivio,* philosophical wisdom, becomes transfigured into the glorified Beatrice, symbol of that wisdom which is revealed and divine.[26] In the *Vita Nuova,* the way of mystical contemplation takes its rise. At first we are dealing with the unrequited human love enkindled at the sight of Beatrice in her ninth year.[27] Dante tells us of "new matter, more noble than the past," and his love for Beatrice becomes unselfish and idealized after her death.[28] In the last sonnet in the *Vita Nuova,* Dante ascends, "a Pilgrim Spirit," [29] beyond this known world, and visualizes his lady, "round whom splendors move in homage." The *Divina Commedia* is in part the story of the contemplation of that pilgrimage.[30] This great poem is also one of the finest expositions of the theory that human and divine love are essentially one, coming from the same divine source, they differ only in degree. This conception is fundamental in Christian mysticism, and it is important for understanding of much Renaissance love poetry.[31]

The *Divina Commedia* belongs to the Pilgrimage of Life *genre* of Christian mystical expositions.[32] The poet, in the midway of life,[33] encounters the beasts which represent the chief passions of man; and, guided by Reason (Virgil), protected by Wisdom (Beatrice), Mercy (Virgin Mary), and Illuminating Grace (Lucia),[34] he sets out upon a new road.[35] It opens before him, long and difficult to negotiate. Discouragement,[36]

[26] Cf. Gardner, pp. 15-19.   [27] *Vita Nuova,* I.

[28] *Ibid.,* XXXV; XL. Cf. Jefferson B. Fletcher, *The Religion of Beauty in Woman* (New York, 1911), pp. 52-66.

[29] *Vita Nuova,* XLII, Canz. 25.

[30] *Ibid.,* XLIII.

[31] "In the thought process of [medieval] symbolism earthly love derived its significance solely and supremely from the fact that it was a type and symbol of the love existing in the court of heaven, and as such a step towards its comprehension and attainment" (H. Flanders Dunbar, *Symbolism in Medieval Thought* [New Haven, 1929], p. 56).

[32] See Part I, pp. 64-70.

[33] *Inf.,* I, 1.

[34] "Poscia che tai tre donne benedette/curan di te nella corte del coelo" (*Inf.,* II, 124-125). "Since three maids, so blest / Thy safety plan, e'en in the court of heaven" (Cary's trans.).

[35] *Inf.,* I, 91-93: "Another way pursue, if thou wouldst scape, / From out that savage wilderness" (Cary's trans.).

[36] *Inf.,* VIII, 100-103.

and sensuality,[37] the vices and virtues,[38] all play their part as they do in the life of Everyman; but Dante follows closely the guidance and instructions of his spiritual aides until he arrives wholly purified and enlightened at the end of the pilgrimage. This spiritual pilgrimage from the Dark Wood of error to the light and freedom of Paradise is by way of the three essential ways of Christian mysticism. The Purgative way includes the *Inferno,* and approximately the first thirty cantos of the *Purgatorio.*[39] The purificatory ministry of Dante's passage through the *Inferno* rests primarily upon the common medieval practice of " meditative examples," [40] i.e., the sight of the victims of the various sins, luxury, gluttony, avarice, etc., and the awful torments which these sins have induced. The evil of sin, its odious nature, and the necessity of work, energy, and personal goodness make up the moral lesson which Hell revealed to Dante. Human effort, even strained to the utmost in accomplishing the journey, could not suffice; and Dante relies constantly on supernatural assistance.[41]

The mystical import of the *Purgatorio* is clear.

> In which the human spirit from sinful blot
> Is purged, and for ascent to Heaven prepares.[42]

The discipline involved in the laborious and painful ascent of the seven terraces and the mount of Purgatory is varied. The letters of the seven capital sins are seared on Dante's brow; [43] and singly purged away as the living personifications of these

[37] *Ibid.,* IX, 55-57.

[38] *Purg.,* Canto X, wherein begins the purification by an exemplification of the vices and their opposite virtues.

[39] Cf. Gardner, p. 90. In view of the overlapping of these divisions in medieval treatises, one does not feel that Dante intended a rigid division such as Mr. Gardner discovers.

[40] Cf. Richard of St. Victor, *P. L.,* CXCVI, 819, 857; St. Bonaventure, *Soliloquium,* XII, 113-116.

[41] *Inf.,* XII, 2; XXXIV, 95; *Purg.,* II, 65-66; IV, 33. "Here in the *Commedia* is a story completely apposite to the mystical tradition of progress through the way of purgation" (Dunbar, *op. cit.,* p. 376).

[42] *Purg.,* I, 5-6 (Cary's trans.), cf. also *ibid.,* I, 94-99.

[43] *Ibid.,* IX, 112-114.

virtues and vices slowly pass before his vision. He advances farther and farther in the way of perfection, while his soul grows lighter and more eager to mount the summit.[44] Finally, the poet passes through the fire that wholly cleanses,[45] and at the Earthly Paradise [46] Reason (Virgil) leaves him in the charge of Beatrice,[47] " she who makes blessed "; and thus conducts him " pure and apt for mounting to the stars," [48] along the Illuminative way.

Thus the end of the Purgative way and the beginning of the Illuminative way are conjoined in *Purg.* XXVII-XXX, wherein the dream vision of Leah and Rachel (representatives of the active and the contemplative life),[49] the instructions given in the Earthly Paradise,[50] and the passage through the water of Lethe, indicate the end of the purificatory period. The presentation of Dante to the seven virtues [51] and to the Christ-Griffon [52] presage the Illuminative way.

The Illuminative way embraces, in general, the first twenty cantos of the *Paradiso*.[53] It is a road infinitely higher than that which Dante has just traversed, and is a way of enlightenment and instruction from blessed saints and sages.[54] The ascent of the spheres is accomplished through supernatural grace, and the love which radiates from the face of Beatrice.[55] This too has its rich allegorical meaning. This portion of the *Paradiso* is eminently the Christocentric type of contemplation.[56] Mr. Gardner notes the " impassioned contemplation of Christ," as well as Dante's debt to such pieces as St. Bonaventure's *Lignum Vitae*.[57] Although the Christ-pattern perme-

[44]   . . . pungeami la fretta
          Per la impacciata via (*ibid.*, XXI, 4-5).
[45] *Ibid.*, XXVII, 49-51.
[46] *Ibid.*, XXVIII.   [47] *Ibid.*, XXX, 49-50; 73-76.
[48] " Puro e disposto a salire alle stelle " (*ibid.*, XXXIII, 145).
[49] *Purg.* XXVII, 100-109.   [51] *Ibid.*, XXXIII, 1-15.
[50] *Ibid.*, XXVIII.   [52] *Ibid.*, XXXI, 112-114.
[53] Mr. Gardner gives over the entire *Paradiso* save the last three cantos to the Illuminative way (*op. cit.*, p. 91).
[54] Cf. for example, *Par.*, X.   [55] *Par.*, XIV, 82-84.
[56] His [Dante's] visionary journey is, however, an allegorical representation of the literal earthly life of Christ " (Dunbar, p. 63).
[57] *Op. cit.*, pp. 216-217.

ates the entire *Paradiso,* it is in the second, seventh, and fourteenth cantos that Christ is considered in vivid, staccato lines.
Of vital bearing on the mystery of the Incarnation are the brief
accounts of the angelic creation,[58] their fall, and the primal
sin of man.[59] The redemption and the crucifixion are explained in relation to the vicarious atonement and the satisfaction of divine justice.[60] In the magnificent close of the fourteenth canto, Dante rises to poetic heights of rapture and
ecstasy which are brought on by the vision of the victorious
cross of Christ; for to Dante and the mystics, the central fact
of Christ's life was his death.

The Unitive way begins approximately with the twenty-first
canto of the *Paradiso.* Dante turns his gaze away from
Beatrice, and comes to perceive the essences of things divine.[61]
He sees the ladder of contemplation which ascends to heaven,
and converses with Peter Damian,[62] Benedict,[63] and hosts of
contemplatives who prepare the poet for the supreme vision reserved for him in the Empyrean. With each successive vision,
new truths impress him. St. Bernard, " quel contemplante,"
takes the place of Beatrice.[64] The sublime song to Mary [65]
records Dante's emotions, and then: " my vision becoming un-
dimmed, more and more entered the beam of light, which itself
is Truth." [66] The veil dropped; the poet enjoyed for a " brief,
trembling glance," the intimacy of divine union:

> Thus my mind, entirely suspended, with marveling was trans-
> fixed, motionless and attentive; and ever enkindled by its gazing. . . .
> My mind was smitten by a flash, and lo, in the high vision all power
> failed me. But already my desire and will were rolled,—even as a
> wheel that moveth equally—by the Love that moves the sun and the
> other stars.[67]

---

[58] *Par.,* VII, 130-133.

[59] *Ibid.,* 25-27.

[60] *Ibid.,* 28-120.

[61] *Par.,* XXI, 16-18; 85-87.

[62] *Ibid.,* 25-90.

[63] *Ibid.,* XXII, 61-72, wherein contemplation alone is said to lead to this
timeless and spaceless life; the ladder of Jacob is planted upon the star of
abstinence and contemplation and reaches to the heavens.

[64] *Ibid.,* XXXII, 1.

[65] *Par.,* XXXIII, 1-39.

[66] *Ibid.,* 52-54.

[67] *Ibid.,* 97-99; 140-145. Translation based upon that of P. H. Wickstead,
Temple Classics (London, 1899).

The Theocentric type of contemplation forms the framework of Dante's ascent from the visible to the invisible heavens, and finally to the contemplation of the attributes and the essence of God. It is a metaphysical pilgrimage fully in keeping with the methodology of the medieval mystics and the cosmology of St. Thomas. Mr. Gardner rightly observes " that Bonaventure and Dante are merely kindred spirits in the same road, working from the same mystical sources. . . . The general conception of the soul's ascent, though differing in details, is essentially the same in both." [68]

Dante represents all nature and all plant and animal life as part of a universal framework wholly attuned to its Creator in a universal harmony. His is the typical ascent of the mind to God familiar to us in the rather cold prose tracts of the mystics, but by Dante enshrined in cantos of magnificent poetry. After his journey through Hell, the poet climbs the hill of Purgatory, and then by actual ascent and contemplation he traverses the nine moving spheres. Here he meets in turn the nine hierarchies of angels, each of whom has in its charge the nine celestial spheres. He pauses briefly on his flight upward, and he looks down upon the little earth which he has left behind. He is moved to smile and to " deem him wisest who esteems it the least, and he whose thoughts are turned from it, is truly good." [69]

In the Primum Mobile, last of the spheres and nearest Paradise, Dante reviews the order and offices of the triple ranks of the angelic " Intelligences," as they had been arranged by the Pseudo-Dionysius, " eye witness to heaven's mysteries." [70] He ascends at last to the Empyrean or motionless heaven of the blessed. He there beholds the saints and martyrs grouped so as to form the deep-set petals of a rose, which glows softly red in the light of the Beatific Vision. Here indeed is the climax of the *Paradiso*: the vision of the attributes and essence of God. Dante had already disclosed the nature of the attributes of

[68] *Op. cit.*, p. 253.
[69] *Par.*, XXII, 133-138. This is an echo of the familiar *Contemptus Mundi* mystical literature.
[70] *Ibid.*, XXVIII, 98-132.

God, and had given priority of place to Love and Wisdom.[71]
Earlier, too, in the poem, Dante had beheld the Deity from
afar off as a point of intensest Light; [72] but now that the great
Experience was his, he, like so many of the mystics, referred
to it no more.   The *Paradiso* closes and Dante's great pilgrimage ends as does the Theocentric form of contemplation in a
rapturous vision, and in a semi-comprehension of the whole
Mystery in the White Light of the One in Three.

PETRARCH

The influence of Petrarch began in English literature with
the poetry of Chaucer,[73] and reached its highest point during
the last decades of the sixteenth century.[74] Sixteenth century
imitators of the great Italian poet were called " Petrarchists ";
and their use of the sonnet form did much to make this mode
of poetic expression a favorite one in the Elizabethan period.[75]
The marked Petrarchian vogue began with the publication in
Tottel's *Miscellany* [76] of thirty-one sonnets by Sir Thomas
Wyatt, of which about a third are either translations or para-
phrases of Petrarch. The fashion of writing sonnets and
sonnet-sequences was at its height in London at the close of
the century, which witnessed the appearance of numerous editions of Petrarch's *Canzoniere*.[77] The *Triumphs* of Petrarch
were translated by Henry Parker Lord Morley in 1554, and
the *De Remediis Utriusque Fortunae* was translated by Thomas

---

[71] *Ibid.*, XV, 73-75.

[72] *Ibid.*, XXVIII, 16-18.

[73]   . . . The laureate poete,
                          . . . Whos rethorike swete
                          Enlumined all Itaille of poetrie "

(*Clerke's Prologue*, 31-33) ; cf. Robert D. French, *Handbook of Chaucer*
(New York, 1927), pp. 55, 290 ff.

[74] Cf. Sydney Lee, *Great Englishmen of the Sixteenth Century* (New York,
1904), pp. 78-79; 16; 196. The general influence of Petrarch on English
literature is treated by Peter Borghesi, *Petrarch and his Influence on English
Literature* (Bologna, 1906). See especially pp. 27 ff.

[75] Raymond M. Alden, *English Verse* (New York, 1903), p. 273.

[76] 1557, the first of four editions; the last in 1574.

[77] Borghesi, *op. cit.*, p. 29.

Twyne in 1579 as *Physick against Fortune*.[78] *The Visions of Petrarch formerly translated* (from Marot's rendering of them) was one of Edmund Spenser's early productions.[79] The somewhat melancholy, moralizing, and didactic nature of these pieces by Petrarch satisfied a taste for this type of literature among English readers. It is noteworthy that much of this is in the spirit of the *Contemptus Mundi* portions of authentic Christian mystical writings.

Lord Morley represented perhaps the general opinion of six- teenth century England when he wrote of " this famous clerke Petrarche," whose *Triumphs* treated of " al moral virtue, all Philosophye, all story, all matters, and briefly many devyne sentences theologicall secretes declared." [80] This statement leads us to inquire into Petrarch's mysticism, and thus discover another aspect of Christian mysticism in the Elizabethan age.

M. Cochin has observed that a book might be written en- titled " Petrarch and Mysticism," which would correspond to the excellent *Petrarch and Humanism* by M. de Nolhac.[81] First of the great humanists, Petrarch was a mystic by nature, and a Platonist by adoption.[82] And at the outset it can be said that Petrarch reflects the mystical spirit of St. Augustine rather than the developed and systematic methodology of the great medieval mystics. The basis for Petrarch's mysticism rests primarily upon his philosophy of love. In the *Canzoniere* human love is celebrated not only as a powerful human passion, but also as a noble desire for union with God. Petrarch's love was " a passion ardent and coarse at the outset, but restrained by the honor and virtue of the lady whom he loved; and this,

---

[78] Morley's *Triumphs* and Twyne's *Physick against Fortune* are found together in one volume now in the British Museum.

[79] Published in Van der Noodt's *Theatre for Worldlings* in 1569, and in *Complaints Containing Sundrie Small Poems of the World's Vanitie* in 1591.

[80] *The Triumphs of Petrarch*, translated by Henry Parker Lord Morley, reprinted by Stafford Henry, Earl of Iddesleigh (London, 1878), p. xxvii.

[81] Henri Cochin, " Le frère de Pétrarque," in *Revue d'histoire et de Litt. Rel.*, 1901, p. 43.

[82] Camillo Pellizi, *Franciscan Thought and Modern Philosophy in St. Francis of Assisi: 1226: 1926: Essays in Commemoration* (London, 1926), p. 209.

purified by sorrow at her death, was raised to an ideal love, and too, finally transformed into the love of God." [83]

This is a working out of that conception which regards all love as of divine origin—the human and the divine differing only in kind, not in degree. In its application to Laura, Petrarch conjoins two potent streams of love-philosophy current in the middle ages: that of the theory and practice of the Provençal poets with the spirit and method of Plato's *Symposium,* and the doctrine of divine love as worked out by the Christian mystics from St. Augustine and the Pseudo-Dionysius to St. Thomas Aquinas.[84] Petrarch was a lineal descendant of the troubadours of Languedoc and Provence, whom he termed his fellow-servants in Love.[85] Their somewhat sophisticated and self-conscious " courtly love " was precedent to Petrarch's adoration *a longe* of his Laura. With this, Petrarch embodied in his poetry a truly mystical love-philosophy which was ulti- mately Platonic, but became codified in Christian writings to such an extent that a possible substitution of *love* for *charity,* of *Eros* for *Amor,* would convert a treatise or poem on divine love into a rhapsody of a human model. The mystics wrote about love which comes from heaven and returns in a " divine circle," [86] which is rather an attraction for the soul or mind than for the body.[87] They analyzed love which induced a rest- less longing for possession,[88] and it became part of their hymns

[83] Henri Cochin, *La Chronologie du Canzoniere de Pétrarque* (Paris, 1898), p. 139.

[84] The authoritative explanations of the nature of love are those of the Pseudo-Dionysius in the famous *Hymns of Hierothaeus* (*P. G.*, III, 713), and the *Commentary* of St. Thomas upon Dionysius' treatise on the *Divine Names.* (*Opusculum* XIV, *Opuscula Omnia,* Ed. by Mandonnet [Paris, 1927], Lect. XII, pp. 403 ff.)

[85] " I miei infelici e miseri conservi " (*Trionfo d'Honore*).

[86] Cf. St. Augustine, *De Quant. Animae, P. L.,* XXXII, 1035 ff.; the Pseudo-Dionysius, *De Divinis Nominibus, P. G.,* III, 714.

[87] Cf. St. Augustine, *De Trinitate, P. L.,* XLII, 960.

[88] " Love yearning for the beloved object is desire," says St. Augustine, " and possessing and enjoying it is happiness " (*De Civit. Dei.,* XIV 7, 9). St. Thomas discusses love, divine, human, and natural in detail (cf. *Summa Theol.* I, QQ. 27-28) and, discussing the effects of love, mentions the joy felt in the presence of the object beloved; sadness in its absence. Other effects are languor, union, ecstasy. (Cf. *ibid.,* Q. 28, *a.* 5.) This teaching

and tracts. Professor Lewis rightly disagrees with those critics who have been repeating without evidence that the religious tone of medieval love poetry was transferred from the cult of the Blessed Virgin. " It is even more likely," he says, " that the coloring of certain hymns to the Virgin has been borrowed from love poetry." [89] The concept of love which is capable of undergoing progressive purification, and ultimately fits the mind for the vision of God, gave to Petrarch's love for Laura, and to Dante's love for Beatrice their peculiar mystic significance. It was Laura who turned the youthful soul of Petrarch " from all that was base, and forced him to look upward; " [90] or, as he expressed it in a sonnet:

Strive then towards heaven, O my tired heart; follow the chaste footsteps, and the divine light through the mists, whilst you are protected by her sweet love.[91]

The end of human love as Petrarch conceived it in his later sonnets, and in the *Secretum*,[92] was not death; death was rather its triumph, the beginning of a more perfect love, the spiritual union to be enjoyed in heaven.[93] Dante made his early love for Beatrice the beginning of that purificatory process which ended with the divine love raptures in the Empyrean. In the age of Petrarch and Dante and earlier, when our modern sharp demarcation between human and divine love was unknown, the mystics in sacred song and sermon perceived no irreverence in applying the language of human love to their relations with the Deity.[94] St. Francis of Assisi is preeminently

of St. Thomas is largely based on the disquisition on love in the Pseudo-Dionysius, *De Divinis Nom.*, cap. IV. See also his *Commentary* on this work of the Pseudo-Dionysius, *op. cit.*, 381-408.

[89] C. S. Lewis, *The Allegory of Love* (London, 1936), p. 8.

[90] *Petrarch's Secret*, trans. by William Draper (London, 1911), p. 121.

[91] Sonnet CCIV, *Anima che diverse cose tante* (*Le Rime di F. Petrarca,* ed. by G. Carducci e S. Ferrari [Firenze, 1899], p. 290).

[92] " The love which I feel for her [Laura] has most certainly led me to God " (*Petrarch's Secret*, p. 124).

[93] *Trionfo dell'Amore*.

[94] Cf. *The Book of the Lover and the Beloved* by Ramon Lull, trans. by E. Allison Peers (New York, 1923); *The Adornment of the Spiritual Marriage* by Ruysbroeck, ed. by Evelyn Underhill (London, 1916); *Sermons on the Canticle of Canticles* by St. Bernard.

the troubadour of divine love; and of him it is said that his
religion was no mere theory, but a love-affair.[95] Thus Richard
Rolle began one of his hymns: " Now I wryte a sang of lufe,
that thou sal delyte in when thou ert lufand Ihesu Christ." It
contains such " Petrarchian " lines as these:

> Now were I pale and wan
> for love of my Leman, . . .
> Langing in me light,
> that binds me day and night
> Till I it have in sight
> his face sa fair and bright.[96]

The turn from the earthly to the heavenly love is expressed
in a number of Petrarch's religious sonnets, as in the final
quatrain of Sonnet CCLXIV:

> Day by day the End nears visibly,
> A thousand times I ask of God those wings
> On which to Heavenly things
> The mind can rise that here is pinioned.[97]

At one time, the poet sees the entrance of Laura into heaven;[98]
at another time, he meets her there.[99] She is the guiding star
of his life.[100] She inspires his prayer for final salvation;[101] or
makes him aware that Christ is the sole way to true rest and
peace.[102]

The heavenward ascent of the soul, which is, indeed, a true
indication of the mystical element in poetry, is a characteristic
note of the sonnets which Petrarch penned in honor of Laura

---

[95] G. K. Chesterton, *St. Francis of Assisi* (London, 1925), p. 22.

[96] " light " = alighted upon me. Cf. Frances M. Comper, *The Life of Richard Rolle,* etc. (London, 1928-1933), Lyric II from " Ego Dormio," pp. 231-234.

[97] Trans. by William Dudley Faulke, *Some Love Songs of Petrarch* (London, 1915), p. 115.

[98] Sonnet CCCXLVI, *Gli angeli eletti, e d'anime beate*; see especially *Il Trionfo della Morte.*

[99] Sonnet CCCII, *Levommi il mio penser.*

[100] Sonnet XCI, *La bella donna che con tanto amavi*; Sonnet XXI, *Mille fiate, o dolce mia guerrera.*

[101] Sonnet CCCLXV, *I'vo piangando i miei passati tempi.*

[102] Sonnet LXXXI, *Io sono stanco sotto il fascio antico.*

after her death. It was her passing which seems to have emphasized those deep religious feelings so markedly present in the writings of his later years.[103] In Petrarch, as in St. Paul and St. Augustine, the carnal and the spiritual man were at perpetual variance; and despite remorseful relapses, sincere was the " conversion " which he experienced in his fortieth year,[104] and genuine was the ascetic attitude toward life which he maintained to the end. Naturally temperate, Petrarch knew by practice the meaning of vigils, fasts, and abstinences;[105] and he led a life which is an admixture of both the active and the contemplative.

The direct influence of the mysticism of St. Augustine and Boethius is apparent in seven of Petrarch's prose treatises. One of these, *The Secretum* or *De Contemptu Mundi,* published in 1344 consists in an imaginary conversation between the poet and St. Augustine, which is presided over by the silent figure of Lady Truth representative of revealed truth or the reality of the unseen world.[106] All the wealth of pagan ethic from classic sources is brought to bear with St. Augustine's Christian philosophy upon the great problems of human existence. The mutability of fortune and a studied contempt for worldly honors reflect the writings of Boethius; the warfare between the flesh and the spirit is considered in the manner of the *Confessions* of St. Augustine. The conclusion that divine grace and personal striving will bring about remedies for the ills of life is likewise typically Augustinian.[107] The meditations on death, and the lesson of purification of the soul place this work among Petrarch's ascetic contributions of the *De Contemptu Mundi* type to Christian mystical literature.

Petrarch reveals another glimpse of the mystical side of his character in the *Letter to Dionysius,* who was his spiritual

---

[103] Cf. H. R. Tatham, *Francesco Petrarca* (London, 1926), II, 114. For the influence of Augustine on Petrarch, *ibid.,* pp. 327-330.

[104] "As soon as I approached my fortieth year, I repelled these [carnal] weaknesses entirely from my thoughts and my remembrance, as if I had never known them " (*Letter to Posterity,* quoted by Draper, *op. cit.,* p. xvii).

[105] Tatham, *op. cit.,* pp. 279-280.   [106] *Petrarch's Secret.*

[107] Cf. Vincenzo Palazzoto, *Sant' Agostino e Petrarca* (Napoli, 1898), pp. 14-24.

director.[108] The *Letter,* written in 1335, is a detailed account of the poet's meditative reflections after having ascended to the summit of Mount Ventoux. Petrarch's love of nature and his fondness for contemplative moralizing brought on an experience not unusual in the mystics. He compared the ascent of the rugged side of the mountain to the difficult journey of the soul to the mount of perfection. " The very thing which has happened to thee in the ascent of this mountain happens to thee and to many of those who seek to arrive at final beatitude." [109] He conceived of life as a pilgrimage to heaven, and a journey along a straight path with many intervening hills, " over which the pilgrim must advance with great strides from virtue to virtue." [110] The summit was finally attained, and Petrarch paused to admire the beauties of nature around and below him. While so engaged, he tells us : " my soul rose to lofty contemplations." [111] Extracting a copy of the *Confessions* from his pocket, his eyes fell upon the significant lines in the tenth book : " There are those who go up to admire the high places of mountains, the great waves of the sea, the wide currents of rivers, the circuit of the ocean, and the orbits of the stars— and who neglect themselves." [112] Amazed, Petrarch concluded that " there is nothing truly great except the soul "; and he descended the mountain in silence. The rugged ascent had taught him a lesson : " I only wish that I may accomplish that journey of the soul, for which I daily and nightly sigh, as well as I have done this day's journey of the feet, after having overcome so many difficulties." [113] This famous letter bears favorable comparison with the Christian mystical treatises in the manner of the Pilgrimage of Life.

The *Vita Solitaria,* written in 1346, and dedicated to Philip, Bishop of Cavaillon, admirably demonstrates Petrarch's acquaintance with the eminent authorities of Christian mysticism. It is a treasury of views and opinions upon the active and contemplative lives which the poet gathered from a wide

[108] *Epist. Famil., lib.* IV, *Ep.* I, trans. by Henry Reeve, *Petrarch* (Philadelphia, n. d.), pp. 83-89.
[109] *Ibid.,* p. 86.   [111] *Ibid.,* p. 87.   [113] *Ibid.*
[110] *Ibid.*   [112] *Ibid.,* p. 88.

reading of classic, Old Testament, and Christian sources. The late Professor Zeitlin, in an admirable study of the background of the literature of the two lives in Christian mysticism, has thrown considerable light upon this aspect of Petrarch's treatise.[114]

The conception of the relative value of the active and contemplative lives as treated by St. Augustine and St. Gregory became the accepted standard during the middle ages. St. Augustine's practical solution of the claims of the two lives was to the effect that, whatsoever be the superior attractions, or the intrinsic worth of contemplation, it must be interrupted at the call of duty. St. Gregory taught that the active life should consist of good works and acts of charity which fill in the intervals of time not spent in contemplation; and St. Bernard reasserted this view in his monastic regulations. The pre-eminence of the contemplative life was held by St. Thomas in the strict sense of being the monastic ideal. Yet he did not undervalue the active life of the ordinary Christian; for there is also a contemplative life which is the life of a man who is serving God and who devotes a certain portion of time to the contemplation of divine things.[115] The view of Petrarch, not contrary to that of St. Thomas, is chiefly based upon the advantages of solitude and contemplation in contrast to the life of care and busy turmoil which must be endured among crowds in cities.[116] He found in the familiar examples of Martha and Mary, " that the contemplative life is placed before the active by the judgment of Christ." [117] In St. Bernard he found a soul who shared his own love for nature and solitude:

He [Bernard] was accustomed to say that all the literature which he knew . . . he had learned in the woods and fields, and not with the aid of human instruction but with prayer and meditation, and that he never had any other instructor than the oaks and beeches.

[114] *The Life of Solitude by Francis Petrarch,* trans. by Jacob Zeitlin (University of Illinois Press, 1924), pp. 25-54.

[115] *Summa Theol.,* II-II, Q. 182. Cf. Hugh Pope, O. P., *On Prayer and the Contemplative Life, by St. Thomas Aquinas* (London, 1912), p. 3; Butler, *Western Mysticism,* p. 248 ff.

[116] Cf. Zeitlin, pp. 105-108 (*lib.* I, cc. 1-3).

[117] *Ibid.,* pp. 253-254 (*lib.* II, cc. 1-3).

"I like to cite this," Petrarch continues, "because I should like to say it truly—that the same thing is true in my case." [118] It is evident that Petrarch leaves to the mystics the task of outlining the matter and the precise methodology of contemplation. He considers contemplation as the ascent of the mind:

. . . with thoughts that are lifted up above yourself to the ethereal region, to meditate on what goes on there and by meditation to inflame your desire, and in turn to encourage and admonish yourself with a fervent spirit as though with burning words—these are not the least important fruits of the solitary life, though those who are without experience in it do not appreciate it.[119]

It seems not unlikely that the poet speaks from personal experience, for the inner fire of the mystic seems to burn in the following description of the joys of the contemplative.

. . . The solitary souls who are friends of God and habituated to pious moods begin in this life to feel the delights of the life eternal. Nor should I say that it is beyond belief that any one of their number to whom there clings no trace of the dust of this world, should be raised up with the assistance of divine mercy to such a height that, though still confined to earth, he may hear the chorus of angels singing harmoniously in heaven, and behold in an ecstasy of mind what he is unable to express when he comes back to himself.[120]

Petrarch presents other instances in this work of the mystical side of his genius which point to his hold, not so much upon the speculative, as upon the practical aspect of Christian mysticism. The treatise *De Otio Religiosorum* which appeared four years after the *Vita Solitaria,* is a reaffirmation of the views expressed in the earlier work. It is in praise of a life of monastic quietude and contemplative absorption. The first book exhibits the ideal of spiritual repose; the second book in the *De Contemptu Mundi* spirit, declares the vanity of human affairs. The lengthy didactic piece, *De Remediis Utriusque Fortunae,* which Elizabethan Englishmen read under the title,

[118] *Ibid.,* p. 224 (*lib.* II, *cap.* 14); cf. St. Bernard, *Vita Prima,* I, iv, 23; *Epist.* CVI, 2. See also Part I, p. 47.
[119] *Ibid.,* p. 150 (*lib.* I, *cap.* 9).   [120] *Ibid.,* p. 148 (*lib.* I, *cap.* 8).

Physick against Fortune in Thomas Twyne's version, is in many ways not unlike the above mentioned works. It has a decided kinship with Boethius. The words which close the *Vita Solitaria* are illuminative of Petrarch both as a humanist and a mystic:

> Differing here from the practice of the ancients whom I follow in many things, I found it grateful in this unassuming book of mine to insert the sacred and glorious name of Christ. If this had been done by those early guides of our intellectual life, if they had added the spark of divinity to their human eloquence, though great the pleasure which they afford, it would then have been still greater . . . there is no approach save through the humility of Christ.[121]

During the long course of the Renaissance, Petrarch presented to his followers and imitators a philosophic conception of love and life from which could be taken as much as suited particular tastes and times. His Christian mysticism is in the background of his poetry and is an integral part of his prose. In the light of his humanism or mysticism or both, one must estimate the popularity of Petrarch in the Elizabethan period.

CHRISTIAN MYSTICISM AND THE ITALIAN NEOPLATONISTS

One of the richest contributions of the philosophers and poets of the late Italian Renaissance to both continental and English literature of the sixteenth century was a definite philosophy of love and beauty. This system was developed by enthusiastic converts to Platonism in the courtly circles of Rome, Florence, and Urbino. In it was a conscious fusion of the diverse elements which had made up the poetry of the troubadours, of Dante's *Canzone*, and Petrarch's *rime*, together with the transcendent principles of Platonic philosophy. The Italian *literati* discussed love and beauty as Socrates had done in the Dialogues; the poets composed hymns celebrating an ethereal love, and the philosophic lover was taught to raise his mind from contemplation of an earthly to that of a heavenly beauty. What has come to be known as a system of Renaissance

---

[121] *Ibid.*, p. 316 (*lib.* II, *cap.* 9).

mysticism arose, which was to influence European literature, especially in sonnet poetry, for more than a century.[122]

This philosophy of love and beauty was popularized chiefly by Marsilio Ficino in his commentaries on the works of Plato, by Pico della Mirandola's learned *Commento* on the *Canzona dello Amor celeste e divino* of Girolamo Benivieni, and through a work of Cardinal Bembo called *Gli Asolani*. It more or less consciously followed a simple formula of ascent from earthly to heavenly beauty which it derived from Plato's rhapsodies in the *Phaedrus* and *Symposium*. Plotinus had initiated the progressive ascent of the mind to the One with the sight of a beautiful lady; the Italian Neoplatonists arranged this ascent to proceed by six steps from the perception of feminine beauty to the enjoyment and contemplation of the Universal Beauty. The first three steps consisted in a gradual idealization and universalization of the beloved object in the mind of the lover; the last three steps involved the unification and identification of this abstract concept with the Beauty of God.[123]

The essential differences between this mysticism and that of the orthodox Christian mystics are apparent, despite a number of elements which both systems have in common. The formula of the Christian mystic: Man—Christ—God gives way to the Platonic " ladder of love." There is an idealized human, not divine, love; and the charity of Christ, repentance for sin, and the contemplation of a personal God are entirely lacking. The definite methodology which has been noted in medieval mysticism is replaced by philosophical disquisitions upon sensuous and noble love, or a treatment of the origin and universality of beauty.

The influence, however, of the traditional mysticism of St. Augustine, St. Bernard, and the Victorines, although diluted

---

[122] See J. B. Fletcher, "A Study in Renaissance Mysticism: Spenser's ' Fower Hymnes '," *Publications of Modern Language Assn.*, XXVI (1911), pp. 452-475.

[123] Cardinal Bembo put the entire process briefly in the third book of *Gli Asolani*: " Love is one, and from particular love we pass to love that is ideal, and from the ideal to love that is divine."

and wrenched from its medieval setting, is recognizable in a number of the representative works of Renaissance mysticism. There is a curious admixture of pagan and Christian elements which is characteristic of the productions of the Christian humanists of Italy. It is seen, mainly, in the employment of part of the phraseology of Christian mysticism to illustrate treatises on both human and divine love and beauty. And in the higher stages of the typical ascent of the lover's mind to Universal Beauty, one can discover the influence of the regular methodology of Christian mysticism.

The definition of love as a " desire for beauty " is the common heritage of both the Renaissance Neoplatonists and the Christian mystics from Plato. The Pseudo-Dionysius had so defined love,[124] and St. Thomas Aquinas approved of this definition in his Commentary on the *Divine Names*.[125] Richard of St. Victor mentions love in similar terms,[126] and Richard Rolle of Hampole adapted it in his *Incendium Amoris*.[127] Ficino taught that love is defined and bounded by the love of beauty,[128] and referred to this conception in the celebrated " Hymns of Hierothaeus " in the *Dionysiaca*.[129] Pico della Mirandola took over the same definition,[130] as did Cardinal Bembo,[131] and Castiglione in *Il Cortegiano*.[132] This community of idea between the Christian mystics and the Neoplatonists is further illustrated by the remarkable popularity of the subject of love and beauty in the purely religious writings produced in Italy during the sixteenth century. Such mystics as Cajetan [133] and St. Catherine of Genoa [134] treated the origin, nature,

[124] *De Div. Nom.*, IV, 18, *P. G.*, III, 712-713.
[125] *Opusculum* XIV.   [126] *Benjamin Minor, P. L.*, CXCVI, 10.
[127] " Amor est magnum desiderium pulchri, boni, et amabilis " (cap. XVII, ed. by Margaret Deanesly [London, 1915], p. 195).
[128] " Cum amorem dicimus, pulchritudinis desiderium intelligite " (*Commentarium in Convivium Platonis, Opera Omnia* [Frankfort, 1611], p. 1139).
[129] *Ibid.*, p. 1100.
[130] " Et cosi nel convivio di Platone e deffinito, Amore e desiderio di bellezza " (*Commento*, in *Opere di G. Benivieni* [Venice, 1524], lib. III, 10).
[131] *Gli Asolani, lib.* III.
[132] *Il Cortegiano, lib.* IV; Hoby's trans. (ed. Everyman), p. 303.
[133] *Opera Omnia* (Lyons, 1639); cf. especially *In Parab. Salomonis* (Rome 1542, Lyons, 1545, Paris, 1587).
[134] For a comprehensive study of mystical love in Catherine's doctrine and

and effects of heavenly love, and stressed its purificatory powers in rendering the soul free from all sensual affection.[135] The renewed interest in Plato during the Italian Renaissance is reflected in the opinions of many who looked upon the *Dialogues* as an introduction to the true mysticism. Stephen Conventuis, for example, a religious of the Congregation of St. Saviour, wrote a treatise of this kind: *De Ascensu Mentis in Deum ex Platonica et Peripatetica Doctrina Libri Sex*.[136] The idea that the visible world was created by the God of love, that it is the reproduction of a design, pre-existing in Him, and that it will ever receive from its Creator its life and movement is good Christian Platonism of the period. So also the view that the human soul is able to expand and to be enlarged, thanks to divine love, is commonly found in the ecclesiastical writings of the sixteenth century.[137] Savonarola, fiery mystic and preacher, composed hymns of Christian love in the manner of the medieval mystic; and expounded the nature of the Beautiful in the terms of Marsilio Ficino and the Christian Neoplatonists:

In what does beauty consist? In colors? No. In features? No. . . . Beauty is a quality which results from the proportions and correspondence of all the members and parts of the body. . . . Whence comes this beauty? If you investigate it, you will find that it comes from the soul. The good participate in the beauty of God and diffuse it in the body. . . . Shall I show you true beauty? Observe some devout woman praying, how the warmth of Divine Beauty illumines her; watch her when she returns from her orisons, you will see the beauty of God shine in her features, and her face will be like that of an angel.[138]

Even the characteristic Neoplatonic " ladder of love," the

---

its sources in Plato, Plotinus, the Pseudo-Dionysius, and Jacopone da Todi, see von Hügel, *The Mystical Element of Religion* (London and New York, 1909), II, 63 ff.

[135] The *Dialogues* attributed to St. Catherine of Genoa, composed in 1548, reflect the teaching of the Christian mystics of the period. Divine love is the cause of all creation; then, in the ' converted ' man it is the agency of complete purification whereby the soul passes through a ' purgatory ' and a ' long martyrdom.' (*Dialogues*, Part III, cap. I [ed. Paris], p. 306; see also Part II, cap. V, p. 285.)

[136] Venice, 1563.   [137] Cf. Pourrat, *op. cit.*, III, 234.

[138] Quoted by Ralph Roeder, *Savonarola* (New York, 1930), p. 180.

six-fold ascent to ideal Beauty, is not without parallel in the writings of Christian mysticism. St. Augustine had laid down six steps of progressive ascent to God; [139] and St. Bonaventure conceived the spiritual ascension in six grades: sense, imagination, reason, intellection (a primary understanding), intelligence, and the *synteresis,* or the final spark in which intelligence and love, reason and will combine to produce not only the image, but the similitude of God.[140] Ficino wrote of a substantial touch of the intellect with God which is a union with Him in an inexplicable manner such as is illustrated in the writings of St. John the Evangelist and St. Paul.[141] The notion of this mysterious union was likewise entertained by Pico della Mirandola. It was for him an intuitive vision of the face of God such as Moses and St. Paul and many other chosen ones had once experienced.[142]

There is a definite tendency in a number of the typical Renaissance mystics to turn away from Neoplatonism in the direction of the Christian mystical tradition. In the *Commento* on Benivieni's *Canzona,* Pico della Mirandola accepted the first three steps of the Neoplatonic *scala* as given in the *Canzona,* but insisted on the necessity of divine grace to bring the soul along the last triad. " The soul is capable of possessing the light of Divine Beauty," says Pico, " not of itself, but only through a gift and communication from another. There is another and higher love which extends beyond the steps of the Neoplatonic ' amorosa via ' by which God is loved *in himself and not as the author of ideal beauty."* [143] Pico explains that the ascent of the mind to the true beauty is indeed " a rare and celestial gift "; so much so that few arrive at such

---

[139] *De Quant. Animae., lib.* I, *cap. 33, P. L.,* XXXII, 1075 ff.

[140] *Itinerarium Mentis in Deum,* cap. VII, p. 20.

[141] *Theol. Platonica, cap.* II, *lib.* XII.

[142] *Commento* on the *Canzona dello Amor celeste e divino.*

[143] " Ne in se, o per se potra l'anima sufficientemente possidere quel lume della bellezza, ilquale da se non ha, ma solo per dono e communicatione di altrui . . . non e licito camminare più innanzi, perchè quelle e il termine della amorosa via, quantunque per via dunaltro amore più oltre si vada, & quello amore colquale si ama Dio in se, & non quanto auttore della ideale bellezza " (*Commento,* III, 10).

exalted height.[144] The influence of Christian mysticism is met again in the fourth book of *Il Cortegiano,* where Castiglione places his discourse on love and beauty in the mouth of Cardinal Bembo, who, in turn, is made to receive counsel from the hermit Lavinello, the narrator of the same philosophy in Bembo's *Gli Asolani.* Castiglione departs from the sheer intellectual *tour de force* of typical Neoplatonic exposition. I quote from Thomas Hoby's translation, which was one of the most popular books in the Elizabethan age.

Let us therefore bend all our force and thoughts of soule to this most holy light, that sheweth us the way which leadeth to heaven: and after it, putting off the affections we were clad at our coming downe, let us climbe up the staires, which at the lowermost steppe have the shadow of sensuall beautie, to the high mansion place where the heavenly, amiable and right beautie dwelleth, which lyeth hidden in the innermost secretes of God . . . and there shall wee finde a most happie end for our desires, true rest for our travels, certain remedies for our miseries.[145]

In the final pages of *The Courtier,* Castiglione describes the ecstatic union of the soul with the true Beauty as an experience once enjoyed by Plato, Plotinus, and among others, " St. Francis, in whom a fervent spirite of love imprinted the most holy seale of five wounds. And nothing but the vertue of love coulde hale up Saint Paule the Apostle to the sight of these secretes, which is not lawful for man to speake of, nor shewe S. Stephen the heavens open." [146] The purely mystical nature of this love is apparent also in the words of Lord Julian that some women " in our age " were worthy to receive the *stigmata,* i.e., the fiery imprints of divine love; and this same " angellike love " burned in Mary Magdalen, who " had many faultes forgiven her, because she loved much." [147] Another indication of the kinship between Renaissance Neoplatonism and Christian mysticism is based upon a common admiration for the works of the Pseudo-Dionysius. Pico spoke of him as the " prince of

[144] " ' Raro e celeste dono,' veramente raro e celeste, perchè pochi sono quelli che ad questo grado pervenghono " (*ibid.,* III, 10).
[145] Everyman ed., pp. 320-321.
[146] *Ibid.,* p. 323.   [147] *Ibid.*

Christian theologians who used the same mode of speaking as Plotinus." [148]   No less than five Italian mystics belonging to a single religious Order published commentaries on the Pseudo-Dionysius during the sixteenth century.[149]   Hence, it is historicaly impracticable to draw a sharp line of demarcation between the writings of the Christian Neoplatonists of late Renaissance Italy and the productions of Christian mysticism.   Both draw from common sources, and one is needed to shed light upon the origin and principles of the other.   In the works of the same poet, Girolamo Benivieni, this can be illustrated.   Benivieni wrote the undoubtedly Neoplatonic *Canzona dello Amore celeste e divino*, and also a poem, in the strict Christian mystical tradition, which is now the subject of brief analysis.

The Advice of Man to His Soul

This long poem, together with a number of fervent religious *laude*, was included in the single-volume edition of Benivieni's works.[150]   The full title of the poem is: " Ammonitione dello Huomo a l'anima per la quale demostra come lei possa per el mezzo delle creature conoscere & consequentemente amare el suo creatore." [151]   As this long title indicates, the poem is cast in the popular dialogue form, and is primarily of the Theocentric type of contemplation.   Nature is conceived in the manner familiar to the mystics as *vestigia* of the Creator; and a contemplation of creatures brings the mind to the knowledge and love of God.   The ascent which Benivieni describes, not without repetition, has its beginning in the consideration of the entire universe, the earth " suspended in the sea," and roll-

[148] " Dionysio Areopagita principe di theologi Christiani . . . usa pero el medesimo modo di parlare che usa Plotino " (*Commento*, I, 1).

[149] Cf. Pourrat, *op. cit.*, II, 251-2.

[150] *Opere di Girolamo Benivieni . . . con una canzona dello Amor celeste e divino, col commento dello ill. S. Conte Giovanni Pico Mirandolano . . .* Venice, 1524.   Other editions of the *Opere*: 1519 (Florence) ; 1522, 1524, 1526, 1535 (Venice).   There are three classes of poems in the volume: *Laude dello amore di Jesu* (p. 138), *Laude di Jesu* (p. 103) ; *Stanze in passione Domini* (p. 140).

[151] This work is reprinted by Professor Padelford in " Spenser's 'Fowre Hymnes,' A Resurvey," *Studies in Philology*, XXIX (1932), pp. 225-230.

ing spheres of the heavens.[152] The visible creation shows forth divinely posited order and beauty so that " without ravishment it cannot be contemplated." To him who contemplates it well, the universe shows forth the divine attributes of Goodness, Sapience, Beauty, and Power. For this task, however, more than ordinary vision is needed; and the poet feels the need of a purer and deeper illumination and insight not only to contemplate divine things, but also to search into the mysteries of Nature. He then proceeds first, to contemplate the visible world as it appears to him in a peaceful and concordant union. Secondly, he reviews the earth teeming with examples of divine beauty and bounty: trees, fruits, mountains and valleys, the sea and the waters of the earth; the fish, the birds and beasts, even the gems hidden under the earth—so vast in all that his powers of description are wholly inadequate. Finally, ascending on high, the heavens, the stars and the sun are objects of contemplation. Then, turning introspective, as mystics were wont to do since the time of St. Augustine, Benivieni considers the human soul, the image of the creator and its three-fold faculties which are figures of the triune God. This is that soul for whose redemption the incarnation and passion of Christ took place. The meditative review of the redemption is purely theological, entirely appropriate in a mystical composition, and remarkably precise and brief:

To the eyes of him who made thee so amiable, thou wast so pleasing that for thee he descended from heaven even to earth, and took up human flesh. Not content with this, he also took thy sins, and thy guilt; and, to wash thy sins away, O my ungrateful soul, he willed to sustain torments, to suffer hunger, pain, vigils, and exhaustion. For thee, he finally loosed that knot by dying: that knot which thy first parent had tied, and which he alone could unloose.

The last stanzas summarize the lesson of the entire poem; and sentiments of sorrow, longing, and love peculiar to mystical compositions make up the final refrain:

Now what excuse hast thou any longer, ungrateful soul, that thou dost not see, know, and love that First and Highest Good

[152] All references are from the 1524 ed., pp. 159-163.

who has created thee; in so many ways has invited thee, and calls thee still. He is that blessed Spouse who is in thee, and outside thee; for Him thou dost ever burn ardently, and when thou wilt, mayst enjoy Him—O unheard-of Love!

The note of the Purgative way is sounded in the opening lines of the dialogue, and is heard again as subject of the final stanzas. The need of illumination, a special divine gift is felt for this species of contemplation; while the notion of divine union is expressed in the familiar figure of the soul as the spouse of God, and its transformation through contemplation. The reflection of the divine attributes in Nature, and the precedence of the attribute of Sapience, is entirely expected in this model in verse of Theocentric contemplation.

CHAPTER V

SPANISH MYSTICISM IN ELIZABETHAN ENGLAND

The writings of Spanish origin which contributed to the mystical movement in the last half of Elizabeth's reign are not numerous, but exceedingly influential. Notable are the English translations of three famous Spanish mystics, Juan Luis de Vives, Diego de Estella, and Luis de Granada. Mr. J. G. Underhill, after careful research, concluded that close communication between the Spanish peninsula and England which followed the awakened interest in things Spanish in the days of Catherine of Aragon, was never afterward diverted. A number of Spanish grammars were printed, and at least in the court group which centered in the Sydney-Pembroke circle, knowledge of the Spanish tongue was a matter of course.[1] The number of English translations of Spanish literary works which began in the reign of Henry VIII gradually increased in number, and among them works of ordinary devotion and mysticism enjoyed an unusual popularity. The Spanish mystics who were read in translations during Elizabeth's reign represent, especially in Luis de Granada, the most influential predecessors of St. Teresa and St. John of the Cross. The weight of this influence together with that of the mystical literature from Italy, must have been felt by the native English writers who are the chief subjects of this study.

JUAN LUIS DE VIVES

Juan Luis de Vives (1492-1540) noted humanist, educator, and writer of numerous moral and religious treatises, was a friend of Erasmus and More and a teacher of rhetoric at Oxford. His influence was greatest in England during the closing years of Henry VIII's reign and a number of his pedagogical works were translated in 1540. Vives' works became the common property of continental Europe and England

---

[1] J. G. Underhill, *Spanish Literature in the England of the Tudors* (New York, 1899), p. 261 ff.

during the first half of the sixteenth century,[2] although, as we shall see, portions of his mystical writings were an integral part of Elizabethan devotional literature.

His most important contribution to the literature of Christian mysticism is the *Excitationes Animi in Deum*, a lengthy work which includes the following separate treatises: *Preliminary Discourse upon Prayer, Preparation of the Soul for Prayer, Daily Prayers and Meditations, General Prayers and Meditations, Commentary on the Lord's Prayer,* and *The Passion of Christ*.[3] Two other important mystical works of Vives are the *Seven Meditations on the Penitential Psalms,* and the *Meditations on the Passion of Christ*.[4]

The *Excitationes Animi in Deum* was translated in part by John Bradford in 1559 in his *Private Prayers and Meditations,* and again in *Godly Meditations,* which appeared in 1562.[5] Part of Bradford's translation was reprinted in the collection called *Christian Prayers,* made by Henry Bull, Powell, and Middleton in 1570, and reappeared in *Queen Elizabeth's Prayer Book* in a number of editions. In the system of Vives, the purificatory and Christocentric elements are predominant, together with a marked emphasis on the mutability and vanity of worldly things.[6] He admits his indebtedness to Cassian's spiritual writings, which were of great importance in the establishment of the active and the contemplative ideal in western mysticism. But the portions of Vives' works which were read in England during Elizabeth's time were mainly devotional in nature, in contrast to the very true spirit of mysticism which came to England in the writings of Luis de Granada.

DIEGO DE ESTELLA

Another Spanish mystic who was read at least in part during the last half of Elizabeth's reign is Diego de Estella,

---

[2] Cf. *Enciclopedia Universal Illustrada* (Madrid, 1930), LXIX, 718-720.

[3] *Opera Omnia,* Antwerp, 1538, 1578; Cologne, 1530; Basle, 1545. My references are from the Basle edition, II, 199-251.

[4] *Ibid.,* pp. 147-199.

[5] Also printed in London, 1569, 1578, 1581, 1590; cf. J. G. Underhill, *op. cit.,* p. 378.

[6] *Excitationes Animi in Deum, ibid.,* p. 199 et *passim.* Also see pp. 201-258.

(1524-1578). One of his works entitled, *De la Vanidad del Mundo* (1574) went through four editions and six translations (into Latin, French, and Italian) before 1600.[7] This treatise was translated into English in 1584, at Douay, by a certain " G. C." with the title, *The contempte of the world and the vanitie thereof.*[8] Four years later, Thomas Rogers published his translation of the same work in London, *Methode unto Mortification, called heretofore the contempt of the world and the vanity thereof.*[9] It is a perfect example of the *Contemptus Mundi* type of mystical literature. Noteworthy also is the fact that Rogers had previously translated the *Imitation of Christ*, which is one of the greatest of all expositions of the ascetic side of Christian mysticism.[10] De Estella's *Contempt of the World* is strikingly similar to à Kempis' *Imitation of Christ*. Both present the Christocentric ideal, and also the lessons of abnegation and detachment from worldly concerns which together with an imitation of Christ make up a very familiar strain in all Christian mysticism. The mystical expositions of both Vives and de Estella served to bring into the England of Elizabeth a genuine body of mystical theology under the unassuming aspect of religious works of merely devotional nature.

LUIS DE GRANADA

The mystical movement of the Elizabethan period received its strongest impulse from the writings of Luis de Granada.[11] One of the most influential of the Spanish mystics, Luis de Sarria, was born at Granada in 1505. He was a Dominican priest, a noted preacher, and during a long life published a large number of spiritual tracts and sermons. His best known works are: *Libro de la Oracion y Meditacion* (1554) in two parts, which went through eleven editions in five years; *Memorial de*

[7] E. Allison Peers, *Spanish Mysticism* (New York, 1924), p. 138.

[8] Underhill, *op. cit.*, p. 391.

[9] Peers, p. 244; cf. also Underhill, p. 393.

[10] For notice of Rogers' translation of certain anonymous treatises which he considered authentic works of St. Augustine, see below, p. 130.

[11] The critical edition of his works is that of Justo Cuervo, *Obras de Fray Luis de Granada* (Madrid, 1906-27).

la Vida Christiana (1566 with *Additions* in 1574), and *Guia de Pecadores* (1567). He died in 1588.

Luis de Granada is an extraordinary figure in the history of mysticism, and unaccountably he enjoyed a most remarkable popularity in Elizabethan England. He was a humanist and a lover of nature; he reminds one of St. Bonaventure in his descriptions of nature and in his desires to make nature the means of ascent to God. The writings of Granada show his intimate knowledge of St. Augustine and the great medieval mystics, and citations from their works abound in his pages. He possessed high literary skill,[12] and his influence upon sixteenth century mysticism cannot be over-estimated. His works were the first religious writings in the peninsular vernacular to be generally read in England,[13] and the translations from the mystical writings of Granada were remarkable both in number and in popularity during the reign of Elizabeth. The works coming from both Protestant and Catholic translators doubtless contributed enormously to the spirit and method of Christian mysticism which is found in the native English mystical writers of the period. Ten translations of Granada's treatises were either printed or licensed to be printed in English during the twenty years beginning with 1582.[14] Richard Hopkins translated the *Libro de la Oracion y Meditacion* in 1582,[15] and the *Memorial* in 1586.[16] In 1598, Francis Meres published his translation of the *Guia de Pecadores,* Part II, as *The Sinners Guyde,*[17] and also the *Libro de la Oracion y Medi-*

[12] The eulogy by Francis Meres, well known to Shakespeare students for his *Palladis Tamia* (1598), refers to Granada in his Preface (see below) to *Granados Devotions*: "That rare and matchless Divine F. Ludovicus Granatensis," whose style is "heavenly and exact."

[13] Underhill, *op. cit.,* p. 182.

[14] *Ibid.,* p. 226.

[15] Paris; Rouen, 1583 and 1584; London, 1592; 1599, Edinburgh, 1600, London, 1601 (cf. Underhill, p. 390).

[16] *A memoriall of a Christian life; wherein are treated all such things, as apperteyne unto a Christian to doe, from the beginning of his conversion, until the ende of his perfection. Divided in seven treatises,* Rouen, 1586; Louvain, 1599. (*ibid.*)

[17] Underhill, p. 403; "*A work contayning the whole regiment of a Christian life* . . . Compiled in the Spanish Tongue . . . And nowe perused, and digested into English, by Francis Meres, London, 1598 " (Brit. Museum).

tacion which he entitled *Granados Devotions.*[18] Another work of Granada was translated and published in London by " J. G." in 1598.[19] " Anthologies " or collections of Granada's writings were popular in Italy and France.[20] Thomas Lodge made a translation of parts of Granada's writings entitled *The Flowers of Lodowicke of Granado,* and what is probably another translation from the same author was licensed in the same year with the title, *A Paradise of prayers gathered out of the works of L. of Granada.*[21] The sprightly simplicity of Granada's style and the warm devotional character of his writings accounts for their extraordinary popularity throughout Europe in the sixteenth and seventeenth centuries.[22] It is significant that contemporaneous with their appearance in England, the production of mystical literature begins with renewed fervor among native writers.

The Methodology of Granada's Mysticism

The three stages of the spiritual life, with the Christocentric and Theocentric types of contemplation, are fully exemplified in the three great works of Luis de Granada.[23] The Purgative way is especially severe in Granada's system. Not only long meditation and prayer is required, but also a sign of the mystic's progress is a " quick and fervent desire to afflict and maltreat the body with fastings, hair-shirts, vigils, disciplines, and other bodily severities." [24] The Illuminative way is essentially a

[18] " *Exactly teaching how a man may truely dedicate and devote himselfe unto God and so become his acceptable Votary* . . . since translated into Latine, Italian, and French. And now perused and englished, by Francis Meres, Master of Arts and student of Divinity. London, 1598 " (Brit. Museum).

[19] *A most fragrant flower; or devoute exposition of the Lordes prayer,* which is a translation of Part III of Granada's *Compendio y Explicacion de la Doctrina Cristiana.* (Underhill, p. 403.)

[20] Cf. Underhill, p. 406.   [21] See Part III, p. 165.

[22] E. Allison Peers, *Studies in the Spanish Mystics* (London, 1927), I, 422-430.

[23] *Libro de la Oracion y Meditacion (Obras,* vol. II) ; *Guia de Pecadores (Obras,* vol. I) ; *Memorial de la Vida Christiana (Obras,* vol. III).

[24] *Memorial of the Christian Life,* Bk. VII, cap. 6, " Show me," says Granada, " a heart that is devout and recollected, and I will show you a

progress of the soul by means of prayer and with the use of the
Christocentric contemplation. The Unitive stage of the mystical life is the end and objective of Theocentric contemplation. Few mystics have described so well the intimate psychological details of the final ascent of the contemplative soul.
The soul is first inflamed with love of God and then we are
told, " there is born a marvelous delight, thence a most ardent
longing for God, from this longing a faint satiety, from the
satiety an holy inebriation, and then a security and a perfect
quiet in God, wherein the soul rests and has its spiritual
Sabbath." [25] The Christocentric type of contemplation is of
greatest moment in preparing the soul for divine union. " It
appeareth," says Granada, " that this first manner of meditating
(by way of taking compassion of the bitter paines of our
Sauiour) is as it were a meane or a ladder unto all others.
And for this very cause S. Bonauenture made great account
of this manner of meditation, because it is sensibly seene, that
this manner of meditation openeth the way vnto all the other
manners of meditating." [26]

The *Libro de la Oracion y Meditacion* is mainly devoted to
the purificatory exercises which are characteristic of the Purgative way, and to the Christocentric type of contemplation.
Since this book emphasizes the traditional principles of asceticism, with preparatory exercises for higher spiritual union, the
usual teaching of mystical theology is confined to a comparatively brief compass. The regular Theocentric contemplation
makes up the meditation assigned to the last day of the week in
the first part; and to the first sections of Part Second. A detailed consideration of the Passion concludes the second part of
this important work. It is, however, in the *Memorial de la Vida
Cristiana*, that Granada presents in truly mystical fashion the
details of the Unitive way as a product of a soul that has
actually experienced whereof it speaks. This treatise with the

body that is restrained with fasting and silence and vigils and discipline,
and measure and moderation in all things (*Book of Prayer and Meditation,*
Bk. III, Sermon I).

[25] *Memorial of the Christian Life,* Bk. VII, cap. 1.

[26] *Of Prayer and Meditation,* English translation by Richard Hopkins
(1611 reprint of 1582 translation), Part II, sect. I, cap. VI, p. 162.

Additions of 1574 brought before a wide variety of readers of the sixteenth century all that is best in the medieval authorities on Unitive mysticism. Less than two years after the *Memorial*, appeared the famous *Guia de Pecadores*. It is a treatise for the " just man," and " contains such rules and instructions as are proper to make a man virtuous." [27] Herein, are treated at length the virtues and vices which make up so much of mystical literature from the ascetic and purgative aspect. The lofty contemplations which are found in the *Book of Meditations,* and are a characteristic of the *Memorial* are intentionally subdued in the *Guia* for a more practical treatment of Christian perfection. Nevertheless, Granada places in his very first chapter the " Contemplation of the Divine Being, and the excellency of the divine attributes as the first motive to virtue and divine service." In so doing, he tells us, he " will make use only of St. Denis, who wrote his treatise of Mystical Divinity . . . to raise up our souls to the contemplation of a Being that exceeds all beings." [28] A purely Theocentric contemplation follows, and is repeated in the ninth chapter which is a consideration of Heaven. *The Sinner's Guide* is a treasury of citations from patristic and medieval authorities to an even greater extent than Granada's other works. His only important translation is the Spanish version of Thomas à Kempis' *Imitation of Christ.* Luis called this work *Contemptus Mundi,* which was the title commonly given the *Imitation* in his time. This translation enjoyed considerable popularity, and passed through more than thirty editions in the course of the sixteenth century.[29]

Granada's *Libro de la Oracion y Meditacion,* popularly known as the *Book of Meditations,* amply illustrates all the cardinal principles of Christian mysticism, and warrants a brief analysis from the pages of an Elizabethan translation.[30] Luis makes

---

[27] *The Sinner's Guide*, Bk. I, cap. I., 1.   [28] *Ibid.*, no. 4.

[29] Cf. Peers, *Studies in the Spanish Mystics*, p. 40.

[30] The following references are from the famous translation made by Richard Hopkins in 1582 and again reprinted in 1583, 1592, 1600, 1601, and still another reprinting is dated 1611. The references which follow are from this 1611 version. The book is divided into two parts. Part I, Of Meditation and Prayer. Part II, Of Consideration and Prayer. Its title page is as follows:

clear at the outset to what extent he will employ the two types of contemplation. Of the Christocentric type, he writes: " All the points in the life and passion of our Saviour Christ," make up the " Meditation of the Imagination. . . . Sometimes agayne, this Meditation is upon things that do rather appertain to the Understanding, then to the Imagination: as when we think upon the benefits of Almighty God, or upon his goodness and mercy, or upon any other of his perfections . . . *we use both the one manner and the other in these exercises.*" [31] The manner of the Christocentric type of Granada is quite conventional.[32] But Granada's contemplation of God as arrived at from creatures is a veritable paean of heavenly Beauty; the beauty of Nature causing the heart to ascend to the uncreated Beauty.

For if almighty God hath created things so wonderful and beautiful in this vale of tears, what wonderful things, trow ye, hath he created in that place which is the seate of his glory, the Throne of his majestic power, the Pallace of his majesty, the house of his Elect, and the Paradise of all delights.[33]

The first object of contemplation is the varied order and beauty of Nature, the mountains and the sea.[34] Then arising to the created heavens, he exclaims: " When one lifts up his eyes to behold the magnitude and number of the stars, he cannot help but be astonished and (in a manner) besides himselfe, considering the passing greatness of that place, and much more of the Soveraign Lorde, that created it out of nothing." [35]

Of Prayer and Meditation / contayning / fourteene Meditations, for / the seven dayes of the weeke; / both for Mornings and Evenings. / Treating the principal matters / and holy Mysteries of / our Faith. / Written by F. Lewis / de Granada. / At London, / Printed by W. I. for Edward White, / and are to be sold at the little / North doore of Paules Church, at / the signe of the gunne. / 1611. /

[31] *Of Prayer and Medit.*, Part II, cap. V, p. 89.

[32] This observation of Granada is significant: " Nowe if thou bee desirous to see a most perfect patterne of the Contempt of the World, and of all honours, riches, pleasures, and delights that be therein, behold our Sauiour vppon the Crosse" (*ibid.*, p. 179).

[33] *Of Prayer and Medit.*, Part. I, sect. V, p. 298.

[34] For Luis' sensibility to the beauties of Nature and its effects upon his mysticism, see E. Allison Peers, *Spanish Mysticism* (New York, 1925), pp. 19 ff., and also his *Studies in the Spanish Mystics*, pp. 62-70.

[35] *Of Prayer and Medit.*, Part. I, sect. V, p. 298.

Leaving the stars, the mind is next brought up to the spiritual heavens and their blessed inhabitants, "whose number, holiness, riches, and beauty are greater than any man can imagine." [36] Then rising yet higher, the angels are the objects of contemplation, especially their beauty and their order. The picturesque description of the duties of the several choirs is noteworthy:

There the Angels go (as it were) in Embassages, the Archangels are occupied in their Ministry, the Principalities triumph, the Powers rejoyce, the Dominations governe, the Virtues shine, the Thrones glister, the Cherubins give light, the Seraphins burne with love, and all of that heavenly Court do sing lauds and praises unto God.[37]

True to this type of Contemplation, the Divine Essence and the attributes of God are brought before the meditative eyes of the soul:

Arise up therefore, (O my soule) advance thyselfe on hye, leave all earthly affaires here beneath, and fly up with the winges of thy spirit, unto the most excellent Noble Lord of Promise.[38]

We hear the first note of the mystical ecstasy in the description, when the wisdom of Solomon is associated with the divine attribute of Wisdom:

Consider, therefore, that the fame of that Heavenly Jerusalem, and of that Supreme King that governeth it, is no lesse than the renowne of Solomon was. Ascend thou now up on hye with thy Spirite unto this noble Citty, to contemplate the wisdome of this Supreme King, the beauty of this Temple . . . for if thou be able to consider everie one of these things; it may be, that thy Spirite shall be lifted up above himselfe, and thou shalt perceive, that there hath not beene declared unto thee so much, as the very least part of his glory.[39]

The above citations from but one of Granada's works could well serve as a commentary upon many English mystical pieces of the last two decades of Elizabeth's reign. Much of this material on Christian mysticism was common property, and the great authorities of Christian mysticism were readily accessible to Elizabethan writers and readers. Yet by no means the least abundant source of this knowledge was Luis de Granada.

[36] *Ibid.*, p. 299.   [37] *Ibid.*, p. 300.   [38] *Ibid.*, p. 306.   [39] *Ibid.*, pp. 306-7.

10

CHAPTER VI

THE CONTEMPLATION OF CHRIST

This study of Elizabethan mysticism from foreign sources would be incomplete without mention of some work from the Latin. The most important Elizabethan translation of a Latin mystical treatise was an anonymous version of the *Manuale seu Libellus de Contemplatione Christi* which was considered a work of St. Augustine,[1] and printed by John Day in 1577. It bore the title, *The Contemplation of Christ,* and another translation of the same work was made by Thomas Rogers in 1582. Other reprints of this work are dated 1591 and 1600.[2] As it was intended for Protestants, three chapters of the original were omitted in the 1577 version, and one in that of 1600.[3] Neither these omissions nor minor twists of the text to convey other than the author's meaning impair the substantial spirit or method of the original. The Latin *Manuale* is an anonymous work of the late medieval period which was printed among the *Opuscula* of St. Augustine at Venice in 1512. Few of the Pseudo-Augustine pieces have been so frequently reproduced either in the original or in translation as this treatise on contemplation.

The Contemplation of Christ [4] may be analyzed according to the chief sources from which the author worked. The preface and first two chapters are taken from the *Confessio Fidei* of Alcuin by way of the *Speculum,* which is another treatise long supposed to be St. Augustine's.[5] The Preface serves as an introduction to the main body of the contemplation, and states that the author's purpose was " to have with me a short summary of the choicest sayings of the holy fathers concerning my God, that by the fire of the reading thereof, the

[1] This treatise is reprinted by Migne, *P. L.,* XL, 951-968.

[2] See the Appendix for list of translations by Rogers and others of mystical treatises wrongly attributed to St. Augustine.

[3] The anonymous English translator of the 1577 edition omitted chapters XI, XVIII, and XXV. Rogers left out the short chapter XXV, "that thy zeal," he writes, "might not be cooled by the reading thereof. For it containeth strange, that I may say not erroneous doctrine" (Introd.).

[4] My references are to *The Contemplation of Christ,* Catholic Truth Society Pub. (London, 1897).

[5] Cf. Migne, *P. L.,* XL, 950-951.

love of Him might be kindled in me as oft as it waxed cold." [6]
The medieval *Codex Mittensis,* probably composed by Arnulf,
Abbot of Metz, furnishes the next portion of the text.[7] It is
entitled in the medieval excerpt a *Meditatio theoretica,* or a
formal disquisition on contemplation. The English heading
for the third chapter, " Of the Longing of the Soul that feeleth
God," reveals the nature of this portion of the work, which
virtually consists of lessons in spiritual aspiration.

Behold, when my mind riseth upward unto Thee, and busieth
itself with thinking upon Thine unspeakable loving kindness, the
weight of my flesh becomes less burdensome unto me . . . all
things are still and all things are calm . . . Let my spirit take wings
as an eagle, and fly without faltering. Let it fly even till it come
to the beauty of Thy house, and to the throne of Thy glory.[8]

The meditative musings of the first half of the work led to
a contemplation in the Theocentric manner of heaven and its
joys, which chapters (XVI-XVII) fairly reproduce a supposititious sermon of St. Augustine. Then follow eight chapters
which make up a Christocentric meditation transcribed chiefly
from St. Bernard's *Sermons on the Canticles* and his *Liber de
Diligendo Deo.* The following excerpt, typical of this portion
of the work, expresses the heart of mystical contemplation.

Through love the soul withdraweth and departeth aside from the
bodily senses, so that it may forget itself in knowing and loving
God. And this is done when the mind, being allured by the
unspeakable sweetness of God, doth after a sort steal away from
itself, or rather is ravished and slippeth away from itself to the
intent it may enjoy God and delight in Him.[9]

The remaining chapters of this illuminating treatise are
taken from the writings of Hugh of St. Victor and St. Anselm.
The speculative nature of the Victorine mysticism is reflected
even in these few excerpts from Hugh's pen.[10] A single work
of St. Anselm furnishes the closing chapters which are in the
typical vein of the *De Contemptu Mundi* literature. They describe with ardent longing the blissful end of contemplation,
which is entirely in keeping with the affective character of the
work as a whole.

[6] *The Contemplation of Christ,* p. 9.
[7] *Ibid.,* pp. 14-28.
[8] *Ibid.,* p. 15; cf. *P. L.,* XL, 953.
[9] *Ibid.,* p. 40; cf. *P. L.,* XL, 960.
[10] Cf. *P. L.,* 964.

The medieval compiler of this tract evidently collected his material with a view to present an attractive and complete text of contemplation. The longing of the soul, the purificatory injunctions, the meditation on Christ, and the final consideration of divine union, compose the framework of his method. The work reproduces not only the spirituality of St. Augustine, but also that of authorities who are among the most representative of medieval mysticism.

Summary

The preceding analysis of Christian mysticism from foreign sources in England during the sixteenth century constitutes a definite literary background for the ensuing study of native mystical literature. How much this literature is dependent upon the foreign influences is not an easy question. Certainly the prevalence of the mystical literature which has already been noted ought to have exerted a significant influence upon mystical productions not only during Elizabeth's reign but also upon the mystical writers of the following century. The subject of foreign mystical literature in England during the sixteenth century is still open for further investigation since, like all merely pioneer work, the preceding pages have indicated the vastness of the field which remains for investigators further to analyze and expand.

It is fairly obvious that the Elizabethans were attracted to the matter and form of Elizabeth's version of Queen Margaret's poem, and that the interest of the learned English Queen in Boethius would have sustained interest in Colville's adaptations of the *Consolation*. Similarly the widespread interest in Dante and Petrarch and the Renaissance Neoplatonists during this period served to bring to perhaps unsuspecting readers the full spirit and method of Christian mysticism from both medieval and Renaissance authorities. In the very popular translations of the Spanish mystics, particularly of Luis de Granada, Elizabethan readers and writers had at hand summaries and numerous citations from the great authorities of the spiritual life, and also in Granada himself there was perfect exemplification of Christian mysticism in its simple and most attractive aspects.

INTRODUCTORY NOTE

Before proceeding with a detailed study of Elizabethan mysticism, a brief general view of the field is essential. First, one notes that native English exponents of Christian mysticism were never numerous, albeit they were not wanting in vitality and power. Rolle, Hilton, Juliana of Norwich, the anonymous author of *The Cloud of Unknowing* and *Dionysius Hid Divinity,* fairly represent the mystical movement of the ages which precede the Tudor period. These works were intimately related to the writings of St. Bernard, St. Bonaventure, the Victorines, Suso, Gerson, and other great continental authorities upon the mystical life.

The Tudor period, as a glance at the Appendix to this study will show, presents two distinct waves of mystical literature: one shortly after the beginning of the sixteenth century, the other during the last two decades of Elizabeth's reign. The trough lies in the middle decades. The first wave of Tudor mysticism is expressed in the numerous printed editions of early English mystics, in printed translations of classic Latin treatises of the golden age of medieval mysticism, and in the few works of the Oxford Reformers. The second and more potent wave of English mysticism reached its crest in the *Fowre Hymnes* of Edmund Spenser. Spenser's *Hymnes* mark the focal point towards which this work on Elizabethan mysticism has aimed. They are a perfect exemplification in English literature of noble, thought-laden poetry, didactic, sacred, and at the same time wholly conformable to the canons of mysticism. Indeed, the methodology of Christian mysticism as developed and illustrated in Part I and Part II of this work appears in a new and practical light in the *Hymnes* of Spenser. He may be said to accompany the revival of English mysticism in the 1580's with his superb handling of the " House of Holiness " in Book One of *The Faerie Queene*; and with his *Fowre Hymnes* he marks the high tide of mystical poetry in the Elizabethan Age.

The lesser mystical writers I shall consider, not in chronological order, but in an ascending scale of approximation to the spirit and method of the *Fowre Hymnes,* with Spenser at the top, as follows:

Chapter I.   The Mystical Sonneteers
Barnabe Barnes—Henry Constable—Henry Lok.

Chapter II.   The Spirit more than the Letter
Alexander Hume—Sir John Davies—Henry Walpole—Gervase Markham—Robert Parsons—John Davies of Hereford — Thomas Lodge — Philip Howard, Earl of Arundel and Surrey.

Chapter III.   The Full Methodology
Robert Southwell — Nicholas Breton — Edmund Spenser.

CHAPTER I

THE MYSTICAL SONNETEERS

The employment of the sonnet apart from its conventional usage for serious, religious purposes took on a new vogue in the mid-sixteenth century, naturally enough, with the appearance of the *Petrarca Spirituale* of Malipieri in 1536.[1] The sonnet was used to express religious sentiment in France by Joachim du Bellay,[2] but more extensively by Abbé Jacques de Billy [3] and Phillippe Desportes.[4] In England, the French influence was undoubtedly felt by Barnabe Barnes and Henry Constable,[5] who with Henry Lok are representative English sonneteers employing this form not only in a religious vein, but also definitely in the spirit of Christian mysticism.[6]

BARNABE BARNES

Barnabe Barnes (1569?-1609), whose father was Bishop of Durham, entered Oxford in 1586, and left without taking a degree.[7] He entered upon an expedition to France, and later wrote a collection of love-poems entitled *Parthenophil and Parthenophe,* which was published in 1593. This was followed in 1595 by what Barnes considered his best work: *A Divine Centurie of Spirituall Sonnetts.* These deeply religious poems

[1] Alfred H. Upham, *The French Influence in English Literature* (New York, 1908), p. 97. Salvatorino published in 1549 his *Tesauro di Sacra Scrittura,* developed from the *Rime* of Petrarch.

[2] See Sonnet VI of " XIII Sonnetz de L'Honneste Amour," *Œuvres Françaises de Joachim du Bellay,* Marty Laveux (Paris, 1860), II, 27. Note also the musings on the mutability of things in his *Les Antiquitez de Rome,* which were translated by Spenser.

[3] The *Sonnets Spirituels* were published in 1573 and 1578.

[4] The *Œuvres Chrétiennes* belong to the *genre.* Cf. Upham, pp. 130-132.

[5] Cf. Upham, pp. 129, 135.

[6] Among the English writers of religious sonnets of this period whose poems are not mystical either in spirit or method are Abraham Fraunce and Fulke-Greville (*Caelica,* from Sonnet 85 to end).

[7] Cf. *Thomas Lodge and Other Elizabethans,* ed. by Charles J. Sisson (Cambridge, 1933), pp. 175-229.

were, according to Barnes, written in the " sure fire of immortall entheusiasme," and " in earnest true motions of the
spirit were they devised . . . to stirre up your spirits to divine
contemplations." [8] Obviously such productions would partake
of the mystical spirit. The opening Sonnet " retracts " former
profane love poetry, and sounds the motif of the entire sonnet
sequence.

> No more lewde laies of lighter loves I sing,
>> Nor teach my lustfull Muse abus'de to flie
>> With sparrowes plumes, and for compassion crie
> To mortall beauties, which no succour bring.
> But my Muse, fethered with an angel's wing,
>> Divinely mounts aloft unto the skie,
>> Where her Love's subjects with my hopes doe lie:
> For Cupid's darts prefigurate Hell's sting;
>> His quenchlesse torch foreshadows Hell's quenchlesse fire,
> Kindling men's wits with lustfull laies of sinne.
> Thy wounds my cure, deare Saviour! I desire
> To pearce my thoughts thy fierie cherubinne,
>> By kindling my desires, true zeale t'infuse,—
> Thy Love my theame, and Holy Ghost my Muse.[9]

The first half of the hundred sonnets approximately accord
with the Christocentric type of contemplation. The remaining
poems are largely of the poet's own consciousness of sin, his
ultimate reliance on faith for salvation, and meditations upon
heaven and God. Petitions for purification and illumination [10]
run through the entire series. One can note a perceptible spiritual development unfolding in the sonnets, which at times exhibits flashes of the mystic vision. The upward flight of soul
which Barnes all too rarely voices distinguishes these sonnets
from merely devotional poetry of this and other periods. Thus

---

[8] " To the Reader," pp. v-vi. References are to *Heliconia,* ed. by T. Park
(London, 1815), vol. II. (Pagination is of the edition of the Sonnets, not
of the volume itself.)

[9] Park, p. 1.

[10] The following lines are fairly typical:
> Rayons of glorie, beames of endlesse joy!
> Cherish my soule, illuminate my wits;
> Ravish my sences with celestiall fits.
>> (Sonnet XXIX, Park, p. 15).

he wrote, " Oh, my deare God! my comfort, my solláce: / My swift soule flies, with my divine thought's wings, /Ev'n to thy bosom." [11] This is not great poetry, for Barnes was not free from the literary excesses of his age; yet one notes, despite the limitations of the sonnet form, the correct upward swing of the mystic soul in flight. This is illustrated in the final sonnet of the series.

> Lighten my pensive soule, which could flie on
>> To thy sweete Mercie's seate, Heaven's Paradise!
> Thy pure Dove's white winges (that my soule may rise
> And mount from this base earth) deare Lorde! tye on.
>> So shall my spirite flye from starre to starre,
> And, in consent of musicke's sweete reporte,
>> Beare thy rich glories forth from farre to farre,
> Where cherubins with seraphins resorte,
>> And angelles with archangelles still, to sing
> The glorious wonders of their Heavenly King! [12]

HENRY CONSTABLE

Henry Constable (1562-1613) graduated at Cambridge in 1579, and he later took up residence in France with other recusant exiles where, for the most part, his two collections of sonnets were written.[13] *Diana,* his first published work, is a series of love sonnets which enjoyed four editions with additional poems included between 1594 and 1604. Constable was popular in England, although his position as leading Catholic exile brought him into conflict with the government. He was a close friend of the Countesses of Warwick and Cumberland and he dedicated some love sonnets to Sydney's " Stella," Lady Rich. Constable's poems were praised by Ben Jonson, Edmund Bolton, Sir John Harrington, Robert Tofte, Drayton, and the author of *The Return from Parnassus,* and he is mentioned by

[11] Son. XXXVII, Park, p. 19.
[12] Son. C, Park, p. 51. See also Sonnets VIII, XVI, XVIII, XIX, XXVII, XLV, XLVI, LXI, LXX.
[13] William C. Hazlitt, *Diana: The Sonnets and Other Poems of Henry Constable, B. A.* (London, 1859), pp. ix-x. And see also Louise Imogen Guiney, *Recusant Poets* (New York, 1939), pp. 303-316.

Francis Meres among others.[14] He closed his *Diana* with a kind of " retractation " to the effect that these were but " vayne poems," and expressed determination to employ the remnant of his wit to calmer thoughts.[15]

Constable's place as a mystical poet depends upon a series of seventeen sonnets which circulated only in manuscript, entitled *Spiritual Sonnettes to the Honour of God and Hys Saintes.* Sir Sydney Lee dates these about the year 1593.[16] They are a minor contribution to Elizabethan mystical literature. The *Sonnettes* are mainly contemplations, as far as the limitations of this form admit, on subjects familiar to the mystics. The first three poems on the Persons of the Blessed Trinity are strictly theological with the mystical ascent expressed in the final sextet.

> True God of Love! from whom all true love sprynges,
> Bestowe upon my love thy wynges and fyre,
> My soule and spyrytt ys, and with thy wynges
> May lyke an aungell fly from earth's desyre,
> And with thy fyre and hart inflam'd may beare,
> And in thy syght a seraphim appeare.[17]

The sonnets " To our Blessed Lady," apart from the usual treatment of this theme, noticeably reflect the prevailing cult of love and beauty. This admixture of mysticism and " Petrarchism " in the following sonnet is a significant warning against driving too sharp a distinction between the poetry of mystical love and verses celebrating earthly love and beauty. The Elizabethans found the difference, if any, exceedingly slight; and they have ample precedent from the Renaissance love and beauty poets.

> Sweete Queene: although thy beuty rayse upp mee
> From ssyght of baser beutyes here belowe:
> Yett lett me not rest there: but higher goe
> To him, who tooke hys shape from God & thee.
> And if thy forme in hym more fayre I see,
> What pleasure from his deity shall flowe,

[14] Guiney, pp. 304, 316; Hazlitt, pp. xv-xviii.
[15] T. Park, *Heliconia*, " Advertisement " to Constable's sonnets, vol. II.
[16] *Life of Shakespeare* (London, 1931), p. 717 cited by Guiney, p. 306.
[17] Son. 3, Hazlitt, p. 51.

By whose fayre beames his beuty shineth so
When I shall yt beholde aeternally.
Then shall my love of pleasure have his fyll,
When beuty self, in whom all pleasure ys,
Shall my enamored sowle embrace & kisse:
And shall newe loves, & newe delyghtes distyll,
Which from my sowle shall gushe into my hart,
And through my body flowe to every part.[18]

The series of pieces in honor of Mary Magdalene are significant in their emphasis upon her " teares " of repentance, and for the familiar distinction between earthly and heavenly beauty, and the distinct note of mystical union in the closing sonnet.

Sweete Saynt, thou better cans't declare to me,
What pleasure ys obtaynt by heavenly love, . . .
For lyke a woman spowse my sowle shall be,
Where synfull passions once to lust did move,
And synce bethrothed to Goddess sonne above,
Should be enamoured with his deity. . . .
And clasped in the arms of God injoye
By sweet conjunction everlasting joye.[19]

HENRY LOK

Henry Lok (1553?-1608?), the son of a London merchant, was engaged by the State on various diplomatic missions to the continent and in the East. He is known only for his religious sonnets, which exhibit a deep spiritual insight. His life was troubled, and he suffered greatly from poverty.[20] He wrote a verse translation of Ecclesiastes, and more than 300 sonnets, all of which belong definitely to sacred and mystical poetry.[21] " The varied and deep religious feeling which throbs in them," wrote a modern critic, " is sufficient of itself to give them an

[18] Son. 12, *ibid.*, pp. 57-58.
[19] Son. 17, Hazlitt, p. 61. This sonnet is omitted by Park, *Heliconia*, vol. II, in the publication of Constable's *Spiritual Sonnettes*. Hence, the poet is usually credited with only sixteen sonnets in this series.
[20] *Poems by Henry Lok, Gentleman,* ed. by A. B. Grosart, *Miscellanies of Fuller Worthies' Library* (London, 1871), pp. 82-88.
[21] Fifty-six other commendatory sonnets composed by Lok were collected by Richard Field, printer of the 1597 edition of Lok's works. Cf. Grosart, pp. 395-389.

honourable place in the religious poetry of the age." [22] Lok's sonnets, dedicated to the Queen, appeared in 1597 under the following title: *Sundrie Christian / Passions, Contained / in Two hundred Sonnets. / Diuided into two equal parts: / The first consisting chiefly of Meditations, Humi / liations and Prayers. / The Second of Comfort, Joy, and / Thanksgiuing.*[23] It appears that the first part of this work at least was written before 1593,[24] and that both series of sonnets were printed before the edition of 1597, since the title-page of the volume containing Lok's complete poems refers to the *Sundrie sonnets of Christian Passions as heretofore printed.*[25] The 1597 edition contains a third series of a hundred sonnets which represent a distinct falling off in inspiration, and probably are of later composition. They are entitled, *Sundry Affectionate Sonnets of a Feeling Conscience.*

Lok's purpose was didactic and he chose the popular sonnet form as more conducive to his purpose than a formal religious treatise.[26] Viewed in respect to their mysticism, the first hundred sonnets follow the Purgative and ascetical way, with sin and repentance as principal themes. The *Sonnets of Comfort, Joy, and Thanksgiuing,* however, are remarkably different in spirit, and make up interesting illustrations of the Illuminative and Unitive ways or stages of the mystical life. Noteworthy is the typical language of the mystical experience.

> Some times with eagles flight aloft I tower,
>   And seeme to see the glorie of the sunne. . . .
>
>   . . . The quiet mind in peace and rest,
>   Possessèd of the thing it most desired,
>   —A thing so precious, nowe durst haue aspirde
>   To gaine, vnlesse the giuer had him blest.[27]

The group of sonnets in praise of heavenly love and beauty,

[22] C. J. Abbey, *Religious Thought in Old English Verse* (London, 1896), p. 159.

[23] Grosart, p. 138.

[24] *The firste parte of christian passions* was licensed to be printed in 1593 Cf. Grosart, p. 74.

[25] *Ibid.,* p. 97.

[26] See " To the Christian Reader," Grosart, pp. 85-88.

[27] Son. LXIII, Grosart, pp. 269-270.

likewise, are truly mystical, and, if read apart from their context, might be erroneously considered as evidence of Lok's acquaintance with Neoplatonism.[28] He who beholds heavenly beauty, says Lok in the first sonnet of the group, will join his voice with angelic praises. Then, in one of his finest sonnets, he chants of divine beauty.

> O heauenly beautie, of loue the fountaine true,
>   Whose shining beames do penetrate my soule,
>   With such a zeale as former thoughts controll,
>   And drawes heart, powre, and will Thee to insue;
> Thou mak'st my fainting sight for to renue,
>   And dazeling eyes new strength thus to attaine;
>   To Whom alone perfection faire is due.
> Thou mak'st Earth's bewteous shadow seeme but vain;
> Thy works of glorie, and of powre remain. . . .
>   Thy loue doth wean my thoughts from baser loue,
>   And mak'st my heart and mind to soare aboue.[29]

The typical contempt of the world and the mutability thereof are treated in a number of sonnets;[30] the pursuit of the mystic quest is present in others, and the contemplation of nature as it reflects the Creator is the subject of two sonnets of which one presents a miniature example of the Theocentric type of contemplation.[31] The large quantity of Lok's poetry and the comparatively small range of subjects to which the mystics have traditionally limited themselves may account for much repetition and tedious self-analysis. The sonnet form does not lend itself to the adoption of the full methodology of Christian mysticism such as one finds in the *Fowre Hymnes* of Spenser; hence one finds in these sonneteers portions only of the three ways or stages of the mystical life and of the Christocentric and Theocentric types of contemplation. The treatment of love and beauty in Lok and even in Constable is significant in view of similar emphasis in Spenser; and it affords further evidence of the partiality of the mystics for noble love and transcendent beauty.

[28] Sonnets XXXI-XXXIV; XXXV-XL. Grosart, pp. 247-249; 250-253.
[29] Son. XXXII, Grosart, pp. 247-248.
[30] Sonnets XLVIII, LVI, LVII, LVIII, LX, Grosart, pp. 259, 265-267.
[31] Sonnets XLVII, LII, Grosart, pp. 259, 262.

CHAPTER II

THE SPIRIT MORE THAN THE LETTER

ALEXANDER HUME

Alexander Hume (1560-1609) was a Scottish clergyman who, in virtue of *A Treatise on the Felicitie of the Life to Come* (1594), and *Hymnes or Sacred Songs* (1599), merits a minor place at least among the poets who exemplified the method of Christian mysticism. Hume's *Treatise of Conscience* (1593), although not mystical, manifests thorough acquaintance with medieval theology.[1] The work on *The Felicitie of the Life to Come,* in prose, is in the manner of mystical treatises with, however, no originality of treatment. The following lines partly descriptive of heaven illustrate his mode of contemplation.

The excellencie of the place is taken from the situation, the fabrick, and the bewtie thereof, from the high stiles that are given vnto it in the Scriptures, and from the worthiness of the architrure [*sic*], and inhabitants thereof. Which is also aggreged by the liuely description of a bewtifull terrestrial place, and consideration of the bewtie of the firmament, the Sunne, the Moone, and the Starres, and the argumentation, from the lesse to the more. The dignitie of the indwellers is manifested by their righteousness, and are the three persons of the Trinitie, the holy Angells, or ministering Spirites, and are the Saintes or elect people of God.[2]

Hume's *Hymnes* are not exceptional in any way; nor do they adequately exemplify the traditional method of Christian mysticism as is the case with the *Fowre Hymnes* of Spenser. The second, " Of God's Benefits Bestowed Vpon Men," has some merit; at least there is spirit in the opening lines.

> My saull is reveist vp fra me, my reson is bereft,
> My sensis are astoniest all, my mind hir use hes left,
> My memorie is quite confusde, transported is mine hart,
> My spreit is in ane extasie, as I were to depart.[3]

[1] *The Poems of Alexander Hume,* ed. by A. Lawson for *The Scottish Text Society* (Edinburgh, 1902), pp. 130-143.
[2] *Ibid.,* p. 144.   [3] *Ibid.,* p. 17.

SIR JOHN DAVIES

There is a trace of Christian mysticism in the famed *Nosce Teipsum* of Sir John Davies (1569-1626), which first appeared in 1599.[4] This long "philosophic" poem in two parts[5] is definitely medieval in its teachings, and, apart from its traditional theology, might be called a versification of scholastic psychology.[6] This introspective poem, derived ultimately from St. Augustine,[7] has the same title as a chapter in Richard of St. Victor's *Benjamin Minor*.[8] The poem is rather an exposition of immortality than of mystical contemplation; yet one of its arguments is based upon the aspirations of the soul for the eternal and immutable, and its joy in such contemplation. God is known through his works;[9] and the human soul, at first content, grows restless of earth. "She lights on that and this, and tasteth all, / But pleased with none, doth rise and soar away."[10] Then, the poet but touches the inner spring of mysticism in the verses of which the following lines are a part.

> But if upon the world's Almighty King,
>   She once doth fix her humble louing thought,
> Who by his picture drawne in ev'ry thing,
>   And sacred messages, her love hath sought;
> Of him she thinks she cannot thinke too much,
>   This honey tasted still in euer sweet;
> The pleasure of her rauish'd thought is such,
>   *As almost here, she with her bliss doth meet:*[11]

HENRY WALPOLE

This little known English poet has a place among the lesser Elizabethan mystical writers in virtue of a single poem which was written in prison while the author, a young recusant,

[4] *The Works of Sir John Davies,* ed. by A. B. Grosart, in *Fuller Worthies' Library* (London, 1869), I, 9-10.

[5] "Of Human Knowledge" and "Of the Immortality of the Soul."

[6] This is inadequately brought out by Mabel Dodge Holmes, *The Poet as a Philosopher. A Study of Three Philosophical Poems* (Univ. of Pennsylvania, 1921).

[7] See, for instance, the *Confessions*, Book X, cc. 7-11; 16, 20, 23, 26.

[8] *Opera Omnia, P. L.,* CXCVI, 55-56.

[9] *Grosart,* p. 121.   [10] *Ibid.,* p. 130.   [11] *Ibid.,* p. 132 (italics mine).

11

awaited execution in 1595. Henry Walpole belonged to an old family of Norfolk, where he was born in 1558. He completed his education at Cambridge and at the English College at Rheims. In 1584 he became a Jesuit and was ordained priest four years later. After serving on the continent for some years, he departed for England in 1593. He was arrested shortly after his arrival and spent the remaining year and more in prison. He was hanged, drawn, and quartered on April 17, 1595.[12]

Walpole's poems remained in manuscript until modern times.[13] They are intensely religious in spirit and are of high poetical quality. His longest poem of ninety-five stanzas bears the title, *The Song of Mary the Mother of Christ*.[14] Another poem, *Upon the Death of M. Edmund Campion* is singularly descriptive of the fate which Walpole himself was soon to suffer.[15] *A Dialogue between a Catholic and Consolation* is in the same religious vein and reminds one of St. Thomas More's *A Dialogue of Comfort against Tribulation*.[16]

A Prisoner's Song is distinctly mystical in character and is based upon a poem wrongly ascribed to St. Augustine, " Jerusalem, my happy home," and the opening stanza of Walpole's poem is similar to a poem by St. Peter Damian, " My Thirsty Soul desires her Draught." These likenesses are brought out in the opening stanzas of the poem which ring with the true mystic's exaltation.

> Jherusalem, thy joyes Devine
>   noe joyes may be compared to them
> noe people blessed soe as thine
>   noe Cittie like hierusalem.
>
> My thirstie soule Desyres her Drought
>   at heavenlie fountains to refreshe

[12] See Guiney, *Recusant Poets*, pp. 255-256 and *Lyra Martyrum*, an anthology of the English martyrs: 1503-1681, by Rev. Sir John O'Connell (London, 1934), pp. 53, 65.

[13] See *Recusant Poets*, pp. 259-267; *Lyra Martyrum*, pp. 53-65, and also notice of printing of Walpole's poems in *Recusant Poets*, p. 257.

[14] Part reprinted in *Recusant Poets*, pp. 266 ff.

[15] Printed in *Lyra Martyrum*, pp. 53 ff.

[16] *Ibid.*, pp. 58-59.

> my prisoned mynd would faine be out
> of chaines and fetters of the flesh.[17]

The poem is typical of numerous mystical treatises both in
prose and verse which attempt to describe the blessed state of
the heavenly city. This we have seen is part of the Theocentric
type of contemplation. Much of the description of the heavenly
joys is taken from the Apocalypse, but noticeably in Walpole's
poem the happiness of heaven is presented as by one who longs
to raise his pinions from this vale of care and thus partake
of the hoped-for bliss of heaven. The verses which follow are
characteristic of a mystical poem and are, moreover, significant
in that they approach closely to certain of Edmund Spenser's
lines in the *Hymne of Heavenly Beautie*.

> Where all the glorious saintes doe see
> the secretes of the Deitie
> The godhead and in persons three
> the super-blessed trinitie.
> The depth of wisdome most profounde
> all puisant high sublimitie
> The breadth of love without all bound
> in endlesse longe eternitie.
>
> The heavy earth belowe by kynde
> above ascendes the mountinge fier
> Be this the Center of my mynd
> and loftie speare of her desyre.[18]

One notes in these lines the end of the Theocentric contemplation with mention of the saints and especially of the Godhead
and the " secretes," that is, the attributes of the Deity. Among
these are wisdom, omnipotence, " sublimity," love, and eternity.
The final quatrain is reminiscent of the mystic ascent of the
contemplative.

GERVASE MARKHAM

Gervase Markham (1565-1637), of the ancient Nottingham
family of Markhams, was educated at Cambridge. He wrote
technical treatises on horticulture, and published a number of
poems on various subjects in a prevailingly serious, didactic

---

[17] *Recusant Poets*, p. 259.   [18] *Ibid.*, 264.

vein.[19] In 1596 appeared his version of Solomon's Song of Songs. The influence of Christian mysticism is seen in *The Teares of the Beloved* (1600) and in its sequel, *Marie Magdalene's Teares* (1601).

The Teares of the Beloved [20] is a meditation on the Gospel narrative of the passion of Christ put by the poet into the mouth of St. John, " the beloved disciple." It is an indifferent treatment of the subject; and reflects somewhat the *Imitation of Christ* by à Kempis, of which work the poet's copy is still extant.[21]

Marie Magdalene's Teares For the Losse of Hir Master Jesus is Markham's contribution to this popular mystical theme. The poem is long, consisting of more than two hundred six-line stanzas; and is made up of a Preface, seven " Lamentations " voiced by the Magdalen, and a Conclusion. It is, briefly, a continuation of the passion-story of the first poem, concluding with Christ's apparition at the Tomb. There is ample evidence of the poet's originality in the work, although it bears unmistakable marks of Southwell's prose treatise on the same subject.[22] The meditation on " the better part " chosen by Mary (Luke x, 42), and the scene with Christ, taken for the gardener,[23] are in the regular tradition of mystical poetry.[24] The sixth " Lamentation " contains a bit of that love-philosophy which is common to mystical and " Platonic " love poetry.

[19] *The Teares of the Beloved and Marie Magdalene's Teares by Gervase Markham,* ed. by A. B. Grosart, *Miscellanies of Fuller Worthies' Library* (London, 1871), II, 466-485.

[20] Its full title is: *The Teares of the Beloved: or The Lamentations of Saint John, Concerning the death and passion of Christ Jesus our Sauiour.* (Grosart, p. 490.)

[21] See *Imitation of Christ,* Bk. II, caps. xi-xii.

[22] See below, p. 171.   [23] Grosart, pp. 569-575.

[24] The following stanza (*ibid.,* p. 574) is an illustration.

But oh ! the great effects of rarest loue !
If loue a languour be, how then live I ?
If life, how do I then such dead fits proue ?
If it bereaueth sence, how did I see
    The angels then ? if it revive the same,
    Why did I not know Jesus when he came ?

For euen as loue, in nature coveteth
To be united, yea transformed whole,
Out of it selfe into the thing it loueth:
So what unites, loue most affecteth sole,
     And still preferreth least coniunction euer
     Before best ioies, which distance seems to seuer.[25]

The poet draws noble resolutions generously throughout the poem which make up a continued Christocentric contemplation. This is particularly true of the " Conclusion " with its plea " to rise out of mortalitie's foule mire," [26] and to profit by the entire meditation.

O Christian soule take Marie to thy mirrour,
And if thou wilt the like effects obtaine,
Then follow her in like affections fervour,
And so with her, like mercie shalt thou gaine.[27]

In this poem, Markham chose one of the most popular subjects with which the mystics dealt. For the most part they associated the New Testament details concerning " the woman who was a sinner " (Luke vii, 37), with Mary, sister of Lazarus and Martha, figure of the contemplative life (Luke x, 39), who anointed the feet of Christ at Bethany (John xii, 3). The mystics identified this woman with Mary Magdalen, who stood weeping at the Tomb and was the first to see the risen Christ (John xx, 1-18).[28] Despite the critical and exegetical warfare waged over the identification of these persons, the mystics, since St. Bernard,[29] found in Mary Magdalen all the essential elements of the mystical life: a conversion and repentance, a devout friendship with Christ, and an ecstatic apparition at the Tomb.

[25] *Ibid.*, p. 582.

[26]   " Crave to be cleane of that same filth sinne urged,
     For who is pure, that Iesus hath not purged? "
                                                  (*ibid.*, p. 594).

[27] *Ibid.*, p. 592.

[28] " To those who identify St. Mary Magdalene with the sister of Martha and Lazarus, and with the ' woman who was a sinner,' she cannot but be the New Testament symbol of the mystic " (E. Allison Peers, *Spanish Mysticism*, p. 31).

[29] Cf. *Serm. on the Cant. of Canticles*, I. 84.

Among the most influential treatises of medieval mysticism, the *Meditationes Vitae Christi* of the Pseudo-Bonaventure took especial pains to present the Magdalen as a subject for fervent mediation.[30] The equally popular *Mystica Theologia* conceived her as a model of prayer for the attainment of " unitiva et mystica sapientia." [31] The medieval mystics were accustomed to give prominence to Mary Magdalen, to her conversion and tears, whenever they treated in detail the life of Christ, particularly the passion and resurrection. An excellent example is found in the anonymous English *The Cloud of Unknowing*.[32]

This theme remained a popular one in the sixteenth and early seventeenth centuries. The chief work of the Spanish mystic, Malon de Chaide, was *The Conversion of the Magdalen*,[33] and the Italian mystic, Battista Verani, wrote extensively on the Magdalen,[34] as did numerous devotional poets of the sixteenth century. Other Elizabethan poets besides Markham took up this subject as will be noted in these pages; and it was celebrated in the early seventeenth century by Thomas Robinson,[35] Crashaw,[36] Herbert,[37] and Henry Vaughan.[38] Another important source of the Mary Magdalen literature is the religious drama. The earliest form of the mystery play, the liturgical trope, assigned to Mary an important role.[39] The lively dialogue and conversation in such mystical works as the *Meditationes Vitae Christi* exercised strong, formative influence upon the dramatic representation of Mary Magdalen

[30] *S. Bonaventurae Opera Omnia*, XII, cap. XXVII, p. 546; cap. LXX, p. 593; cap. LXXXVIII, p. 618.

[31] *Op. cit.*, XII, cap. III, part III, p. 35.

[32] Ed. by Justin McCann (London, 1924), Chapters XVI-XXIII, pp. 49-67.

[33] This work was published only in 1592, although it had been written many years previous. (Cf. Peers, *Spanish Mysticism*, p. 30.)

[34] *Dolori mentali di cristo, Acta Sanctorum*, May, vol. VII, pp. 488 ff.

[35] *Life and Death of Mary Magdalen*, ed. by H. O. Sommers (Marburg, 1887).

[36] *Sainte Mary Magdalena*, or *The Weeper, Complete Work*, ed. by Grosart (London, 1874), I, 3-18; cf. also II, 40.

[37] *Marie Magdalene, Works of George Herbert*, ed. by Grosart (London, 1874), I, 199.

[38] *Mary Magdalen, Works* (Oxford, ed. 1914), II, 507.

[39] Cf. E. K. Chambers, *Medieval Stage* (Oxford, 1903), II, 75-76.

and the Virgin.[40] There is a parallel treatment of these characters by the mystics and by the authors of the mystery and morality dramas. Professor Carpenter has outlined the history of Magdalen in the continental and English drama, omitting, however, the important influence of the mystics.[41] Thus, we see in Markham an Elizabethan contribution to this popular theme of the Magdalen. His treatment is in reality a case of focusing attention upon a subject which is found to a greater or less degree in numerous mystical treatises.

PARSONS' CHRISTIAN DIRECTORY

The Christian Directory or Booke of Resolution by Robert Parsons [42] was one of the most important spiritual treatises to appear during the reign of Elizabeth. It was a complete handbook of Christian fundamentals combined with ascetical and mystical theology. This work was printed at Rouen in 1582 and went through a second and enlarged edition which appeared in 1585; it was reprinted in 1587. In 1584 the first London edition appeared under the editorship of Edmund Bunny with changes in accord with reform doctrines. Of this work twelve separate editions of the First Part, and at least eight editions of the Second Part are dated between the years 1584 and 1600.[43] Gabriel Harvey, the good friend of Spenser, praised the work, and Nash recommended it as a cure for atheism.[44] Robert Greene alleged this treatise as a cause of his famous repentance,[45] and it converted Richard Baxter

[40] E. Male, *L'art religieux de la fin du moyen âge en France*, cc. I-III. This work gives evidence of the influence which the *Meditationes Vitae Christi* had on the drama at the end of the Middle Ages. Cf. also P. Pourrat, *Christian Spirituality*, II, 184-187.

[41] *Introduction to The Life and Repentance of Marie Magdalen*, by Lewis *Wager*, ed. by Frederick Ives Carpenter (Chicago, 1904), pp. xxxii-xxxviii.

[42] Robert Parsons was born in Somersetshire in 1546, educated at Oxford, became a Jesuit in 1575, and returned from Louvain to England in 1579. He remained in England nearly two years in the service of the recusants. He died at Rome in 1610.

[43] Cf. Herbert Thurston, " Father Parsons' ' Christian Directory,' " *The Month* (Dec. 1894), 457-476.

[44] *Ibid.*, pp. 468-472.

[45] " The Repentance of Robert Greene," *Life and Works of Robert Greene*, ed. by A. B. Grosart (London, 1886), p. 165.

at the age of fifteen to a " Holy Life." [46] Parsons classed his
book with the great mystical productions of the past, and named
such writers of " devotion, pietie, and contemplation " as St.
Bernard, St. Bonaventure, Gerson, à Kempis, Granada, and
others,[47] but for the most part the work belongs properly to
Elizabethan devotional literature.

The First Part of the *Christian Directory* is essentially in
the Purgative way or stage of mystical methodology; and
specifically concerned with removal of *impedimenta* to the soul's
progress.[48] Numerous quotations from Augustine are included
in the typical Theocentric contemplation which closes the First
Part.[49] The mystical exaltation is found in the following excerpt.

Let us heare St. Augustine once more breathing out his sense of
it in these most affectionate expressions, " O Joy, above all joys,
and without which there is no joy. When shall I enter into thee,
to see my God that dwelleth in thee. O everlasting Kingdom! O
Light Eternal! " Would we who live in these days, and read these
Meditations employ our thoughts as this holy man did, we should
no doubt feel ourselves more inflamed with ardent love, and desires
of this our heavenly bliss.[50]

The second Part of the treatise, containing " added incentives

[46] *Reliquiae Baxterianae,* p. 3, cited by Helen C. White, *English Devotional
Literature (Prose) 1600-1640* (Univ. of Wisconsin Studies, No. 29, 1931),
p. 143.
[47] Quoted from the 1585 edition by Thurston, p. 471.
[48] ". . . And thus released from sin, be supported by inward consolation
of God's holy Spirit, proceed to the Exercises of good works" (*Parsons,
His Christian Directory, Being a Treatise of Holy Resolution in two parts,*
Anon. [London, 1700], p. 223).
[49] The attention given to the divine attributes and Wisdom is significant
in view of Spenser's employment of *Sapience* in his *Hymne of Heavenly
Beautie.* "Were all the excellencies of heaven and earth united in one, the
beauty, the wisdom, the virtue, the greatness, the goodness, the usefulness and
advantage of any creature, yet still that Lord and Saviour is infinitely more
to be valued and admired. For he does not as they do, partake only of all
these perfections, but is the very things in the abstract; Beauty and Wisdom,
and Greatness, and Goodness, and Happiness itself, the Source of all these.
. . . *The Wisdom of God will then appear in her native Beauty and full
lustre, and be acknowledged the true and only Wisdom"* (*ibid.,* pp. 181-2;
185). (Italics mine.)
[50] *Ibid.,* pp. 239-240.

for advancing and persevering to the end " follows most closely the Illuminative way of the mystics. It aims directly to point the " passage to Heaven " for those who have made their " resolution." [51] The regular *Contemptus Mundi* counsels are important in Parsons' method; and the reference to beauty is the familiar one. Earthly beauty is a source of vanity as well as a mirror of divine beauty. " God has imparted some degrees of loveliness to his creatures; thereby to draw us to love and admiration of the Creatour by these rays and shadows of his own essential goodness." [52] The plea for perfection is undisguised throughout the second Part of the work. They are numbered among the perfect " who love the singular advantage of being directed more effectually than common men in spiritual matters." [53] Such men enjoy an inward, secret light and consolation which they alone know " who have received it and felt it." [54] This is characteristic of the higher ways or stages of mystical progress. Mystical perfection, indeed, is explained as

Lifting us above the world and all that it can do for us, while fixing our eyes upon objects certain, though distant and eternal; it exercises and inflames our charity by reviving in us the remembrance of the love of Christ, while conforming us to his example.[55]

The value of Parsons' work for the historian of Elizabethan mysticism lies in the great amount of material in form of citations taken from authorities ancient and medieval on the spiritual life. The range of the author's reading was enormous, going from Plato and Aristotle, the Neoplatonists, through the Fathers, and including numerous quotations from spiritual writers of the middle ages. The clear and complete analysis of contemplation in the first part taken mainly from St. Bernard's treatise, *De Consideratione*, is important in that it placed before the Elizabethan reader fundamental notions of the importance and the method of meditation and contemplation.

[51] *Ibid.*, p. 252.
[52] *Ibid.*, p. 356. Compare with Spenser's *Hymne of Heavenly Beautie*, 15-21 and especially 127-132.
[53] *Ibid.*, p. 304.   [54] *Ibid.*, p. 307.   [55] *Ibid.*, p. 343.

Noteworthy also are Parsons' contemplations of God and His attributes, and the familiar view that the mind arrives at the knowledge of God by means of His works. In general, this work is by no means a treatise on the higher reaches of the mystical life; it is elementary and colored by the evident need to present simply the main points of Christian doctrine and the fundamental motives for salvation and perfection.

The *Christian Directory* ranks somewhat below the English versions of Granada in the history of English mysticism, but they are alike in their unprecedented appeal to all classes and creeds of Elizabethan England.

JOHN DAVIES OF HEREFORD

John Davies, noted member of the Countess of Pembroke's circle, was a voluminous and altogether prolix writer of sacred and profane poetry. Born at Hereford about 1565, he taught penmanship and worked on his verse, the first of which appeared in 1602. He died at London in 1618.[56] In the long list of Davies' religious and didactic poetry only three compositions have to do with Christian mysticism: *Mirum in Modum* (1602), *The Holy Roode* (1609), and *The Muses Sacrifice* (1612).

Mirum in Modum, A Glimpse of God's Glorie is a poem of 311 nine-line stanzas. It is apparently drawn from treatises of scholastic psychology based on Aristotle, orthodox theology, medieval physiology, and Christian mysticism. As with so much of Davies' writings, this poem abounds in repetitions and extravagant similes, and on the whole is difficult to read. Taking for his basis a familiar scholastic division of knowledge into sensuous and supra-sensuous,[57] Davies proceeds to versify medieval epistemology. This part, he says, belongs to philosophy. There is, however, knowledge of God which is supra-sensuous in origin, based on revelation, and acquired only through contemplation. This is proper to mysticism. " Contemplation then doth ruminate / on *Truth,* and none but Truth."

---

[56] *The Complete Works of John Davies of Hereford,* ed. by A. B. Grosart, in *Chertsey Worthies Library* (London, 1878), vol. I, pp. ix-xx.
[57] *Ibid.,* p. 13.

> She (*divine Pow're*) consociates Pow'res divine,
> Gliding through Heau'n on hir celestiall wings,
> And to the *Angells* Hymnes hir eares incline,
> And all the Host of *Heav'n* together brings
> At once, to view those bright-eye-blinding things.
> Yet staies not here, but doth hir selfe intrude,
> Into the presence of the King of Kings,
> To see th' *Objective* sole *Beatitude*.[58]

Davies gives other remarkable evidence of familiarity with Christian mysticism.[59] He affirms that contemplation by force of love brings the aspiring soul, while yet body-bound, into such close proximity to the " heavenly flame " that it experiences the " holy kisse of the Spouse," which must needs be " short as lightnings leame " as the mystical union is effected.

> As if the fire and it were one,
> So is the loving *Soule* through loues desire,
> With *God* in *Contemplation* made intire.[60]

Only death or a special gift of grace will vouchsafe sight of the Vision which was enjoyed once by Moses, St. Paul, and St. John.[61] The soul, too, must be wary of illusions in the higher spiritual life.

The means of the contemplative ascent is the conventional one: " For in thy workes thy steppes do plaine appeare." [62] The poet presents in due order the contemplation of the divine attributes. Of interest is his thoroughly correct account of them.

> Men beeing most vnable to finde out
>   The substance of the God-head by their sence,
>   Haue with the highest titles gone about
>   To explicate that Super-*excellence*. . . .
> He is vnmou'd, vnchang'd, pure, bodilesse,
>   Most simple, subtile, endlesse infinite.
>   All-wise, all good, all great, beginninglesse:

---

[58] *Ibid.*

[59] See *Wits Pilgrimage,* sonnet 36, for reference to Martha and Mary and the two Lives. Grosart, II, 26.

[60] Grosart, I, 14.

[61] *Ibid.,* p. 15.   [62] *Ibid.,* p. 16.

> All these are names by which we do recite,
> Not what he is, but what he is not, right.[63]

This is a good illustration of this part of the Theocentric type of contemplation. Davies' relation of the *Processions* in the Trinity, *Generation* and *Spiration*,[64] is more complete, yet not less precise than Spenser's account in his *Fowre Hymnes*.[65] The Christocentric meditation in *Mirum in Modum* is brief, and confined to mention of the hypostatic union.[66] This type of contemplation, however, to the exclusion of the Theocentric type, characterises *The Holy Roode or Christ's Crosse* which consists of 401 six-line stanzas.[67]

Davies published, four years before his death, a work exhibiting the full methodology of Christian mysticism, which consists of more than forty poems called *The Muse's Sacrifice*, or *Diuine Meditations*. One poem only, that out of St. Augustine, mentions its mystical source. As for the others, Davies' own statement holds true: " Here are no Nouels nor ought unusuall; but, here shall you see what hath been said of old in new Attire." [68] The same may be said for most of the mystical works of the Elizabethan period.

[63] Again, in full accord with theological tradition, he says,
> Those *Attributes* are borrowed from our Kinde,
> To lend our *Reason* light, that *Light* to see:
> But those essentially to him assigned,
> Of his owne Nature and existence bee.
> Namely, *Vbiquity, Simplicity,*
> *Eternity,* and sole *Omnipotence*
> Consorted all with perfect Vnity. . . .
> Then *Wisdome, Knowledge,* and *Intelligence.*
> (As in their Subject) are in him alone. (*Ibid.,* p. 19.)

[64] *Ibid.,* pp. 17-18. " ' By Procession' we understand ' the origination of one Divine Person from another.' There are two such Processions, viz. Generation (generatio, γέννησις) and Spiration (spiratio, πνεῦσις) " (Arthur Preuss, *The Divine Trinity* [St. Louis, 1915], p. 161). The Son proceeds from the Father by *Generation*; the Holy Spirit proceeds from the Father and the Son by what theologians call *Spiration.*

[65] *Hymne of Heavenly Love,* 27-39. See below, p. 211. Davies' reference to " Deities that in the Starres doe dwell " (*ibid.,* p. 17) illustrates Spenser's *Intelligences* in the *Hymne of Heavenly Beautie,* 84. But see below, p. 218.

[66] *Ibid.,* pp. 21-22.

[67] Grosart, I, 1-29.

[68] " To ouer-curious Critiques," *ibid.,* p. 8.

THOMAS LODGE

Thomas Lodge (1558-1625) [69] holds a most important place in the history of Christian mysticism in Elizabethan England. He was educated at the Merchant Taylor's School, and at Oxford, where he received his Bachelor's degree in 1577.[70] His recusancy,[71] his unsettled temperament, and his undoubted genius go to make him one of the most interesting and baffling characters of his time. He was a poet, dramatist, traveler, and physician; and a pioneer in the composition of prose romance and the heroic satire. Lodge is said " to have lived under the tyranny of a gnawing sense of neglect," [72] and his literary reputation now rests upon his *Rosalynde,* not so much for what it actually is, as for what Shakespeare took from it in *As You Like It.* Our interest in Lodge lies in that moral and didactic quality which appears with greater or less emphasis in all his works.[73] He was widely read in the lore of the ancients, both pagan and Christian; and was fond of citing as authorities in his moral works the greatest names of classic, patristic, and medieval literature.[74] Lodge's devotional temperament and his reading brought him into sympathetic and intimate contact with Christian mysticism. His life, as far as we know it, was

[69] The most probable date of Lodge's birth is placed at 1558 by Mr. N. Burton Paradise, in *Thomas Lodge, The History of an Elizabethan* (Yale University Press, 1931), p. 10.

[70] *The Complete Works of Thomas Lodge,* edited with a *Memoir* by Edmund W. Gosse, published by the Hunterian Club (Glasgow, 1883), p. 47. All references to Lodge's individual works are to this edition.

[71] Lodge was converted to Catholicism some time subsequent to his sojourn at Oxford. "He had," remarks Professor Paradise, "doubtless been subject to the influence of Rome ever since his Oxford days " (*op. cit.,* p. 17).

[72] Paradise, Preface, p. v.

[73] The religious element is strongest in the following *non*-mystical works: *Catharsis* (1591), *Robert the Divell* (1591), "wherein is contained his dissoluble life in his youth, his devout reconcilement and vertues in his age "; *The Life and Death of William Longbeard* (1593) and its poems which show "how sweet the fruits be of a reconciled and penitent soule "; the translations of *Seneca's Moral and Natural Works* (1614), and the *Summary Upon the Famous Poeme of William of Saluste Lorde of Bartas* (1621).

[74] See Miss Alice Walker's discussion of Lodge's sources in the *Review of English Studies,* VIII (1932), where she notes the origin of much of Lodge's non-mystical material.

a sort of mystic quest, a search for something which the London of his time denied him. He went from one profession to another, from one *genre* of literature to another; and died in the exercise of his final profession, that of doctor of physic, most probably of the plague in 1625 at the age of 67.[75]

Three of Lodge's works are in the direct tradition of Christian mysticism: *The Diuel coniured,* and *Prosopopeia,* both of which appeared in 1596,[76] and the *Flowers of Lodowicke of Granado,* which was printed in 1601. However, as early as 1589 Lodge revealed his love for contemplation in a poem, *In Commendation of a solitaire life* which was printed in the edition of *Glaucus and Scilla.* It contains the germinal thought later developed in *The Diuel coniured.*

The Diuel coniured

This work is a lengthy conversation of St. Anthony, famed hermit and contemplative of Egypt, with three worthy seekers after truth: a learned philosopher, named Metrodorus, an exiled magician, called Asterius, and a young Indian Prince. Anthony the hermit is hardly more than a symbol of the contemplative life, through whom Lodge argues so effectively that " both Metrodorus and Asterius, the one forsaking curiosity, and the other renouncing both astronomy and magicke, cast away their vainnesse of Philosophy, and humbly submitted them to *Anthony,* and euer after, from worldly minded men, became zealous and contemplative fathers." This work, when viewed apart from the tradition which it revives, is dull enough and heavy reading;[77] nevertheless, it is a document of Elizabethan mysticism of no little importance. Lodge himself valued this work highly; it represented the fruits of his own experi-

[75] "A new devotion made Thomas Lodge, doctor as well as poet, with a fine sense of professional duty, which was then rare, remain at his post to attend the poor during the plague in London" (Lewis D. Einstein, *Tudor Ideals* [London, 1921], p. 282.

[76] These works may have been written earlier, in view of the publication of no less than four books by Lodge during the year 1596.

[77] " It is," says Edmund Gosse, " a tedious soliloquy on virtue, put into the mouth of a ' virtuous and solitary Hermit called Anthony ' " (*Memoir,* p. 36, *Works,* vol. I).

ence, and his previous writings compared to it were but so much weeds and cockle.[78] It implies a " conversion," not unusual in writers of our period, and a frequent prelude to devotional compositions. Lodge was fully in sympathy with the philosophy which the hermit Anthony expounds in this work. In the preface to the hermit's instruction on the contemplative life, he says:

> But where found they thee, O holie *Anthony*? What office becomming thy happy spirite? What exercise wert thou occustomed in? Truly (as Gregorie saith) slaying, and sacrificing thy will; by obedience, pouring out, and offering thy soule in praier, testifying thy contrition by thy trickling teares: thus in thy earthly bodie didst thou practice an immortal worke, and with the immoved eie of thy mind, didst thou behold God in faith.[79]

The arguments of the philosopher in reproof of Anthony's stern mode of life only moved the hermit to extol his life of solitude and contemplation, and to review the three ways or stages to mystical perfection: mortification of the flesh, enlightenment of the soul, and a direct " walke to the celestial Paradise." The mystical life is well described in the following brief summary which Lodge put into the mouth of Anthony:

> What then letteth me (O Metrodorus) to imitate Christ? Whose life is a law to mine, and whose abstinence a lesson to instruct me? . . . The solitarie man (I tell thee) liuing on the earth, forsaketh the same, and mortified in the flesh is planted in heaven by the spirit: he burneth in the loue of God, to banish the loue of the world, he weepeth transitorie tears, to receiue eternal consolation: he fasteth in bodie, to be fed in soul: he depresseth himselfe, to be lifted up to heauen: he watcheth and thirsteth, to be refreshed in Paradise. . . . O happy contemplative men.[80]

The hermit's discourse left Metrodorus wholly confounded, and " he sat eying the ground." Then, after a lengthy discussion with the learned Asterius on the errors of magic and

---

[78] " Courteous sith you haue long time drawn the weeds of my wit, and fed yourselves with the cockle of my conceits, I have at last made you gleaners of my haruest and partakers of my experience " (*To the Reader, Works,* III, 3).

[79] *The Diuel coniured,* p. 5.   [80] *Ibid.,* p. 10.

astrology, Anthony resumed his disquisition on the contemplative life. This part of the work is a collection of opinions upon
the spiritual life garnered from patristic and medieval authorities.[81]   The effect upon Elizabethan readers resulting from this
armament of authorities on the spiritual life must have been
impressive. Lodge cites his sources throughout the work, and
unhesitatingly places these quotations in the mouth of Anthony,
quite oblivious of the curious anachronisms which are involved.
Anthony states that the beauty of nature reflects the beauty
of its celestial Source, and compares the purified love to the
feather which " except steeped in water, is easily lifted vp into
the aire with the least puff of wind, so mans spirit (except
soiled by vices, and detained by worldly infirmities) is still
mounting vp to heauen, as being a portion of the same." [82]
Lodge's final words are from St. Augustine's *Confessions*, and
the passage is significant in presenting perhaps for the first
time to English readers a translation of St. Augustine's
important description of mystical love.

What loue I, when I loue Thee? Not the beauty, forme, or fauer
of the bodie, not the ornament of time, not the brightnesse of light,
befriending the eyes [istis amicum oculis], not the sweet melody
of delightful songs, not the odoriferous smell of flowers, spices, and
ointments, not Manna, not hony, not soft pleasing members, fit for
fleshly embraces: I loue not these, when I loue my God, and yet I
loue a certaine light, and a certaine voice, and a certaine smell, and
a certaine meat [cibum], and a certaine embrace when I loue my
God: the light, the voice, the odour, the food, the embrace of my
inferior [interior: interioris hominis] man: where that shineth to
my mind, the place comprehendeth not [which no place can contain: quod non capit locus] and where that soundeth, which time
carieth not away, and where that smelleth which breath disperseth
not; and where that favoreth, which eating diminisheth not; and
where that sticketh which sacietie [satietas] pulleth not away.
This is that which I loue when I loue my God.[83]

[81] Lodge quotes these authorities eighteen times in reference to the spiritual
life. St. Augustine is mentioned seven times; St. Bernard on four occasions.
[82] *Ibid.,* p. 70.
[83] *Ibid.,* p. 71. The bracketed emendations to Lodge's translation are from
text of the *Confessions* in Migne, *P. L.,* XXXII, 782-783. Compare with
Pusey's translation, Book X, 8 (Everyman ed.), p. 208.

The spirit and general framework of this book is strongly suggestive of Petrarch's *Vita Solitaria* with which Lodge may have been acquainted, in view of his familiarity with other writings of the Italian poet.[84] Petrarch, too, conceived of the contemplative life, as apart from life in cities, to be highly conducive to virtue. He, as well as Lodge, was attracted by the philosophy of the desert solitaires of which Anthony was the first Christian exponent.

Prosopopeia

The full title of this work is *Prosopopeia Containing the Teares of the holy, blessed, and sanctified Marie, the Mother of God. Luke 2. And moreover, the swoord shall pearce the soule, that the thoughts of many hearts be opened.*[85] This book was printed in 1596 by Edward White, a lifelong friend of Lodge,[86] and was jointly dedicated to the Mother Countess of Darby, and the Countess of Cumberland.[87]

The initials T. L. at the close of the dedication in the Lambeth copy of *Prosopopeia* are our only external evidence of Lodge's authorship; indeed, in two of the three extant copies these initials are transposed.[88] Collier unhesitatingly attributed the work to Lodge,[89] although David Laing [90] suggested Laurence Twine as possible author, in accordance with the dedication initials. Professor Paradise, however, well observes that " the transposition of initials means little when the vagaries of Elizabethan printing are considered." [91] He is convinced moreover, from considerations of style, subject-matter, and

---

[84] Cf. Alice Walker, " Italian Sources of Lyrics of Thomas Lodge," *Modern Language Review,* XXII, 75-79.

[85] Cf. *Bibliographical Index, Works,* I, pp. 18-19.

[86] Paradise, p. 125. White also printed the English translations of Luis de Granada's *Book of Prayer and Meditation.* (See above, p. 128.)

[87] Edmund Spenser, in the same year, dedicated his *Fowre Hymnes* to the Countess of Cumberland and to her sister, the Countess of Warwick.

[88] In the copies at the Bodleian, and in the Drummond collection, Edinburgh, the dedication is signed L. T.

[89] See *Bibliog. Index, Works,* I, 18-21.

[90] Introduction to " The Defense of Poetry, Music and Stage-Plays," *Shakespeare Society* (London, 1853).

[91] *Op. cit.,* p. 127.

method, that Lodge is the author of *Prosopopeia.*[92] One may add that the frequent quotations from patristic and medieval mystical authorities in this work are in keeping with Lodge's similar treatment in *The Diuel coniured,* and in *The Flowers of Lodowicke of Granado.* A typical " retractation " of former " lewd lines," more pronounced than usual, is contained in the address " To the Readers." [93] Although one finds small justification in either Lodge's poetry or prose for this repentant attitude, the treatise on " Marie's Teares " indicates a complete " conversion," and a familiarity with a most difficult form of contemplation. The dedicatory letter sounds the note which pervades the entire book. " I doubt not," he observes, " but that they will proue holy motives of meditation. . . . Use them as the goldsmith his mettal, trie them at the test of your contemplation, and so prise them." [94]

Lodge announced the purpose of his work, which is fully in accord with the numerous treatments in medieval mysticism of the theme of Mary's compassion for the sufferings of Christ. " In meditating with Marie," he says, " you shall finde Iesus : in knowing Christ's sufferance, you shall be inflamed in his loue." [95] In final analysis, this is a work of Christocentric contemplation; and what is most significant, it is a veritable treasury of quotations, most of them marginally annotated, from both the Scriptures and the greatest authorities on the spiritual life. St. Bernard alone is quoted sixteen times,[96] St. Anselm thrice,[97] including a mention of St. Bonaventure. St. Augustine is cited on eleven occasions,[98] while Luis de Granada furnishes three different quotations.[99] The Pseudo-Dionysius

---

[92] " The internal evidence is overwhelmingly in the poet's favor," wrote Louise Imogen Guiney in attributing this work to Lodge. (*Recusant Poets, op. cit.,* p. 232.)

[93] " Now at last I have wounded the world with too much surfeit of vanitie, I may bee by the true Helizeus, cleansed from the leprosie of my lewd lines, & beeing washed in the Jordan of grace, imploy my labour to the comfort of the faithfull " (*Prosopopeia,* p. 13, *Works,* vol. III).

[94] *Ibid.,* pp. 5-7.   [95] *Ibid.,* p. 12.

[96] *Ibid.,* pp. 5, 6 (three times), 11, 19, 22, 23, 29, 47, 48, 50, 62, 63, 98, 106.

[97] *Ibid.,* pp. 49, 51, 74.

[98] *Ibid.,* pp. 13, 42 (twice), 44 (twice), 46, 82, 83, 84, 87, 113.

[99] *Ibid.,* pp. 24, 29, 93.

is noted but once, that in a paraphrase of the *Divine Names.*[100] " I have written nothing without example," said Lodge of his sources, " I build no waies on mine owne abilitie." [101]

Although Lodge followed no regular order throughout this lengthy treatise, it divides itself according to different aspects and considerations of the central theme—the Passion of Christ. There is, first, a praise of Mary herself, for which Lodge is heavily indebted to St. Bernard.[102] Then follows a lamentation spoken by her upon sin, which is the basic cause of her " teares," [103] a meditation upon the actual sufferings of Christ, at one time in the first person, and again " personating her son." [104] The personal note of repentance follows the consideration of Christ as Man, and as God.[105] Among allusions to mystical union, the following is noteworthy : " She was touched with an unspeakable affection of love, whereby being united to God, we seeme to be converted & made one with him " ; [106] or this adaptation from the Pseudo-Dionysius : " First loue him, for loue uniteth things together, drawing all mans interest from himself, and placing it in another." [107] To analyze the treatise further would merely involve repetition of the typical Christocentric characteristics of mystical writings. Lodge adhered strictly to the limitations placed upon him by his subject, by the authorities whom he uses, and above all by the particular form which this species of meditation had already developed in mystical literature.

The Background of Prosopopeia

The Christocentric contemplations of medieval mysticism were frequently accompanied by meditations on the *compassion* of Mary. " It is impossible," writes Abbé Pourrat, " to meditate on the passion of Christ without thinking of the sorrows of his mother. So great were these sorrows that it is not, say the mystics, in our power to understand them." [108] St. Bernard

---

[100] *Ibid.*, p. 80.
[101] *Ibid.*, pp. 11-12.
[102] *Ibid.*, p. 18.
[103] *Ibid.*, pp. 22-39.
[104] *Ibid.*, pp. 39-71.

[105] *Ibid.*, pp. 76; 87-90.
[106] *Ibid.*, p. 48.
[107] *Ibid.*, p. 80.
[108] *Christian Spirituality*, II, 32.

was the first of the medieval mystics to give current to this form of meditation,[109] and the probable source for much of the writing on the subject of Mary's "teares" is the *Liber de Passione Christi et Doloribus et Planctibus Matris ejus* which was written in the thirteenth century, and circulated as a work of St. Bernard.[110] The famed *Stabat Mater* of Jacopone da Todi was a rimed version of the same subject. The most influential of the medieval mystics glorified the tears and dolors of the Virgin.[111]   Richard of St. Victor,[112] Suso,[113] and Gerson [114] follow with a remarkable sameness the spirit and the method of the above-mentioned Pseudo-Bernard. Similarly, fervent meditations on the sorrows of Mary are included in the *Stimulus Amoris*,[115] and the *Meditationes Vitae Christi*,[116] which were long known as works of St. Bonaventure. The lamentations of Mary also came to be represented in the Mystery plays and gained altogether the widest possible currency.[116a]

In view of the universality of the subject-matter of *Prosopopeia,* as well as the "teares" literature of Mary Magdalen and St. Peter, it is obviously impossible to consider any particular work as Lodge's source.[117] This is especially true in

[109] See, for example, "Sermon for the Feast of the Assumption," St. Bernard's *Sermons on the Cant. of Canticles,* trans. by a Priest of Mt. Melleray (Dublin, 1925), III, 277-279.

[110] *P. L.,* CLXXXII, 1134-1142.

[111] To the writings of the mystics is due the origin of the devotion to the Seven Dolors of Mary. (Cf. Pourrat, p. 321; J. Dissord, "La Transfixion de Notre Dame," Études [de la Compagnie de Jesus], May 5, 1918, pp. 264 ff.)

[112] *De Sacrificio Abrahae et B. Mariae, P. L.,* CXCVI, 1043 ff.

[113] *Book of Eternal Wisdom,* pp. 99-111.

[114] *Sermo Alius in Coena Domini; Expositio in Passionem Domini, Opera Omnia,* vol. III, pp. 1134, 1193-1196.

[115] "Meditatio compassiva, in Parasceve, doloris quem tunc habuit beata Virgo Maria." *Op. cit.,* cap. III, p. 638.

[116] "Lamentum virginis," also "Meditatio de Domina et sociabus." *Ibid.,* cc. LXXXIII, LXXXIV, pp. 610-612.

[116a] Professor Carleton Brown calls attention to the Marian Lament, which reached its highest development in English literature in the fifteenth century, and he suggests that the religious drama may also have served to stimulate and vitalize the religious lyric. (*Religious Lyrics of the XVth Century* [London, 1939], p. xxi.)

[117] Professor Paradise (p. 126) believes that the immediate inspiration for *Prosopopeia* were Southwell's *Marie Magdalen's Teares* (1591) and *Saint*

view of his own copious source references. His book stands first among the Elizabethan examples of this type of mystical literature.[118]

The Flowers of Lodowicke of Granado

In 1601, Lodge published another volume in the strict tradition of Christian mysticism entitled, *The Flowers of Lodowicke of Granado*.[119] It is a unified compilation of material gathered from the writings of the popular Spanish mystic, Luis de Granada,[120] which Lodge translated not directly from Granada but from a Latin compilation of Granada's works. This work of Lodge also contains translated passages from two medieval Pseudo-Augustine treatises. What may have been a sequel to this work, called *The Paradise of Praiers*, also " gathered out of the spiritual workes of Lewis of Granado and Englished by T. L." was entered in the Stationers' Register nearly a month later.[121] This book is not extant unless it be identical with the fourth edition of a work dated 1633 without the name or

Peters Complaint (written before 1595). Collier (p. 156) observed that Lodge was influenced also by Nicholas Breton's (?) *Marie Magdalens Loue* (1596). The basis for these conjectures is Lodge's remarks in the *Epistle to the Readers* (p. 10), "For other that Love wept (as Peter his apostasie, Marie her losse & misse of Christ), their teares wrought from them either repent or loue."

[118] Constable's sonnets and Walpole's poem on this subject have already been noted. (See above.) Two *post*-Elizabethan examples of this tradition are Amelia Lanyer's, *The Salutation and Sorrow of the Virgine Marie* in *Salve Rex Judaeorum* (1611), (Corser, *Collect. Anglo-Poet.*, Part VIII, p. 346), and Crashaw's, *Quaeret Jesum suum Maria; Santa Maria Dolorum or the Mother of Sorrows, Complete Poems* (Oxford Edition, 1927), pp. 379, 284.

[119] It was entered in the Stationers' Register on April 23, 1601. (Arber's *Transcrit*, III 183.) The work bore the following title: The / Flowers of Lodowicke / of Granado./ The first part./ In which is handled / the conuer- / sion of a Sinner./ Translated out of Latine in- / to English, by T. L. Doctor / of Physicke./ At London, / Printed by I. R. for Tho- / mas Heyes, and are to be sold / in Paules church-yeard, at the signe / of the Greene-dragon. / 1601./

This book was not reissued in the Hunterian Club reprint of Lodge's work. Copies of this book are in the British Museum and in the John Newberry Library, Chicago. For a further discussion of it, see A. H. Arkle, *Notes and Queries,* 10th Series, V (1906), p. 246.

[120] See Part II, pp. 123-129.   [121] Arber's *Transcript*, III, 184.

initials of Lodge, but similarly entitled and compiled from the treatises of Luis de Granada.[122]

Lodge probably took as his immediate source for *The Flowers of Lodowicke of Granado,* one of two Latin compilations from the Spanish writings of Granada;[123] and his marginal notes and references at the ends of chapters show that he had direct recourse to Latin texts of the *Sinners Guide,* the *Manual of Christian Life,* and chiefly, the *Book of Prayer and Meditation.* Although Lodge explicitly states that "this is a worke of the learned and spirituall Granado, aptly translated into English,"[124] he also availed himself of other sources, notably the Pseudo-Augustine's *Meditations,* and *Soliloquia,*[125] both medieval treatises of highly contemplative nature.

The Flowers of Granado is not alone an accurate rendition of the ascetic mysticism of the popular Spaniard, but it reflects the pure medieval spirituality of the works attributed to St. Augustine. We are already familiar with the medievalism of Thomas Lodge, and through his mystical writings it is not the Renaissance, but the middle ages that live again for Elizabethan readers.

PHILIP HOWARD, EARL OF ARUNDEL AND SURREY

Blessed Philip Howard, Earl of Arundel and Surrey, born in 1557, was a grandson of Henry, Earl of Surrey, the poet. Tutored by John Foxe and educated at Cambridge, Philip Howard incurred the hostility of Elizabeth when he became a Catholic in 1584. In the following year, he was imprisoned in

---

[122] *A Paradise of Praiers: containing the purity of Devotion and Meditation: Gathered out of all the spirituall exercises of Lewes of Granado: and Englished for the benefit of the Christian Reader.* Professor Paradise (p. 166) feels there is a possibility that this work and the book described in the Stationer's Register as "Englished by T. L." are the same.

[123] Henry Cogmon made such a collection entitled, *Flores ex Omnibus Opusculis Spiritualibus* (Ludovici Granatensis) Colon., 1585. Another work was, *Flores Lodovici Granatensis ex omnibus ejus opusculis spiritualibus summa fide excepta, et in octo partes distributi,* by Michael ab Isselt, Colon., 1598. (Cf. Underhill, *Span. Lit. in England of the Tudors* [*New York, 1889*], p. 406.)

[124] *The Flowers of Lodowicke of Granado,* "To the Reader," A₃.

[125] Cf. *P. L.,* XL, 863-898 and 901-942.

the Tower, where he remained until his death in 1595.[126] The
Earl spent the greater part of his ten years' confinement in
meditation, in composing spiritual pieces, and in translating
spiritual works.[127] Of these works, but five are extant. They
are: *The Foure-Fould Meditation of the foure last things,*
" Through Thy Cross and Passion," an *Epistle of Jesus Christ
to the Faithful Soule,* and two short poems translated from
Lanspergius.[128]

" Through Thy Cross and Passion " is an untitled poem in
four-line stanzas. It was written before 1590 since it was
included in the *Sydenham Prayer Book* of that date.[129] This
work is a meditative prayer on the passion of Christ and hardly
lifts itself into the class of mystical verse.

The Foure-Fould Meditation of the foure last things is a
long poem of at least 126 six-line stanzas. It was entered in
the Stationers' Register in 1606, and published as Robert
Southwell's in the same year. Philip Howard's authorship of
this work, however, is now beyond dispute.[130] Four transcripts
of this poem, written after the Earl's " attaynder " in 1585,
are still extant,[131] and the printed version of 1606 has now
been lost save a small brochure consisting of only a fragment, which at present is in the British Museum. Herbert
Thurston printed the fragment and other extracts of the work
in *The Month.*[132] The poem reflects a careful study of the

[126] *Lives of Philip Howard, Earl of Arundel, and of Anne Dacres, his Wife.*
Edited by Henry Howard, Duke of Norfolk (London, 1857). See also Cecil
Kerr, *The Life of Ven. Philip Howard, Earl of Arundel and Surrey* (London,
1926).

[127] Cf. Kerr, p. 122.

[128] Three treatises on the " Excellency of Virtue " were never published.

[129] From this source the poem was printed in the *Transactions of the
Catholic Record Society, Miscellanea,* VI (1909), pp. 29-30. Miss Guiney
also reprinted the poem in *Recusant Poets,* pp. 227-228.

[130] Miss Guiney agreed with the evidence of Father Thurston in *The Month*
(January, 1896, LXXXVI, 32-50), that the poem is by Philip Howard. See
also H. J. L. Robbie in *Review of English Studies,* April, 1929, V, 201-202.

[131] An early manuscript has the following sub-title: " Memorare novissima
tua et in aeternum non peccabis. A poeme of the Contempte of the worlde
and an exhortation to prepare to dye made by Phillipe, Earl of Arundel after
his attaynder " (Kerr, p. 144). A prose work, *The Four Last Things,* by
St. Thomas More treat of the same subjects. See above, p. 77.

[132] October, 1893, LXXXII, 230-245; January, 1896, LXXXVI, 40-42.

writings of Luis de Granada; [133] and as one would expect, much of it is devoted to subjects common to the *Contemptus Mundi* type of literature. There are numerous indications that this work has value as another sample of Elizabethan mysticism, but complete analysis must await its publication in full.

The most important of the Earl of Arundel's works are three translations from the well-known German mystic, John Lanspergius (1489?-1539). His *Alloquium Jesu Christi ad Animam Fidelem* [134] was rendered into English by the Earl and printed before 1595. A second edition appeared in 1596, and a reprint of this was made in 1610.

The work has the following title-page: " An epistle of Jesus Christ to the Faithful Soul, that is devoutly affected towards Him: Wherein are contained divine inspirations teaching a man to know himself, and intrusting him in the perfection of true Piety. Written in Latin, by the devout servant of Christ, Joannes Lanspergius, a Charter-House Monk; and translated into *English* by Lord Philip, xixth. Earl of Arundel." Although the first edition bears no place of printing, it was probably printed at London; the second edition, although it bears the imprint " Antwerp," was likely also printed at London.[135]

This lengthy treatise, with its repeated pleas for detachment from the world and for genuine growth toward perfection, embodies the essential ways or stages of the mystical life. More than half the work is of regulations and motives consistent with complete transformation of self.

A Hymne of the Life and Passion of our Saviour Christ, also translated from Lanspergius [136] by the Earl of Arundel,[137]

---

[133] " He used to read the Spirituall Books of Father Luis de Granada very frequently " (*The Lives of Philip Howard . . . and Anne Dacres his Wife,* p. 106).

[134] Printed at Antwerp, 1547, Louvain, 1572, and translated into several other languages. This work was included in the *Opera Omnia* of Lanspergius, Cologne, 1693, and in the modern critical edition, *D. Joannis Justi Lanspergii Carthusiani, Opera Omnia in quinque libros distributa,* Montreuil-sur-Mer, 1888.

[135] See *An Epistle of Jesus Christ to the Soul,* edited by a Monk of Parkminster (London, 1926), Introd., p. xxvi. This is a reprint of the London, 1610 edition.

[136] See *Opera Omnia* (Montreuil-sur-Mer), V, 395 ff.

[137] Cf. *An Epistle,* etc. 1926 edition, Introd., pp. xxviii-xxix.

appeared with the second (1595) edition of the *Epistle*. This *Hymne* is definitely a Christocentric contemplation.

A Hymne wherein the praises of all Creatures are offered up unto the Creatour is in eighteen eight-line stanzas, and is likewise a translation from the Latin of Lanspergius.[138] As the title indicates, this *Hymne* is in the formal manner of the Theocentric type of contemplation.[139]

These contributions of Philip Howard, Earl of Arundel and Surrey, to English mysticism rightfully place him with Southwell, Breton, and Spenser. His poems do not possess great literary merit; certainly he was not so gifted as Southwell nor so forceful as Breton, and he lacks the great literary power and beauty of Spenser. *An Epistle of Jesus Christ to the Faithful Soul* added its modest share to the English mystical movement; and it is significant that the two final *Hymnes* appeared in manuscript before the *Fowre Hymnes* of Spenser, and like Spenser's poems are excellent exemplifications of Christian mysticism.

---

[138] See *Opera Omnia*, V, 414 ff.
[139] Reprinted by H. J. Thurston, "Catholic Writers and Elizabethan Readers," *The Month*, LXXXVI (1896), 43-44.

CHAPTER III

THE FULL METHODOLOGY

ROBERT SOUTHWELL

Blessed Robert Southwell, of the ancient Norfolk family of Southwells, was born in 1561 and educated at Douai and Rome, where he entered the Society of Jesus in 1578. He was sent on the English mission in 1586 and from that date until his execution at Tyburn in February, 1595, was engaged in intercourse with the English Catholics and in composition of his literary works, which circulated widely in manuscript before publication.[1]

Southwell earned an honored place among the truly great religious writers of the Elizabethan period with a fairly large amount of verse and prose which appeared between the years 1591 and 1595. Southwell's prose, conformed to popular Euphuistic standards, and the plaintive, lyrical strain of his sacred poetry attracted readers irrespective of creedal differences.[2] The merits of his writings were recognized by Mars-

---

[1] Southwell's poetry is edited by A. B. Grosart, *The Complete Poems of Robert Southwell, S.J.,* in *Fuller Worthies' Library,* 1872. There is no complete edition of the prose. W. Joseph Walter edited *Mary Magdalene's Funerall Teares,* the *Epistle of Comfort,* and *Triumphs over Death* in *The Prose Works of Robert Southwell* (London, 1828); J. M. De Buck translated and edited from unpublished MSS. the *Spiritual Exercises and Devotions* (London, 1931).

[2] All these works were printed in London: *Mary Magdalene's Funerall Teares,* in prose, appeared in 1591, 1594, 1602, 1607, 1630, etc. *The Triumphs over Death,* written in 1589, was published in 1595, 1596. *St. Peter's Complaint,* a long poem of 132 six-line stanzas, went through the following editions: 1595 (twice), 1596, 1597, 1599, 1602, at London; and at Edinburgh in 1602. A collection of twenty-four shorter poems which Grosart calls *Myrtae* were printed (with a few poems excepted) in the 1595 editions of *St. Peter's Complaint;* the remaining pieces were added in 1596 and in subsequent editions. Southwell gave the name *Maeoniae* to another collection of twenty-four poems which appeared in 1595 (two editions), 1596 and 1598. Other works in verse and prose are printed by Grosart; some still remain in manuscript. See Grosart, pp. lxvi-lxxii; also Herbert Thurston, "Father Southwell, the Popular Poet," *The Month* (Feb. 1895), pp. 231-246.

170

ton,[3] Lodge,[4] Gabriel Harvey,[5] and reputedly also by Ben Jonson.[6]

The relation of Southwell to Christian mysticism was of life-long duration. He had for teacher at Douai the noted theologian and mystic, Leonard Lessius;[7] and he was early imbued with the thoroughly ascetical and mystical *Spiritual Exercises* of St. Ignatius.[8] During his imprisonment he was allowed the Bible and the works of St. Bernard, the only books for which he petitioned the Queen.[9] In his student days Southwell wrote a series of seventy-three meditative exercises of varying length and of undoubted spiritual value.[10] He made an English version of Diego de Estella's important mystical treatise, *Meditaciones Devotissimos del Amor de Dios*,[11] which he entitled *A Hundred Meditations of the Love of God*. Although the work circulated only in manuscript,[12] it added to the already impressive volume of English mysticism from Spanish sources.[13] *The Foure-Fould Meditation*, written by Philip Howard, may have been revised by Southwell, who was the intimate friend and counsellor of the Earl during their imprisonment.

Mary Magdalene's Funerall Teares in prose antedates all other Elizabethan mystical treatment of this subject.[14] South-

---

[3] *Certayne Satyres,* Sat. IV.

[4] See above, influence of Southwell on Lodge, p. 164, f. n.

[5] "Mary Magdalen's Tears," wrote Harvey, "was elegantly and pathetically written" (*Letters of Gabriel Harvey, Works,* ed. by Grosart [London, 1882], II, 291).

[6] In the *Conversations with Drummond,* "That Southwell was hanged; yet so he (Jonson) had written that piece of his, the Burning Babe, he would have been content to destroy many of his" (quoted by Grosart, p. xciii).

[7] Cf. *Spiritual Exercises and Devotions,* ed. by De Buck, p. 3.

[8] E. Allison Peers, *Studies of the Spanish Mystics* (London, 1927), p. 15 ff.

[9] Quoted from Challoner by Grosart, p. lvii.

[10] *Spiritual Exercises and Devotions,* p. 11. Another manuscript of Southwell's early period is now lost. It was apparently written in the formal traditional method of Christian mystical treatises, since its title read: *Meditationes Roberti Sotvelli Martyris de Attributis Divinis ad amorem Dei excitantes—Exercitia et Devotiones ejusdem* (cf. *ibid.,* p. 15).

[11] First published at Salamanca, 1576. See *The Month* (Nov. 1925), pp. 443-445.

[12] Edited in 1875 (London) by John Morris.

[13] See above, Part II, p. 122.

[14] Gervase Markham's work appeared in 1601. See above.

well's work is a paraphrase of John xx, 1-8, which is cast in
meditative form and interspersed with ejaculations and spiritual
fruit drawn from the sufferings and death of Christ. There
is a markedly gradual development until a mystical ravishment
is reached in the apparition of Christ to Mary at the Tomb.
Southwell, who wrote that " none can express a passion that
he does not feel," [15] closed this long prose treatise with a
glimpse of the mystical vision.

If, with Mary, thou cravest no other solace of Jesus, but Jesus
himself, he will answer thy tears with his presence, and assure thee
of his presence with his own words; that having seen him thyself,
thou mayest make him known to others—saying with Mary, " I
have seen the Lord." [16]

St. Peter's Complaint [17] is a companion piece in verse to the
earlier meditation of the Magdalen. Seen through the eye of
repentant Peter, the denial of Christ and subsequent forgive-
ness by the Master are enlarged in perspective by the poet to
include the universal lot of human kind, sin and folly, and the
spiritual readjustments which follow upon a penitent conversion and change of life.

The Myrtae

The shorter poems called " *Myrtae* " were published in the
editions of *St. Peter's Complaint.* They manifest a similar tone
of detachment, of soul-purification, but less of " tears " and a
more exalted fervor and transcendence. They express a longing
for release from a life of suffering as in the following lines,
which may have an autobiographical interest.

> Not where I breathe, but where I love, I live,
> Not where I love, but where I am, I die.

The reciprocal love of God and man is the subject of " Life's
Death, Love's Life " [18] which is in the typical strain of the
mystics. " Synne's Heavy Load " [19] is a meditation on the

---

[15] Introd. to *Mary Magdalene's Funerall Teares,* ed. by Walter, p. II.
[16] *Ibid.,* p. 83.   [18] Grosart, pp. 86-87.
[17] Grosart, pp. 11-44.   [19] *Ibid.,* pp. 105-106.

Passion, a favorite subject with Southwell. The well-known " Burning Babe " [20] is a mystical vision poem of universal power and charm.

The Maeoniae

The *Maeoniae* or *Certaine Excellent Poems and Spirituall Hymnes* are, as the printer of the 1595 edition affirms, " divine Meditations." [21] Southwell is here in the tradition of the great medieval poets of mysticism, Adam of St. Victor and Jacopone da Todi and Dante. Taking the chief mysteries of Christ's life from the Conception of the Virgin Mary to the Passion, he treated these subjects in short poems expressive of moral reflection. Such contemplations make up the mystical *Meditationes Vitae Christi,* and embrace the usual subjects of Christocentric contemplation. Southwell not infrequently allowed his soul to rise on the wings of contemplation as in these lines,

> My hoveringe thoughtes woulde fly to heaven,
> And quiet nestle in the skye;
> Fayne would my shipp in Vertue's shore
> Without remove at anker lye.[22]

Again, in " Seeke Flowers of Heaven " one notes the spiritual ascent, the celestial beauty, and the mystical ravishment. Since this short poem is one of the poet's finest achievements in verse, it deserves a citation in full.

> Soare up my soule unto thy rest, cast off this
> loathsome loade.
> Long is the date of thy exile, too long the
> strickt abode.
> Graze not on worldly withered weede, it fitteth
> not thy taste,
> The flowers of everlasting spring, doe grow
> for thy repast.
> Their leaves are staind in beauties die, and
> blazed with their beams.
> Their stalks enameled with delight, and
> limbde with glorious gleams,

---

[20] *Ibid.,* p. 109. [21] *Ibid.,* p. 114.
[22] " Man's Civill Warre," Grosart, pp. 165-166.

> Life giving juice of living love, their sugred
>   veines doth fill,
> And watred with eternall showers, their nectared
>   drops distill.
> These flowers do spring from fertile soile,
>   though from unmanured field,
> Most glittring gold in lieu of glebe,
>   these fragrant flowers do yeeld.
> Whose soveraigne sent surpassing sense,
>   so ravisheth the mind,
> That worldly weedes needs must be loath, that
>   can these flowers find.[23]

Southwell's " Platonism "

This series of poems reflects in particular the poetic fashion
of Southwell's time. Apart from the alliteration, the antithesis
and forced conceits, he, like Spenser later in the *Fowre Hymnes,*
took over certain expressions and modes of thought from
the " Platonic " love and beauty poetry. These expressions
are not, as has been pointed out, foreign to mystical treatment of divine love and beauty. The verses on the eyes of
Christ in *St. Peter's Complaint* take over the concept of courtly
poets that love enters through the eyes and inflames the heart;
and Southwell retains the imagery with obviously different
effects.[24] He countered the over-emphasis on merely human
love with poetry which celebrated its heavenly counterpart.
He believed that love is a form of Charity, that there is a
kinship and amity between human love and divine; and his
aim, unlike that of " present wits," is to elevate the object of

[23] From *Recusant Poets,* p. 297. Also in Grosart, pp. 167-168.

[24] *Ibid.,* pp. 24-29. Southwell turned a poem of Sir Edward Dyer to his
own deeply religious purpose, and justified his familiarity with current love
poetry. Thus he wrote in " Dyer's Phancy turned to Complainte," (Grosart,
p. 102) :

> And though I seeme to use
>   The feyning poet's stile,
> To figure forth my careful plight,
>   My fall and my exile.
> Yet is my griefe not fayn'd,
>   Wherein I sterve and pine,
> Who feeleth most shall thinke it least;
>   If his compare with mine.

human passion.[25] With the singers of " Platonic " love, South-well inveighed against " lewd lines," and, similarly, many of his poems are veritable hymns of heavenly beauty. Both these qualities are illustrated in " Lewd Love is Losse," notably in its second stanza:

> If picture move, more should the paterne please;
>   No shadow can with shadowed thing compare,
> And fayrest shapes, whereon our loves do ceaze,
>   But sely signes of God's high beautye's are,
> Go, sterving sense, feede thou on earthly mast;
> Trewe love, in heaven seeke thou thy sweete repast.[26]

Southwell sought and found the true image of heavenly beauty within his own soul; and with the mystics since St. Augustine, he expressed it in Platonic terms.

> Man's soule of endles bewtye's image is,
> Drawen by the worke of endless skil and might.[27]

Similarly in another poem he wrote,

> I seeke and finde a light that ever shynes:
>   Whose glorious beames display such heavenly sightes,
> As yeld my soule the summe of all delightes.[28]

Robert Southwell figures as a pioneer of greatest importance in the mystical movement in English literature of the 1590's. He produced more devotional and mystical verse than any other poet of the period save Breton, and his poetic quality and dignity is second only to Spenser's. The mystical writings are distinguished from those only devotional by a spirit of exaltation, a genuine uplift of soul, and the burning love of the true mystic which appears throughout his lines like a flame

[25] *Mary Magdalene's Funerall Teares,* ed. by Walter, p. 111.

[26] Grosart, p. 90; see also "At Home in Heaven" (pp. 88-89), wherein the poet explains in "Neoplatonic" fashion that true beauty is of the soul, not existent merely in "the features of a pleasing face." This indicates what Spenser exemplified in the *Fowre Hymnes,* the kinship in terms and certain modes of thought between Christian mysticism and Platonic love and beauty philosophy.

[27] "Looke Home," Grosart, pp. 65-66.

[28] "From Fortune's reach," *ibid.,* pp. 94-95.

from glowing embers.   This love-longing for union with God so marked in Southwell's poems is exemplified in the closing quatrain of " To the Wound in Christ's Side."

> O happie soule that flies so hie,
>   As to attaine this sacred cave:
> Lord send me wings that I may flie,
>   And in this harbour quiet have.[29]

Southwell's prose writings added to the body of formal mysticism in English; and he moreover sought to refine and elevate poetry of love to a higher degree of literary as well as spiritual excellence.[30]   He wrote at the same time as Breton, whose poems on the divine " passion " of love are in Southwell's vein.   He certainly influenced Lodge, and his poems bear striking affinity to the *Fowre Hymnes* of Spenser, not alone in their diction but also in a common praise of heavenly love and beauty cast in the mould made familiar to the Christian mystics.

NICHOLAS BRETON

The main facts of Breton's life are unknown; even the exact dates of his birth and death, generally given as 1545-1626, are matter of conjecture.   The son of a London merchant, Breton was well educated,[31] and he was a prolific writer of considerable versatility, whose works appeared in rapid succession over a period of nearly fifty years.   He wrote satirical,[32]

---

[29] *Recusant Poets,* p. 298.

[30] This was Southwell's poetic creed,

> It is the sweetest note that man can sing,
> When grace in Vertue's key tunes Nature's string.

(Lines prefixed to the volume of poems containing *St. Peter's Complaint* and the *Myrtae,* Grosart, p. 7.)

[31] From a reference to a contemporary diary, Grosart concluded that Breton attended Oriel College, Oxford.   See Memorial-Introduction, *Nicholas Breton* in *Chertsey Worthies' Library,* ed. by A. B. Grosart, I, xx.   All references are to this edition of Breton's works.

[32] *Pasquil's Madcappe, Pasquil's Foole's Cappe, Pasquil's Pass and Passeth Not* are in the typical satirical vein of Breton; they lack the " saeva indignatio " of contemporary satire.

pastoral,[33] romantic,[34] and religious prose and verse, all marked by a habitual refinement and high moral tone, though never wholly free from the euphuism and conceits prevalent in the literature of the closing decades of the Elizabethan period. He reflects chiefly in his writings the influence of Gascoigne;[35] with traces of Sidney, Spenser, Southwell, and Drayton.[36]

Religious poetry makes up a large part of the Breton canon. Out of a total of forty-six separate published works, ten are of definite and highly transcendental religious character. The deep piety and pronounced devotional nature of Breton's writings mark an important contribution to the mystical literature of the period. This is rarely if ever pointed out, together with the fact that Breton is one of the immediate forerunners of Crashaw, Vaughan, Traherne, and other mystical writers of the next century.[37] Mr. G. B. Harris observed that Breton was a mystic whose religious poetry with its expressions of " passionate longing for mystical union with Christ in the hereafter " was deep and genuine.[38] Breton was sensitive to the claims of the spirit over the appetites of the flesh, and was possessed of a missionary zeal for human betterment. Qualities such as these, conjoined with meek patience under affliction,[39] produced in Breton a melancholy quite different from that which is apparent in so many Elizabethan records. It is the melancholy of the unsatisfied soul, expressed in poignant feelings of sorrow and regret and longing. Such melancholy enters into the writings of all genuine mystics. It springs from

[33] *Arbor of Amorous Delightes* (1594) ; *The Passionate Shepherd* (1604) ; *A sweete Pastorall* in *England's Helicon* (1600).

[34] *Arbor of Amorous Deuices* (1597) ; *Melancholike Humours* (1610) are among the most representative of this species of Breton's poetry.

[35] Gascoigne was Breton's step-father for nine years. The didactic, moral, and satirical works of Breton's early years are in the vein of Gascoigne, as are, likewise, his lyrical and pastoral poetry. Cf. Oskar Heidrich, *Nicholas Breton, Sein Leben und seine Gedichte* (Leipsic, *n. d.*), p. 17.

[36] Cf. Grosart, " Memorial-Introduction," p. lxxi.

[37] Cf. Heidrich, p. 47.

[38] *Nicholas Breton, Melancholike Humours,* edited with an *Essay on Elizabethan Melancholy* (London, 1929), p. 84.

[39] Breton reveals the sorrows and trials of his life in a letter written in his declining years to *H. W.* See Grosart, vol. II, *A Packet of Letters,* p. 38.

13

a contempt of the world and a love longing of the soul for union and rest with God.

Breton's mysticism appeared early in his literary career. In 1577 he published a collection of romantic love pieces to which he added a short poem called, *A Solempne and repentant Prayer, for a former life mispent.*[40] More than a decade elapsed before the appearance in 1592 of *The Pilgrimage to Paradise* and its companion piece *The Countesse of Penbrookes loue,* both of which he rightly regards as " heavenly meditations." [41] His philosophy of life, which he expressed in *Brittons Diuinitie,* remained unchanged through the years and is definitely that of a mystic. " The contemplative life," he wrote, " is most neere vnto the angelicall nature"; and he felt that " the world is but a base corner when the King of Kings with the brightnesse of His glorie doth rauish the soules of His beloved.[42] His detailed analysis of contemplation in *Diuine Considerations* is the fruit of earnest mystical communion.[43] ' Contemplation ' and ' consideration ' were synonymous terms for Breton as they were also to the medieval mystics and their followers before the analysis of the mystical states by St. Teresa of Avila and the modern authorities on the spiritual life.

The word Consider, in a few letters containeth a large volume. . . . Yea, and the best parte of the moste perfect and diuine contemplation, of the most gracious and blessed spirites in the worlde: for if it please the Almighty God of his infinite goodness, so farr to inspire the soule of man with the grace of his holy spirite, as that being by the heavenly power thereof, drawn from the worlde to beholde the courses of higher comforts, when leauing the delights of fading vanities, he shall be rauished with the pleasures of Eternall life.[44]

" Breton does not merely prate of texts," observes his editor, " but is writing from personal experience."

[40] *A Floorish upon Fancie,* I, 59.

[41] *To the Gentlemen students and Scholers of Oxforde* prefaced to *The Pilgrimage to Paradise,* I, 4.

[42] *To the Readers of Auspicante Iehoua: Marie's Exercise.* Grosart, vol. II.

[43] Published in 1608. Grosart, vol. II. This work may have been inspired by Granada's popular work upon the same subject. (*Of Prayer and Meditation,* Part II, " Of Consideration.") This treatise follows the principles of St. Bernard's *De Consideratione.* (*P. L.,* CLXXXII.)

[44] *The First part of consideration concerning God,* Grosart, II, 7.

Five of Breton's works were dedicated to Mary Sidney, the Countess of Pembroke.[45] This illustrious patroness of letters exerted unquestioned influence upon religious literature of the period, not so much through her own writings,[46] as in the encouragement which she gave to productions of religious nature by other poets. Occupying alone the position in letters once shared with her brother, Sir Philip Sidney, the Countess included in her circle the most eminent contributors to the religious-mystical movement in the Elizabethan age. Spenser, Abraham Fraunce, and John Davies of Hereford are among the poets who gratefully acknowledged her friendship and patronage.[47] Breton's mysticism will now be pointed out in the most important of his works, and all will be treated in chronological order.

The Pilgrimage to Paradise and *The Countesse of Penbrookes Loue*

These poems were entered in the Stationers' Register in 1591,[48] and published in 1592. The first poem is a long allegory of Man conceived as a pilgrim on the journey of life which ends in Paradise; the second is a glowing rhapsody on mystical love. Breton's pilgrim sets out upon his journey accompanied not only by his five senses, which are personified as servants, but also by Reason their only trustworthy guide. These servants are carefully instructed ere they begin the "trauail that should neuer ende." [49] The first part of the poem relates the

[45] *The Pilgrimage to Paradise* (1592) ; *The Countesse of Penbrookes Loue* (1592) ; *The Countesse of Penbroke's Passion* (1592-7) ; *Auspicante Iehoua: Marie's Exercise* (1597) ; *The Rauisht Soule; The Blessed Weeper* (1601).

[46] She collaborated with her brother in a translation of the Psalms, published in 1580; and rendered into English a work from the French of Plessis du Mornay, *A Discourse of Life and Death* (1593). Sidney had translated from du Mornay a treatise entitled, *A Work concerning the Trewnesse of the Christian Religion* (1587).

[47] Spenser dedicated his *Ruines of Time* (c. 1590) to the Countess of Pembroke; as did Abraham Fraunce his *Countess of Pembroke's Ivychurch,* and *Countess of Pembroke's Emmanuel* (1591). All of which are non-mystical works.

[48] Arber's *Reprint,* II, 573.

[49] *The Pilgrimage to Paradise,* p. 7. Grosart, I, 7.

temptations which test the resolution and fibre of each sense. First, Venus and fair Diana appear to tempt the eyes; but these trusty servants are proof against all sensual blandishments, as are the ears against the charms of earthly music. Flora's lovely flowers aimed to attract the sense of smell, and Ceres with her cornucopia of sense delights are ultimately passed by in triumph. Even the road, the highway of Life, is strewn with obstacles and crosses, but "feeling" clears the pathway, and the heaven-sent trials of the senses of Man are over.[50]

The second part [51] of *The Pilgrimage to Paradise* reveals the temptations of a more subtle and persistent nature, viz., those which tend to turn the *mind* and *soul* of the pilgrim from the road to Paradise. Passing through the "wood of Worldly desire," the traveler perceives the outcome of selfish indulgence where souls are transformed into the bestial shapes of their shameful pleasures. The pilgrim then enters upon the "way of virtue," where he encounters the most dangerous of all his enemies, a terrible monster, "the sien of sinne, the fiende of hell, the deuil," whose seven heads represent the seven deadly sins. From here to the end of the poem the metaphysical and the mystical elements become the deciding factors in the Pilgrim's ultimate victory. Reason is powerless unless aided from on high, and straightway, a heavenly messenger, Mercy, is sent to lead the poor traveler against his supernatural foes.

> The happie staie, whereon thy hope doth stande,
> Where humble praier but pittie doth aspire:
> Have got thee grace in Mercies glorious eies,
> To finde the path that leads to Paradise,
> Where life doth go on pilgrimage to loue.[52]

Humility, fasting, prayer, and repentance now discipline the spirit of the wayfarer so that the seven deadly sins are finally slain, and he emerges victorious from the wood. Other and equally severe trials are encountered on the allegorical sea of life in the staunch ship *Buonaventura;* but Man, fully tried and tested, needs but the spirit of detachment from the world to

---

[50] *Ibid.*, p. 8.   [51] *Ibid.*, pp. 8-15.   [52] *Ibid.*, p. 9.

be wholly perfect. This is accomplished by a journey through the " worldly city," and in witnessing the vanity of a regal court—preludes to the glories of the devout life. The last portion of life's pilgrimage ends in a church " not built of lime or stone." [53]

> Whose head is Christ, whose martirs are his pillers.

The poet lifts the pilgrim to Paradise, which is described in the manner of the visions of heaven, and in this strain the poem ends.

The Pilgrimage to Paradise belongs definitely to the Pilgrimage of Life *genre* of Christian mystical literature. Breton was perhaps influenced by the ethical allegory of the first book of Spenser's *The Faerie Queene*. The framework of the journey of Redcrosse and Una is similar to that of Breton's pilgrim in that both reflect the trials and temptations of the *genus Homo* on his journey through life to his proper end. The wilderness of error in *The Faerie Queene* (I, i) corresponds to the woods which initiate Breton's pilgrimage. Redcrosse repelled the advances of the pseudo-Una; the pilgrim disdained Venus and Diana. Redcrosse encountered the seven deadly sins in the House of Pride (*F.Q.* I, iv), whereas the pilgrim encountered them as represented in the seven heads of the Monster, which, in turn, is described not unlike Spenser's Beast which Arthur wounded (*F.Q.* I, viii). The ascetic discipline, the personified virtues, and the supernatural agencies of Spenser's Canto X are reflected in the less elaborate purification of the pilgrim. Finally, the arrival at the allegorical Church-Heaven in Breton is akin to the progress of Redcrosse through the House of Holiness to the vision of the celestial Jerusalem.[54]

The Countesse of Penbrookes Loue is " joyned to " and complementary to *The Pilgrimage to Paradise*. It is a meditation upon that heavenly love which constitutes the impelling force of *The Pilgrimage to Paradise*.

---

[53] *Ibid.*, p. 20.
[54] See pp. 64-70 for detailed consideration of the Pilgrimage of Life.

Where life doth goe on pilgrimage to loue:
Whose humble hart, the holy spirite leads.[55]

The mystical nature of this poem was pointed out by John
Case, M.D., in his commendatory letter published with these
two poems of Breton. He described the prevailing literary
fashion of " exalting wanton loue and dalliance," and observed
the nature of the love that Breton lauds:

Loue is the name; but God is the marke, and matter at which it
aimeth. This Loue is not the Loue of Martha, but the Loue of
Mary who loued so much, who loueth Christ. This loue made
Mary Magdalen's teares, and maketh the best Mary liuing to
ascend to *Jerusalem* and there to seeke her louer in the Temple.
But finding him not among the Doctors shee taketh the wings of
an Eagle, and in her sacred thoughts flieth aboue the Sunne, never
ceasing to seeke, till shee have founde her Louer.[56]

A modern student of Breton has observed that the contrast
between divine love and merely romantic affection runs through
all Breton's religious poetry; and, furthermore, that such too
is the essential theme of Spenser's *Fowre Hymnes,* which appeared four years after this poem of Breton.[57]

The Countesse of Penbrookes Loue is, in essence, a prayer
in praise of heavenly love placed on the lips of the devout
Countess, who is seen to spurn the presents and honors which
an admiring world lays at her feet. Breton clothes her soul's
preference in fervent, and often stilted and euphuistic diction.
The following lines on reciprocal love, a favorite subject in
mystical poetry, are characteristic of the poem as a whole:

But what shoulde I? shall I? or can I giue?
To thee, for all that thou hast giuen to me:
When, by thy loue, my soule doth only loue,
And hath her being wholy but in thee:

[55] *The Pilgrimage to Paradise*, p. 9.
[56] *Ibid.*, p. 5.
[57] Oskar Heidrich, *Nicholas Breton, sein Leben und seine Gedichte,* p.
17. The author is of the opinion that Breton's *The Countess of Pembrokes
Loue* does not yield precedence of merit even to Spenser's immortal *Hymnes*:
" Er fühlt dies auch selbst und sucht durch eine ausserordentlich bilderreiche
Sprache dem abzuhelfen, worin er seinem Vorbild Spenser nicht nachsteht "
(*ibid.*, p. 49). One is inclined to demur.

Nothing I haue, but, if that ought be mine,
All doe I giue vnto that loue of thine.[58]

The first half of the poem is a contemplation of the effects of divine love as seen in Nature, and in the heart detached from the world. These reflections take on the typical character of the *De Contemptu Mundi* literature, in the composition of which Breton is comparable to such ascetic writers as Luis de Granada, with whose works he may have been familiar.[59] The characteristics of the Purgative way pervade the latter half of the poem in stanzas of undoubted mystical power. Careful order, however, and progressive development are lacking here; a fault far less noticeable in Breton's later poems. The closing description of the vision is an expression of mystical ecstasy and marks the climax to the longing for divine union upon which the entire poem rests.

A Solemne Passion of the Sovles Loue

This poem was entered in the Stationers' Register,[60] September 20, 1595, and published in the same year together with a prose commentary on John xx, 10-18, entitled *Mary Magdalen's Loue*. Corser [61] assigned both works to Breton, although Grosart [62] believed the latter work to be from another hand solely because of its " strong Catholic viewpoint." [63] His

---

[58] *The Countesse of Penbrookes Loue*, p. 23.

[59] Compare, for example, Breton's " What thing is Man? a clodde of miry claye / Slime of the earth, a slave to filthy sinne / Springes like a weede and so doth weare away / Goes to the earth, where first he did begin." with ". . . the affinities that men haue with weeds and slimy dirt which is the common father but to weeds and men " (*Of Prayer and Meditation*, p. 58).

[60] Arber's *Reprint*, III, 48.   [61] *Collect. Anglo-Poet.*, Part VIII, p. 160.

[62] Memorial-Introduction, p. lxxiii; see also *Dictionary of National Biography*, art. Breton.

[63] Breton's religious affiliation is uncertain: Corser discerned strong Catholic tendency in a number of his poems, but undeniably Protestant expressions appear on occasion in his prose. Breton refers to the Massacre of St. Bartholomew " *where the deuill and the Pope made the Duke of Guise the chiefe murtherer* " (*Wit's Trenchmour*, Grosart, II, 16). He considered it a grave misfortune to be cast into utter darkness: " while the Buls of *Rome* shal breed too many calues in Britanie " (*A murmurer*, Grosart, II, 5). For other illustrations, see Grosart, vol. I, p. xxix.

evidence, however, is by no means conclusive. The subject of Mary Magdalen was, indeed, a favorite one with devotional and mystical writers.[64]

A Solemne Passion of the Sovles Loue was separately reprinted in 1598 and again in 1623. It marks a distinct advance in range and power over Breton's earlier poems. This work is a rimed exposition of the regular methodology of Christian mysticism. Breton seems to have used all his " notes " and no essential element is omitted. The first part is a detailed contemplation of the divine attributes [65] as they are manifested in the primal act of creation, in the order of Nature, and in man. Wisdom, Power, and Love receive especial attention, and he challenges the poets to compare their romantic love with his.

> Ye that fill the world with fancies,
> Whose faining Muses shew but madding fits; . . .
> Lay downe your lines, compare your loue with mine,
> And say whose vertue is the true diuine.[66]

Reviewing the beauty of the earth, " where glorious works vnto the world doth shew thee," Breton draws the usual conclusion :

> And if He so hath deckt the earth below,
> Imagine then the glory of His seat.
> . . .
> For where the sunne, the moone and stars haue light,
> For Nature's eyes the beauty is too bright.[67]

Directly follows a contemplation of the Divine Essence :

The nature of Christian mysticism is such that it takes for granted life in accordance with the Church and its Sacraments, and hence it is chiefly concerned with expressions of purification, of imitation of Christ, of contemplation, and the experimental Vision of God. Mystical writing by itself, therefore, does not necessarily warrant a definite conclusion relative to the external religious belief of the writers themselves. In Breton's case, however, there seems no doubt of his adherence to the Established Church.

[64] See above, p. 148 relative to Markham's *Marie Magdalene's Teares,* and prevalence of the Mary Magdalen literature.

[65] Nine attributes are mentioned: goodness, justice, love, mercy, glory, ire, power, truth, wisdom.

[66] *A Solemne Passion of the Sovles Loue,* Grosart, I, 5.

[67] *Ibid.,* p. 6.

And of His essence, this is all we finde,
A Spirit fully incomprehensible;
A louing God vnto His servants kinde,
And in His humane nature sensible:
In wisedome's wonder, knowledge, quintessence,
And in that essence highest excellence.[68]

Meditation on love leads directly to a full Christocentric contemplation in the second part of the poem. Divine love unites
the four elements, and is the " mould " out of which all things
were made and are preserved. This love brought about the
entire history of Christ's life and death.[69] The latter part of
the poem is in the strict purgative mood, and contains a longing for divine union. The lines are composed at white heat,
and indicate the nature of Breton's mystical fire. This is one
of the final stanzas:

And I (alas) of many thousand soules,
Vnworthy most of His high worth to write:
Who in His mercie's true record inroules
The louing substance of the soule's delight:
Must mercy cry, for feare of loue's presuming
Of too high sence, may be my soule's consuming.[70]

The Countesse of Penbroke's Passion

This poem, according to Grosart, was written not later than
1597,[71] but it circulated only in manuscript, of which three
copies are known to be extant.[72] It was first printed as the un-

---

[68] *Ibid.*, p. 7.
[69] The following stanza is typical of this part of the meditation:

In loue He came, that he might comfort doe vs,
In loue went from vs to prouide our places;
In loue He sent His Comforter vnto vs,
In loue He guides vs with His holy graces:
In loue He made, bought, keepes, and guides
vs thus,
And shall not we loue Him that so lou'd vs?
Ibid., p. 8.

[70] *Ibid.* (Italics mine.)   [71] Memorial-Introduction, p. xlvii.
[72] The Sloane MS., that used by Halliwell-Phillips, and one described by
an anonymous writer in *Notes and Queries*, 1st. Series, V. 487. A version
of the poem with the title, *The Passions of the Spirit*, was printed at London

doubted work of Breton in 1853 by Halliwell-Phillips whose text is the basis of Grosart's reprint.[73]

This poem is a companion piece to the earlier *Countesse of Penbrookes Loue,* and furthermore, it adds nothing to the spirit and method of *A Solemne Passion of the Soules Loue* except a more definite order, and a remarkably well developed sequence of thought. Grosart, unfortunately, does not preserve the canto divisions of his manuscript. Each canto marks a unit of development and gradual progress of the soul from a sense of sorrow, melancholy, and grief to a joyful and exultant union with God. The poem illustrates admirably the traditional three ways of the mystical life. Canto I (stanzas 1-46) is intensely purificatory in nature; the second and third cantos (47-80) embrace the way of grace and illumination through a two-fold meditation on Christ; and the final cantos (81-110) are essentially of the Unitive way.

The theme of the opening canto, poignant sorrow and grief, is seen to arise not from regret over a misspent life (stanzas 11-12), but chiefly because there has been no place for a life and a love which are of Christ:

> But such a lacke, and such a losse, aye me!
> Must neds the sorrowe of all sorrowes be.[74]

Then follows a detailed consideration of this love and of this

by Thomas Eske in 1599. This rare work is now in the Huntington Library. Cf. Jean Robertson, " The Passions of the Spirit (1599) and Nicholas Breton," *The Huntington Library Quarterly,* III (1939), 69-75.

[73] The Sloane MS. was the chief basis for a reprint made in 1862 by N. G. B. under the title, *A Poem on our Saviour's Passion by Mary Sidney, Countess of Pembroke.* Both this title and its attribution to Mary Sidney are unwarranted. The Breton authorship is practically indisputable both on external and internal evidence.

[74] *Ibid.,* p. 4 (stanza 19). This is the peculiar meaning of *passion* in Breton's mystical poetry. It is a deep and fervent emotion of love and longing for Christ commingled with regret over personal sin. Thus, in stanza 18 (p. 4), he says:

> Ther is a lacke that tels me of a life,
> Ther is a losse that tels me of a love;
> Betwixt them both a state of such a strife
> As makes my spirite such a passion prove;
>> That lacke of t'one and th'other's losse, alas!
>> Makes me the woefulest wretche that ever was.

life which fit into the typical Christocentric type of contemplation. In the second and third cantos, this is first a *visual* meditation upon the scenes of the Passion, with repeated appeals to the eyes; then, another account of the same details furnishes food for the mind, and elicits appropriate devout ejaculations, as in the following stanza:

> Butt can I leave to thinke upon the thinge,
> That I can never put out of my thought?
> Or can I cease of his sweet love to singe,
> Who by his blood his creature's comfort wrought?
> Or can I live to thinke that he should dye,
> In whom the hope of all my life doth lye? [75]

The transition from the Passion to its effects, i.e., to assurance of eternal bliss, leads Breton to the regular Theocentric contemplation in cantos four and five. A note of joy accompanies the consideration of the celestial inhabitants in the " holy city," and the contemplation of the divine attributes. The experience is overwhelming, yet the soul ascends still higher to adore the essence of the Deity in the final canto. There the divine glory is beheld only in reflections of it in the order of Nature, where each work surpasses the other in beauty. Though the closing prayer and song are hardly a successful attempt to express the appropriate emotions of the soul in the intimacy of divine union, nevertheless the entire poem is an admirable illustration of the union of the two types of contemplation.

Other Mystical Works of Breton

The other poems of Breton which are in the strict tradition of Christian mysticism do not require especial analysis, since they present but minor divergence from his customary manner. *Britton's Diuinitie* is important in that it was published after *The Pilgrimage to Paradise* and *The Countesse of Penbrookes Loue.* It was Breton's sole contribution to the *Arbour of Amorous Delights* in 1594. It is a concise declaration of the poet's mystical philosophy expressed in the longer poems.

Auspicante Iehoua: Marie's Exercise, published in 1597, is

[75] *Ibid.,* p. 7 (stanza 67).

a spiritual exercise designed for the Countess of Pembroke, consisting of a series of meditations on pious and valiant women of Scripture story. A special " fruict " for the meditative soul is drawn from each example; and the closing " Prayer upon Magnificate " with its lesson, " The joy of the sovle is rauished withe the loue of Christ " [76] is a brief but complete expression of the mystical experience.

In 1601, Breton published three mystical works and still another which, if the title is an indication, also is a mystical piece. This last poem, entitled, *The Soules Heavenly Exercise, set down in diverse godly meditations,* was discovered by the editors of the *Dictionary of National Biography,* and a copy of it is not included in Breton's collected works.[77] The other three works of the year 1601 present Breton's favorite spiritual themes. They are clearly mystical poems, yet of indifferent merit (with the exception of *The Blessed Weeper*), especially in comparison with the longer poems which have already been considered.

The Rauisht Soule, dedicated to Mary Sidney, presents nothing new. It is made up of two distinct poems; one is in the Theocentric manner, the other is aptly entitled, " Il christiano al honore di Christo." [78] Both poems, observes Breton, make up " the diuine humour of a ravisht sovle." [79]

The Blessed Weeper, printed with the above work, is in the form of a dream-vision of Mary Magdalen at the tomb of Christ. This may be Breton's second poem on this subject, if *Mary Magdalen's Loue* is actually his. *The Blessed Weeper* is in the manner of the devout meditations of the mystics on the familiar theme of the sinful life, the conversion, and the repentance of Mary Magdalen.[80] All this is recounted by the Magdalen in a tearful monologue supposedly spoken before

[76] *Marie's Exercise,* Grosart, II, 12.

[77] Cf. *DNB,* art. Breton. An apparently unique copy, dated 1601, stamped with the Queen's crest, is in a private library.

[78] The use of the Italian title could suggest that Breton had recourse to an original in that language.

[79] Dedicatory Letter, Grosart, I, 5.

[80] See above, re Markham, p. 148, and recall Southwell's work on this subject.

the appearance of Christ to her on the Resurrection morn. This event Breton presents in his best poetry.

The Longing of a Blessed Heart which loathing the World doth long to be with Christ is the third work to appear in 1601. The title indicates the character of these " humble meditations of no worldly mind." [81] It is an expression of the fervent love-longing of the soul wherein the vain and futile desires of worldly minds in all conditions of life are contrasted with that divine longing which Breton felt should possess the souls of men.[82]

The Soule's Harmony (1602) is another excellent poem in the mystical tradition. It is Breton's last mystical composition in verse.[83] The typical note of repentance and detachment give way in the course of this poem to a triumphant song of divine praise which embraces the subjects of the Theocentric contemplation.

Nicholas Breton was the most prolific writer of religious poetry of the Elizabethan period. Who his chief authorities were, or from what sources his ideas are derived cannot be determined since he, unlike Lodge, gives no clues; and his subject-matter is common to mystical literature. The motif which runs through his religious poetry and prose is an exaltation of heavenly love in contrast to its earthly counterpart. He spurns the reaches of the merely erotic with the zeal of Rolle or Granada; and decries the amorous conceits of the " Petrarchist " and the Platonist.[84] Breton's manner was to embody the Christocentric and Theocentric types of contemplation, to unite them in his own way, and to stress the Purgative and the Unitive ways of the mystical life. He was fond of expressing ecstasy, rapture, or ravishment in the concluding

---

[81] Dedicatory letter.

[82] Compare, for instance, the identical spirit in the Pseudo-Augustinian (medieval) *The Contemplation of Christ* (see Part II, p. 130), with these lines of Breton: " My heart gloweth, my mind rejoiceth, my memory is fresh, my understanding is clear, *and my whole spirit kindled with desire to see Thee, findeth herself ravished with the love of things invisible*" (Grosart, I, 15). (Italics mine.)

[83] In 1608 appeared *Diuine Considerations* in prose. See above.

[84] Cf. " What is Love," in *The Longing of a Blessed Heart*, pp. 12-14.

stanzas of his poems, and thus the increase of emotional fervor brought on by his contemplations constituted the climax of the mystic experience.

We do not know much of Breton's life from external documents, but the internal evidence of those writings which we have just examined would indicate a noble, God-fearing man, whose life was lived on a spiritual plane above the majority of his fellows. The invitation to the more perfect life extended to all men, but answered only by the mystics, was also answered by Nicholas Breton. He reflects this in his writings, and of such is the literature of Christian mysticism: an expression of personal experience. He perfectly understood that the heart of Christian mysticism was embodied in purification of soul and detachment from the world, and in cooperation with grace, and above all in fervent love which gives substance to the mystic's inner fire. This has not been sufficiently noted in Breton's literary productions. Indeed, they are rarely read. One feels that this unpopularity of Breton is not due mainly to lack of literary excellence, but to misunderstanding of the *genre* to which his religious pieces belong.

Nicholas Breton is closest of all the English mystical writers to Spenser. Both poets were members of the Countess of Pembroke's circle. Breton's most important works were published before Spenser's *Fowre Hymnes* appeared in 1596; and in the light of these poems of Breton the *Fowre Hymnes* of Spenser can be more fully understood and appreciated. It is fitting that in this study, Breton stand closest to the summit of that pyramid upon whose peak Edmund Spenser rests securely.

EDMUND SPENSER

It is fitting that Edmund Spenser should rank highest in the history of Christian mysticism in the Elizabethan age. Because of their great literary merit and high spiritual import the House of Holiness and the *Fowre Hymnes* deserve a crowning place in this study. The specific mystical character and excellence of the House of Holiness is second only to the full spirit and methodology of Christian mysticism which is found in the *Fowre Hymnes.*

The Faerie Queene is a composite work drawn from many sources, chiefly medieval, which are harmonized and fused through meditation and assimilation with a purpose " to fashion a gentleman or noble person in vertuous and gentle discipline." [1] Spenser scholars have progressively succeeded in drawing out these varied elements in Spenser's poem; and, in general, have allocated them in the wide range of his source material. The debt which Spenser owed to the Bible, to the classics, to Plato and Aristotle, as well as to the romantic epics of Ariosto and Tasso, is now amply illustrated, as is the general relation of the Arthurian romances to *The Faerie Queene*. The implications of the political and ecclesiastical allegory have also been brought to light not, however, with entirely unanimous conclusions. The moral and spiritual allegory is capable of more ready and palpable explanation in accordance with the didactic aim and method expressly stated in the celebrated letter to Raleigh. For Spenser was primarily a teacher; indeed, Milton, Spenser's spiritual son, considered him " a better teacher than Scotus or Aquinas." [2] He was, moreover, unwilling that his lessons be " delivered plainly in way of precepts, or sermons at large," but that they be " clowdily enwrapped in allegorical devices." [3] Under cover of this allegory or " darke conceit," each book of *The Faerie Queene* has a moral unity of its own without detracting from the development and illustration of those virtues " which Aristotle hath devised," but to which Spenser gave a decidedly medieval and scholastic cast.[4] As to the import of the spiritual allegory in the first book of Spenser's great poem, called the " Legend of Holiness," scholars are generally in basic agreement.[5] Professor

[1] " Letter to Raleigh," *The Works of Edmund Spenser, Variorum Edition,* edited by Edwin Greenlaw, C. G. Osgood, F. M. Padelford (Baltimore, 1932), I, 167.

[2] See Professor Greenlaw's interpretation of Milton's phrase in *Studies in Philology*, XIV (1917), pp. 203 ff.

[3] Letter to Raleigh.

[4] Cf. R. E. N. Dodge, *The Complete Poetical Works of Edmund Spenser* (Boston, 1908), pp. 132-133, and also H. S. V. Jones, *Studies in Philology*, XXIX (1932), 200-206.

[5] See the explanations of the moral and spiritual allegory of the first book in *Variorum Edition*, Vol. I, 422-488.

Padelford interprets it as a portrayal of " the growth in grace, through experience and instruction, of a Christian gentleman. Interpreted in this last sense the book is a pilgrim's progress." [6] And Dr. Tillyard says, " In sum the first book of the *Faerie Queene* is a Divine Comedy in miniature." [7]

The House of Holiness

With these views in mind, and fully recognizing the manifold origins of particular figures, phrases, and episodes in *The Faerie Queene,* we are now prepared to interpret the spiritual allegory of Book One in the light of the Pilgrimage of Life type of Christian mystical treatises.[8] This already has been noted by Professor Padelford and more recently by Dr. Tillyard, but the definite connection between the Pilgrimage of Life literature and Christian mysticism has received no attention.[9] In keeping with the fundamental conceptions of the type, the greater part of the Legend of Holiness in Book One, viz., the first nine cantos, depicts the successes and failures of the struggle of man, represented by the Red Cross knight, against evil forces.   In the House of Holiness, the specific discipline of Christian mysticism is prescribed to bring about a spiritual regeneration and final arrival at the sublime heights of mystical

[6] " The Spiritual Allegory of the Faerie Queene, Book One," *ibid.*, p. 431.
[7] " Milton and the English Epic Tradition " in *Seventeenth Century Studies presented to Sir Herbert Grierson* (London, 1938), p. 221.
[8] For the development of this type of mystical literature, see pp. 64-70.
[9] F. M. Padelford, " The Pilgrimage of the Life of Man," *Variorum Edition,* I, 414. E. M. W. Tillyard, " Milton and the English Epic Tradition," in *Seventeenth Century Studies presented to Sir Herbert Grierson* (London, 1938), p. 220. The following works, with one exception, written in the sixteenth century, are strictly in the Christian mystical tradition of the Pilgrimage of Life *genre,* and can readily be classed as mystical treatises. *Desiderius, or the Original Pilgrim: A divine dialogue, Shewing the most compendious Way to arrive at the Love of God.* Written originally in Spanish by an unknown author, this work was translated into Italian, French, High and Low Dutch, and, about 1587, was rendered into Latin by Surius. It was translated into English only in 1717. (Cf. James B. Wharey, *A Study of the Sources of Bunyan's Allegories* [Baltimore, 1904], p. 134.) *The Palice of Honour* (1501) by Gavin Douglas. *The Pylgrimage of Perfection,* anonymous, is one of the works printed by Pynson. *Philothea's Pilgrimage to Perfection* (1668) is a work by John of the Holy Cross.

contemplation.   Thus, the House of Holiness in the tenth canto stands apart from the other cantos as an allegory complete in itself of man's conversion and training toward spiritual perfection.   And, moreover, it is an excellent exemplification, in form of allegory, of the methodology of Christian mysticism.

The tenth canto of Book One, bears a two-fold relation to the whole book of which it is an essential part.   First, it marks the dramatic ascent of the fortunes of the Red Cross Knight, which had reached their nadir in the dungeon of Orgoglio. Secondly, this canto is an essential unit in the larger plan which conceives of the knight as a Christian pilgrim on his way to heaven.   After fitful lapses and some successes, ever sustained from on high, the pilgrim is finally regenerated in the House of Holiness and he manfully climbs the mystical mount which leads to the haven of every pilgrim—the new Jerusalem.   This canto is capable of self-subsistence as a treatise of Christian mysticism, and as such may stand apart from the rest of the first book.[10]

Canto ten may be divided into three parts: the House of Holiness, the Hospital of Mercy, and the Mountain of Contemplation.   Thus, Spenser's allegorical parallels to the familiar mystical units are Repentance, Good Works, and Contemplation; and they correspond, as we shall point out, to the three ways or stages of the mystical life, viz., Purgation, Illumination, and Perfection or Union.   Spenser reveals the requisite behavior of the Christian, who, regardless of age or particular sect, is " converted " and gives himself over to a definite and

[10] " We can nowhere," says Aubrey de Vere, " meet an exposition of the Christian religion in its completeness and proportions, doctrinal, devotional, and practical, more searching, while so brief, than exists in the tenth canto of his first book, describing the visit of the Redcross knight to the House of Holiness " (" The Two Chief Schools of English Poetry," in *Essays Chiefly on Poetry* [London, 1881], p. 140 ff.).   Writing elsewhere on the same subject, he said: " This canto is a poem so complete in itself that no extracts can do it justice.   It is one in which Plato, could he have returned to earth, would have found the realization of his loftiest dreams; in which St. Thomas Aquinas would have discovered no fault; and in which St. Augustine would have rejoiced as though he had felt once more that evening breeze which played about him as he stood at the window on the seaside at Ostia " (Grosart, *The Complete Works . . . of Edmund Spenser* [London, 1882], I, 300).

14

traditional spiritual discipline. This is Spenser's method of embodying the essential condition of Holiness as the mystics for centuries had conceived it.

In illustrating the ascetic character of the experiences of the knight, it is noteworthy how Spenser brings out the parallel between physical and moral health, between physical debility and spiritual weakness, and to what extent wounds of the body have a spiritual counterpart in the wounds engendered by sin in the soul.[11] This " soule-diseased " knight [12] whom Despayre had termed a " man of sin " [13] was by Una herself called a " fraile, feeble, fleshly wight." [14] Only a special training will rid the knight of sin, and recover for him his spiritual strength. In the House of Holiness, which Spenser also calls the " house of penance," [15] is incorporated the typical Purgative way of Christian mysticism. Under the familiar usage of personified abstraction, Spenser achieves the end-result of all ascetic regulations, i. e., the gradual purification of the Christian who has finally turned and entered upon the " narrow road " [16] which leads to perfect and lasting Holiness. Caelia or Heaven, " thought from heaven to come or thither to arise," [17] is mother of the theological virtues Faith, Hope, and Charity. These ladies assume their traditional attributes, and unfold to the knight the specific training of the three-fold ways or stages of the mystical life. This procedure has direct mystical ancestry in such statements as the following from the *Itinerarium Mentis in Deum*: " It is necessary, therefore, if we would reenter into the fullness of Truth, as in a Paradise, that we do so through Faith, Hope and Charity. . . . Our minds must be clothed with the three theological virtues, by which the soul is purified, illuminated, and perfected, and thus made fit for the supernal Jerusalem." [18] Gerson insists on the training of the soul in these virtues. He refers to this discipline as the specific work of " mystical theology which is a school, not of the intellect but of the affections, whereby the soul is exercised in the moral and

---

[11] *F. Q.*, I, x, 2. Compare *F. Q.*, VI, v. 31, and vi, 1-3.
[12] I, x, 24, 1.   [14] I, ix, 53, 1.   [16] I, x, 5, 9; 10, 4.
[13] I, ix, 46, 1.   [15] I, x, 32, 8.   [17] I, x, 4, 2.
[18] *S. Bonaventurae Opera Omnia*, XII, 13-14.

theological virtues, and by them is properly disposed to Purification, Illumination, and Perfection." [19]

Spenser's designation of Humiltá as Porter of the House of Holiness has fullest possible authorization in Christian mysticism, beginning with the outline of the " Twelve Stages of Humility " by St. Benedict.[20] Humility was an elemental virtue in St. Augustine's spiritual philosophy.[21] Hugh of St. Victor took humility, in direct contrast to pride, as the source of the fruits of the spirit. " Humility is the foundation of all the virtues because ' everyone that humbleth himself shall be exalted.' " [22] Gerson, similarly, made humility the essential virtue of the mystic. " It is impossible," he said, " to arrive at true contemplation by any other road than that of humility." [23] This virtue, which has no place in Greek ethics, was nurtured by Judaism and embraced by the Christian mystics; it constituted for them the beginning of all spiritual progress in the other virtues which Spenser makes preceptors of the knight in his growth in holiness. " Stouping low," he follows Humiltá on the " streight and narrow way," [24] and thereby opens his soul to the salutary influence of the heaven-born, infused virtues, of which Faith is first.[25]

[19] *Opera Omnia*, III, 385. See description of the Purgative way in Part I.
[20] *The Rule of St. Benedict*, ed. by Cuthbert Butler (London, St. Louis, 1912), and see also Cuthbert Butler, *Benedictine Monachism* (London, 1919), pp. 51 ff.
[21] " Dost thou wish to rise? " he asks. " Begin by descending. You plan to rear a tower to pierce the clouds? Lay first the foundations in humility " (*Serm. X*).
[22] *De Fructibus Carnis et Spiritus*, P. L., CLXXVI, 997-998.
[23] *Opera Omnia*, III, 545.
[24] *F. Q.*, I, x, 5, 8-9; compare the words of Caelia: " So few there bee/ That chose the narrow path, or see the right " (*ibid.*, 10, 3-4). Originally from Matt. vi, 13-14, this observation is a mystical commonplace.
[25] It is noteworthy that Spenser accords these virtues their traditional relationship. The accepted teaching, following St. Thomas, was as follows: " Order is two-fold: order of generation, and order of perfection. . . . In the order of generation, faith precedes hope and charity. . . . But in the order of perfection, charity precedes faith and hope, because faith and hope are given life by charity. For charity is the mother and root of all the virtues " (*Summa Theol.*, I-II, Q. 62, a. 4). Cf. also *ibid.*, II-II, Q. 23, a. 8: " Since a mother is one who conceives within herself and by another, charity is called the mother of the other virtues." St. Catherine of Sienna, speaking of the virtue of discretion, says it is wedded to charity and has

In the " schoolehouse " of Faith, the knight is taught " celestiall discipline," and the dull eyes of his soul are opened to her
great mysteries: " God, justice, grace, and free will." The
knight grew in holiness through this instruction, and, moved
by grace, began to feel contempt for the world, and even for
his own life as the memory of his sins grieved and dismayed
his soul.[26] So sincerely did he detest his faults that only Hope
could calm and assure him; and Caelia, unalarmed at this usual
purgative procedure, in due time dispatched a Leech, a physician of the soul, who was skillful in curing a grieved conscience.
His name was Patience.[27] This personage was known in earlier
allegories as Shrift or Confession. Thus, as Todd observes,
an interesting parallel is found " in the old Morality of Everyman for Confession." [28]

Everyman.   Where dwelleth that holy man, *Confession.*
Knowledge.   In the house of salvation:
                We shall find him in that place,
                That shall us comfort by God's grace. . . .
Everyman.   Now, I pray you, *Shrift*, mother of salvation,
                Help my good deeds for my piteous exclamation.[29]

With this in mind, one observes how this venerable character
comes to Redcrosse and

Could hardly him intreat, *to tell his griefe*;
Which knowne, and all that noyd his heauie spright
Well searcht, eftsoones he gan apply reliefe
Of salues and med'cines, which had passing priefe,
And *thereto added words of wondrous might*:
By which to ease he him recured briefe,
And much asswag'd the passion of his plight,
That he his paine endur'd, as seeming now more light.[30]

---

many descendants. (*The Dialogues of Catherine of Sienna,* trans. by Algar
Thorold [London, 1907], p. 51.) Compare the foregoing with Spenser's
delineation of the maternal character of Charissa. (*F. Q.* I, x, 16; *ibid.,*
29-31.)

[26] For discussion of conversion and compunction in medieval mysticism,
see F. Vernet, *Medieval Spirituality* (London and St. Louis, 1930), pp.
117-125.

[27] Patience, according to St. Paul, is a virtue of the ministers of God.
(II Cor., vi, 4.)

[28] Cf. *Variorum Edition,* I, 287.

[29] *Everyman,* Everyman edition, p. 16.   [30] *F. Q.,* I, x, 24, 2-9.

In the italicized phrases of this exceedingly compressed stanza, there is an apparent reference to the operation and effects of a confession of sins which is frequently prescribed as part of the purificatory exercises in mystical treatises;[31] and was a practice literally included both in Anglican and Calvinistic ecclesiastical regulations.[32] Spenser, in view of the prevailing sanction of the Reform relative to confession and absolution, would not have deemed it out of place to include this as a work of his Leech, Patience, in the purification of the knight.

> But yet the cause and root of all his ill,
>   Inward corruption, and infected sin,
>   Not purg'd nor heald, behind remained still,
>   And festring sore did rankle yet within.[33]

To remove the *residua peccati,* i. e., the baneful effects of sin in his soul, the knight underwent the usual rigorous discipline enjoined by traditional ascetic rules. In solitude and in fasting, clad in sackcloth and ashes, he prayed early and late with firm purpose of Amendment ready at hand. He also resorted to corporal Penance; and would daily discipline himself, while Remorse for his faults as well as Repentance gradually restored his soul to such health that with a " cured conscience " Una joyfully brought him to Charity. Remorse and repentance for sin, the one naturally and the other supernaturally motivated, are important concomitants of this regeneration of the soul to a new life. All these activities of spiritual purgation have dis-

[31] Cf. *Imitation of Christ,* Bk. IV, cap. 7; *The Scale of Perfection,* Bk. II, cap. 3; The Pseudo-Rolle's *The Dread and Love of God,* ed. by F. M. Comper (London, 1916), p. 71; Luis de Granada's *Memorial of a Christian Life,* Bk. II.

[32] Cf. *The Book of Common Prayer with Notes,* edited by Archibald John Stephens (London, 1849), I, Introd. pp. viii-ix, xl; Henry Gee and W. J. Hardy, *Documents Illustrative of English Church History* (London, 1921), p. 306. See also *The Book of Common Prayer,* edition of 1549, and " Office for the Visitation of the Sick " in edition of 1549 and 1552. There was, as the above evidence points out, a gradual change in the official attitude of the Anglican Church relative to auricular confession of sins. Calvin conceded that ministers as witnesses and sponsors render more assured the consciences of sinners, and thus are said to remit sins and absolve souls. Cf. *Jo. Calvini Institutionis Lib.* III, cap. IV, 12, 22; and *Jo. Calvini Epist.,* ed. Genevae, 1617, p. 452.

[33] *F. Q.,* I, x, 25.

tinct place in the growth of the soul in its mystical progress to perfection; and penitential acts and resolutions of amendment are part of the Purgative way. The conception of the doctor, Spenser's Leech, with his sharp remedies is not so uncommon after St. Bernard's classic exposition.

The Physician has come to the wounded man, the Holy Spirit to the soul which says, " My sores are putrified and corrupted. What is the first thing to be done? Surely, to cut away any ulcerous growth which may have appeared in the wound, and which would prevent or retard its healing. Hence let the keen knife of Compunction remove the tumour of sinful habit. The pain indeed will be sharp. . . . Next is applied the medicine of Penance, a healing poultice of watchings, fastings, and prayers, and all other kinds of penitential exercises.[34]

Walter Hilton advised a bitter repentance such as that which the knight endured, in the following extract from *The Scale of Perfection*.

In the beginning of conversion of such a man, his thought is most upon his sins, with great compunction and sorrow of heart. . . . And if he be touched sharply, our Lord will make him soon clean, him shall think that his sins are aye in his sight, so foul and so horrible that hardly shall he be able to bear himself; and though he shrive him never so clearly, yet shall he feel biting and fretting of conscience.[35]

[34] *Serm. on the Cant. of Canticles*, XVII, Eng. trans. I, 180. These instructions of St. Bernard are fully incorporated in the *Meditationes Vitae Christi* (*S. Bonaventurae Opera Omnia*, XII, cap. XLVII, p. 572). Clement of Alexandria and St. Augustine discuss the purgative training in terms similar to St. Bernard's. (See Part I, p. 23.) Henry Suso similarly refers to the doctor of the soul and his remedies (cf. *Little Book of Eternal Wisdom*, cap. XXIII, p. 137), as does the Pseudo-Bonaventure, *De Sex Alis Seraphim* (*S. Bonaventurae Opera Omnia*, XII, 133).

[35] Bk. I, cap. 2, p. 39; cf. also the directions for the Purgative way in the Pseudo-Bonaventure, *Mystica Theologia, S. Bonaventurae Opera Omnia*, XII, Part II, cap. 1, 5; Gerson, *Opera*, III, 555-556; Luis de Granada, see Part II, p. 125. And note in the Morality *Everyman* that " Confession " gives Everyman " a precious jewel called penance."

> Therewith shall your body chastened be,
> With abstinence and perseverance in God's service:
> Here shall you receive that scourge of me,
> Which is penance strong, that ye must endure.
> . . . Give me the scourge of penance,
> My flesh therewith shall give a quittance.

(Everyman edition, pp. 16-17.)

Notwithstanding the severe discipline of the Purgative way or stage of the mystical method, the final effect is such that, under the effulgence of grace, a warm charity floods the soul, and the second way, the Illuminative way, has its inception. Thus, St. Bonaventure taught that the Purgative way was exercised in pain, but ended in love.[36] So also, Redcrosse had endured sharp treatment " in that sad house of Penance," and then, at the hands of Charity, he received his second course of instruction. Hers is the school of virtue,[37]

> Of loue, and righteousnesse, and well to donne,
> And wrath, and hatrid warely to shonne, . . .
> In which when him she well instructed hath,
> From thence to heauen she teacheth him the ready path.[38]

Charity, or divine love, is the guiding spirit of the Illuminative way, just as Faith sustains the penitent during his period of conversion and repentance. Love, righteousness, and good works are the essentials of the second stage of the growth of the soul in holiness, and make up the ready path to heaven. Spenser rightly considers Mercy and her corporal works as significant part of this stage of the knight's regeneration. Accordingly, after Redcrosse has accomplished the painful and cleansing exercises of the Purgative way he is taught the salutary meaning of the Illuminative way by the kindly Charissa, and then she turns him over to Mercy and her seven works to demonstrate that love of neighbor is part of love for God or Charity. Mercy, daughter of Charity,[39] is a virtue most needfully invoked by the Christian pilgrim as he walks the narrow, thorny way.[40]

Spenser illustrates the practice of the seven corporal works of mercy in the " holy Hospitall " of Mercy with its seven men

[36] *Opera Omnia*, XII, cap. 1, 25.

[37] *F. Q.*, I, x, 32, 6.

[38] *Ibid.*, I, x, 33, 4-9.

[39] " Charity is called the mother of the other virtues " (see footnote above, p. 195).

[40] In itself, mercy takes precedence of other virtues, for it belongs to mercy to be bountiful to others, and to help them in their needs (*Summa Theol.* II-II, Q. 30, a. 4).

of prayer and charity.[41]   Redcrosse, therefore, observes their
individual properties. He thereby learns another important
lesson of the active life in the Illuminative way. It is noteworthy that the Illuminative way is not a stage of quiet or of
inaction, but one of working and doing good. It must include
the requirements of the active life, which of necessity involves
the seven corporal works.

The traditional ideal of the mystical life is a harmonious
union of the active and the contemplative life. The active life
must precede that of pure contemplation, just as a contemplative must first be a good Christian, yet the two lives are not
mutually exclusive. " No one should form an impression,"
says Gerson, " that in the active life no room is left for the
thought of God, no more than that in the contemplative life no
concern is to be had for the work of purgation." [42] The two
lives must go together and assist one another. " The active
life," according to Walter Hilton, " consisteth in love and
charity exercised by good corporal works, in fulfilling of God's
commandments, and the seven works of mercy. . . .   These
works though they be but active, yet dispose a man in the
beginning to attain afterwards to contemplation." [43]   And the
author of the *Meditationes Vitae Christi* summarized the three
mystical ways or stages with St. Bernard's statement: " But
whilst engaged in the labors of penance, we must not forget the
meat of good works," and then he goes on to say that, having
partaken of this food and drink, after the labor of action, one
ought to rest in the quiet of contemplation.[44]

The Red Cross knight, well instructed by Mercy, remained
awhile in the " Hospitall of Mercy."

---

[41] " The sum total of the Christian religion in respect to external works
consists in the exercise of mercy," wrote St. Thomas. (*Summa Theol.*,
II-II, *Q*. 30, *a*. 4, *ad* 2.) He gives the traditional enumeration in *Summa
Theol.*, *Q*. 32, *a*. 2. The " eighth " work of mercy: to care for widows and
orphans, mentioned by Spenser, is found in patristic writings but it is infrequently included in medieval lists. For a medieval description of mercy and
its corporal works which includes care of widows and orphans, see *Sermones ad Fratres in Eremo*, attributed to St. Augustine. (*P. L.*, XL, 1246-
1248.)

[42] *Opera*, III, 556.

[43] *The Scale of Perfection*, Bk. I, cap. II, p. 3; cf. also p. 264.

[44] Cap. XLVII, p. 572.

During which time, in euery good behest
And godly worke of Almes and charitee
She him instructed with great industree;
Shortly therein so perfect he became,
That from the first vnto the last degree,
His mortall life he learned had to frame
In holy righteousnes, without rebuke or blame.[45]

The Illuminative way whereon the knight has trod now merges gradually into the way of union or perfection and its high contemplation, for there is no sharp demarcation in the spiritual development of the soul in holiness. This last stage or way begins for Redcrosse at the foot of the Mount at whose summit dwells the " aged holy man " named Contemplation.[46] This old man had oft seen God with the eyes of his soul; [47] and the knight is brought to him by kindly Mercy. The difficult ascent to Contemplation is finally accomplished, and the aged contemplative leads the knight, purified a last time, as St. Bernard led Dante,[48] to the highest Mount. There in contemplative ecstasy is pointed out the ravishing view of the heavenly Jerusalem—the city wherein dwell the redeemed by the blood of Christ.[49] Loath to leave this exalted place, the knight will return here again, once his work is accomplished, and he will " walk this way in Pilgrim's poor estate." [50] His pilgrimage to perfection is ended.

In the ascent of the Mount of Contemplation,[51] in the description of the Hermit,[52] in the last complete purification of the knight,[53] and in the vision of the celestial Jerusalem,[54] Spenser has sketched the essential marks of the final stage or way of the mystical life, and has retained its basic conception of a pilgrimage.[55]

---

[45] *F. Q.*, I, x, 45, 3-9.   [46] *Ibid.*, 46.

[47] The comparison of the eye of the contemplative beholding the eternal sun, with that of the eagle's eye capable of looking at the material sun is frequently found in mystical writings. Cf. Richard of St. Victor, *Benjamin Major, P. L.*, CXCVI, 91; *De Septem Itineribus Aeternitatis*, p. 469.

[48] *Paradiso*, canto xxxi.

[49] *F. Q.*, II, x, 57.   [51] *Ibid.*, 46, 50, 52, 54.   [53] *Ibid.*, 52, 8-10.

[50] *Ibid.*, 63-64.   [52] *Ibid.*, 47.   [54] *Ibid.*, 55-56.

[55]   Then seeke this path, that I to thee presage,
Which after all to heauen shall thee send;
Then peaceably thy painefull pilgrimage
To yonder same Hierusalem do bend.   (*Ibid.*, 61, 1-4.)

The qualities of the Unitive way received detailed attention in mystical writings notably in Gerson's *De Monte Contemplationis*, wherein the three mystical ways are part of the allegorical Pilgrimage of Life. In Gerson, the last part of the pilgrim's journey, coinciding with the Unitive way, consists of an ascent to the summit of the Mount of Contemplation. Here he pictures a high mountain with the three virtues, Faith, Hope, and Charity, located at the bottom, midway, and summit respectively. The pilgrim makes the ascent directed progressively by each of these virtues; and at the apex, Charity directs the thoughts of the true contemplative, now fully perfected, to God.[56]

The exalted nature of the Unitive way is such that its representation as a hill or mount was unusually attractive to the mystics. The imagery of the mount was frequently associated with St. John's Apocalyptic vision of the New Jerusalem. The *Stimulus Amoris* introduced the Unitive way with advice to those " who wish to come by contemplation to the top of the mount of God." [57]   Spenser's comparison of the Mount of Contemplation with Sinai, Olivet, and Parnassus, is significant in that direct communion with God is scripturally associated with Moses and with Christ on these two mountains; whilst the source of poetic inspiration, itself a supposedly divine gift, had its mythical origin on Parnassus. John Tauler, great German mystic of the fourteenth century, has this interesting interpretation both of the Mount and of the celestial city. " The place where Christ ascended up to heaven was the Mount of Olives. On this mount grows the olive tree by which is signified true

---

[56] *Opera*, III, 540-578. An interesting miniature was made to illustrate Gerson's Mount of Contemplation. Two beautiful ladies, Faith and Hope, with books in hand, are seen directing pilgrims up the steep pathway. An old man, seated, with beads and book, points the way upward. Pilgrims ascend; some, overcome by temptations, fall backward. At the summit of the mount, Charity, crowned, bends over an aged contemplative, whose face is uplifted in ecstasy toward a representation of the Deity surrounded by the nine-fold angelic choir. In MS. fr. 990 in Bibl. Nationale. For a reproduction of this miniature, see *John Gerson, Reformer and Mystic* (Louvain, 1928), p. 272.

[57] Part III, cap. IV, p. 678. The final chapter of this treatise is devoted to an ecstatic description of the heavenly City.

godly devotions. . . . But he who would experience in himself all that I have said, should have his face towards Jerusalem, the city of peace." [58] Similarly, Hilton's *Parable of the Pilgrim* is based on the mystical journey which ends at the " celestial Jerusalem, that is, at the sight of peace and contemplation." [59] Finally it is noteworthy that the author of *Pearl* [60] besides Chaucer [61] and Spenser,[62] were familiar with the vision of the celestial city. And by all this rich and varied tradition in medieval mystical literature, Spenser, sympathetic mystic and critical artist, brought his knight to perfect holiness.

The Fowre Hymnes

Spenser's *Fowre Hymnes,* which receive the crowning place in this study of Elizabethan mystical literature, were published in 1596.[1] These wholly fresh and moving poems present Spenser's mature genius for instilling poetic beauty and high seriousness into small compass. They are, in brief, four poems of seven-line stanzas averaging forty-two stanzas in length with the following titles : *An Hymne in Honour of Love, An Hymne in Honour of Beautie,* which Spenser described as treating " natural love and beautie ; " and *An Hymne of Heavenly Love, An Hymne of Heavenly Beautie,* which he tells us, celebrate " heavenly and celestiall " love and beauty.[2] The literary ances-

---

[58] " Sermon for Ascension Day," in *Life and Twenty-five Sermons by John Tauler,* trans. by S. Winkworth (London, 1858), pp. 323-326.

[59] *The Scale of Perfection,* p. 169.

[60] Professor Osgood, in his edition of *The Pearl (Belles-Lettres Series,* 1906, note, p. 90), calls attention to the passage in that poem (ll. 973 ff.) which bears comparison with the vision of the Red Cross knight on the Mount of Contemplation. That *The Pearl* is a poem in the direct tradition and spirit of Christian mysticism has been pointed out in Sister Madeleva's *Pearl, A Study in Spiritual Dryness* (New York, 1926).

[61]   " And Jhesu, for his grace, wit me send

             To shewe yow the wey, in this viage,

             Of thilke parfit, glorious pilgrymage,

             That highte Jerusalem celestial." (Prol. to *Persone's Tale.*)

[62] The last sonnet in *A Theatre for Worldlings* is a vision of the New Jerusalem in the manner of the Apocalyptic vision of St. John (XXI, 10).

[1] The joint dedication to Margaret, Duchess of Cumberland, and her sister, Duchess of Warwick, bears the date September 1, 1596.

[2] Dedicatory Epistle.

try of the *Fowre Hymnes* has been, since earliest Spenser criticism, almost entirely allocated in Petrarchian and Platonic literature of the Renaissance. The element of Christian mysticism, however, notably in the second pair of *Hymnes,* has already been detected by Professors Greenlaw [3] and Padelford; [4] and the view that other elements in the *Hymnes* " are merged with the mystical tradition of Christianity " is expressed by Professor Charles G. Osgood. [5] In the following study, the *Fowre Hymnes* will be analyzed and interpreted exclusively in the light of the traditional spirit and methodology of Christian mysticism. This treatment is arranged in the following order.

> The Unity of the *Fowre Hymnes.*
> Mystical Elements in the First Pair.
> The Hymnes of Heavenly Love and Heavenly Beautie.
> The Nature of Sapience.
> The Theology of the *Hymnes.*

The Unity of the ' Fowre Hymnes '

The unity of theme and purpose in the *Fowre Hymnes* depends, of course, upon the relations which the first two *Hymnes* bear to the second pair, as well as upon the inner spirit which binds each *Hymne* to the other and to the composition as a whole. It is the usual practice of modern scholars with few exceptions to take each pair of *Hymnes* separately. Miss Lilian Winstanley, in an elaborate introduction to her edition of the *Fowre Hymnes*, found the first pair to reflect an earlier, purely Platonic period in Spenser's poetry, while " the later ' Hymnes ' differ in their mentality, being fundamentally Neo-Platonist." [6] Professor Renwick, likewise, considered the second pair a new

[3] " Spenser's Hymns," wrote Professor Greenlaw, " are the first expression in English literature of that Mysticism which grows out of Neoplatonic impulses developed into a transcendental philosophy that has been a continuous and pervasive element in our poetry " (" Spenser's Influence on ' Paradise Lost,' " *Studies in Philology*, XVII [1920], 347 ff.). See also, *Modern Language Notes*, XLV (1930), 326 ff.

[4] " Spenser's *Fowre Hymnes*: A Resurvey," *Studies in Philology*, XXIX (1932), 207 ff.

[5] *The Voice of England* (New York and London, 1935), p. 166.

[6] *The Fowre Hymnes* (Cambridge, 1916), p. lxxii.

start and a breaking away to set down the central tenets of Christianity; in the last *Hymne,* however, Spenser returns " to his Platonists, and remembering his Bible, he begins again." [7] Professor Fletcher says that the " later " *Hymnes* are a sequel or complement to the first pair in which Neoplatonism, chiefly that of Benivieni, is overlaid with the theology of Calvin.[8]

Professor Osgood is the first Spenser scholar to see in the four poems a unity commensurate with their subject-matter. " The essential unity and symmetry of the four hymns is accompanied by an external symmetry," wrote Dr. Osgood. " In each one the poet has rendered the abstract subject of the hymn concrete by presenting a central figure to embody the subject, and in each case exalting it to a certain degree of apotheosis." [9] The continuity of the *Fowre Hymnes* was firmly believed by Professor Greenlaw. He based his view upon their Christian mysticism. The three-fold ways or stages of the mystical method, Purification, Illumination, and Perfection, run through the pairs of *Hymnes,* uniting them in an organic whole,[10] and presenting at the same time Spenser's mature philosophy of love.[11] Mrs. Josephine Waters Bennett, in a careful study of the *Fowre Hymnes* in the light of Pico della Mirandola and Benivieni, traced a distinct unity in the four poems, and observed a gradual turning in the final pair from Renaissance Neoplatonism to that of Plotinus and the

[7] W. L. Renwick, *Daphnaïda and Other Poems* (London, 1929), p. 212.

[8] " A Study in Renaissance Mysticism: Spenser's ' Fowre Hymnes,' " *Publications of the Modern Language Assn.,* XIX (1911), 452 ff.

[9] " Spenser's Sapience," *Studies in Philology,* XIV (1917), 167 ff.

[10] " Spenser's Influence on ' Paradise Lost,' " p. 350; Dr. Greenlaw repeated his opinion in a review of Professor Renwick's *Daphnaïda* (*Modern Language Notes,* XLV, pp. 326-328) and concluded as follows: " Taken as a whole, therefore, there is unity. The first hymns are imperfect, earthly, like the speeches of Phaedrus, Pausanius, and Agathon; for the speech of Socrates he substitutes what is equally characteristic of his method, the method of the Christian mystics; contemplation of Christ's Passion; contrition; contemplation of the cosmic order; the Vision of God."

[11] " To him," wrote Dr. Greenlaw, " love is the source of the universe, of every living thing, and of every spiritual value in this world and in the world to come. . . . In this he parallels Dante. His theme throughout his poetry was L'amor che move el sole e l'altre stelle " (" Some Old Religious Cults in Spenser," *Studies in Philology,* XX [1923], 243).

Pseudo-Dionysius.[12]   There is, then, a structural unity in the *Fowre Hymnes*, not a new beginning or fresh start with the second pair ; and, furthermore, the underlying philosophy which conduces to their unity is not Platonic only but a wider concept of the all-embracing nature of love, which was developed not alone in Platonic but also in Christian mystical discourses of love and beauty.[13]   The *Fowre Hymnes* present a development and intrinsic growth from pure, idealized love to its heavenly counterpart in God.[14]

Mystical Elements in the First Pair

A number of vital passages in the first two *Hymnes* refer to a purification and ascent which indicate the poet's conception of love and beauty, exalted and idealized, which is a lower degree of that which makes up the burden of the *Hymnes* of heavenly love and beauty.   The *Hymne in Honour of Love* (176-189) has repeated denunciations of ignoble passion together with praise of love capable of ascent " out of the lowly dust / Of heavie earth, up to the heavens hight."

This ascent is marked in the stanzas of both *Hymnes* which contain the much-discussed steps of the " Neoplatonic scale." [15] Here Spenser has been over-subtly analyzed by critics.[16]   He has related quite freely the process of idealization of human love ; and embodied therein the steps which are basic in Aristotelian psychology,[17] and used by Dante as well as later by the

---

[12] " The theme of Spenser's *Fowre Hymnes*," *Studies in Philology*, XXVIII (1931), 25-26.

[13] " There are, of course," says Miss Winstanley, " certain sides of Plato's genius which have no parallel in Spenser. . . . And even when he follows Plato most closely, it is with a certain difference " (pp. xi-xii).

[14] Continued reference to Parts I and II of this study will be generally avoided, although the basic evidence for these conclusions is pointed out in the preceding chapters.   But note in Dante (above, Part II) the essential unity of his great poems on human and divine love ; and the same is marked in Petrarch, etc.

[15] *Hymne in Honour of Love*, 120-196; *Hymne in Honour of Beautie*, 210-224.

[16] Cf. Mrs. Bennett, *op. cit.*

[17] The Aristotelian-Scholastic theory of universalization may be stated briefly : An object produces an impression on a sense organ, viz., the eyes. This results in a sensuous phantasm in the imagination, and here the work

Renaissance Neoplatonists.[18] This is illustrated most fully in the second *Hymne* (211-224).

> But they which loue indeede, looke otherwise,
> With pure regard and spotlesse true intent,
> Drawing out of the obiect of their eyes,
> A more refyned forme, which they present
> Vnto their mind, voide of all blemishment;
> Which it reducing to her first perfection,
> Beholdeth free from fleshes frayle infection.
>
> And then conforming it vnto the light
> Which in it selfe it hath remaining still,
> Of that first Sunne, yet sparckling in his sight,
> Thereof he fashions in his higher skill,
> An heauenly beautie to his fancies will,
> And it embracing in his mind entyre,
> The mirrour of his owne thought doth admyre.[19]

Here Spenser outlines the first sense-perception (211-212), then the formation of the phantasm (213-217), which by the abstractive powers of the intellect is refined, dispossessed of concrete particulars, compared with the primal universal concept (218-220) and, finally, is idealized into an intellectual image fairer even than its fleshly prototype (221-224). Spenser goes no higher in the ascent. Had he in mind the typical Neoplatonic scale, he would have identified his idealized image with the universal beauty. Instead, he reserves his treatment of divine love and beauty for the last pair of *Hymnes*.

That he would continue his theme and celebrate the higher as well as the lower love and beauty, Spenser promised in the concluding stanza of the first *Hymne,*

of the lower power ends. The presence of the phantasm forms the condition of rational activity, and the intellect abstracts the essence; that is, by its own active and passive capabilities generates the concept which expresses in the abstract the essense of the object. By a further reflective act it views this abstract concept as capable of representing any number of the class, and thus constitutes it a formally universal idea. Cf. for detailed exposition of this act of idealization, *Summa Theol.*, I, *QQ*. 79, 84, 85.

[18] Read, for example, Pico della Mirandola's detailed explanation of the Neoplatonic steps according to the psychology of Aristotle and St. Thomas in the *Commento* on Benivieni's *Canzona dello amor celeste e divino, lib.* III, x.

[19] Spenser compresses the four psychological steps in the first *Hymne* (190-196), and gives them more at length in the second.

> Then would I sing of thine immortall praise
> An heauenly Hymne, such as the Angels sing.[20]

This intent is likewise apparent in the Dedicatory Epistle, wherein Spenser had purposed to sing the praises of true and noble human love and beauty as well as that which is celestial and heavenly, and to dedicate the same to the ladies who are " most excellent and rare ornaments of all true love and beautie, both in the one and the other kind." [21]

All this is noteworthy in view of the traditional love-philosophy relating to the " divine circle of love," [22] and the belief that human and divine love differ not in kind but in degree. Petrarch and Dante so conceived of love, as did also the Christian Platonists of Florence and Urbino.[23] One finds the same ideas embodied in Christian mystical treatises of the patristic and medieval periods and throughout the sixteenth century.

Hence the progressive development of human love to divine with the idealized conception of the one, and the mystical treatment of the other, constitute the basic framework of the *Fowre Hymnes*; and accordingly, Spenser never entirely leaves his earthly ideal in the first two *Hymnes*, or descends again to human love in the *Hymnes* of heavenly love and beauty. " The saints," wrote Professor Watkin, " have not fled passion, they have transformed it and raised it to a higher level where it is freed from the limitations of sense." [24] That the following words written by a great mystic upon divine love could be applied also to human love, shows the close proximity of one to the other in the mystical philosophy of love.

For, love having aroused our attention to contemplate its object, this attention in turn gives birth to a greater and stronger love which finally attains its crowning perfection when it enjoys the

[20] *Hymne in Honour of Love*, 301-302; cf. Mrs. Bennett, *op. cit.*, p. 36.

[21] This conclusion rests on the belief that Spenser's dedication followed revision and reformation of the first two *Hymnes* and composition of the final pair.

[22] Cf. the Pseudo-Dionysius, *De Divin. Nomin.*, cap. IV, 14; *P. G.*, III, 713; St. Augustine, *De Quantitate Animae, P. L.*, XXXII, 1035; St. Thomas, *Summa Theol.*, I-II, Q. 26, a. 2. Cf. also above, Part I.

[23] See Part II, pp. 112-118.

[24] E. I. Watkin, *Philosophy of Mysticism* (New York, 1920), p. 398.

possession of the object loved. Love urges on the mind to the ever more attentive contemplation of the beloved beauty, and the sight impels the heart to love it ever more ardently.[25]

In this strain of thought the *Fowre Hymnes* are written. Closely akin to them in spirit are the *Canzoniere* of Petrarch, not only with an adoration *a longe* of a beautiful and disdainful lady, but also in the manner of the poet's mystical exaltation. Similarly, the *Vita Nuova* and the *Paradiso* mark for Dante the beginning and the end of his praise of love and beauty.

The Renaissance Neoplatonists, undoubted sources of many of Spenser's ideas, were imbued with a spiritual love-philosophy developed in its higher reaches by the Christian mystics, who, in turn, composed works of love and beauty exhibiting Platonic impulses which had never been wholly foreign to Christian mysticism. There are, moreover, in the first two *Hymnes*, important concepts not to be found solely in Platonic literature. Love conceived as capable of reconciling the warring elements,[26] was, through Boethius, wholly Christianized in the middle ages.[27] That love is a desire for beauty,[28] was a familiar notion to the Christian mystics, who, likewise, took from scholastic disquisitions on love [29] those " effects " or complaints, generally termed Petrarchian, which make up a large part of the first pair of *Hymnes*. The belief that created beauty is an image of the ultimate Pattern of Beauty was a medieval commonplace; and the opinion that beauty is essentially of the soul, not alone resident in physical form or in ordered parts and color, was asserted by St. Augustine [30] and repeatedly affirmed by the mystics as late as Bellarmine in the late sixteenth century.[31]

[25] St. Francis de Sales, *Treatise on the Love of God*, Bk. VI, cap. 3.

[26] *Hymne in Honour of Love*, 78-91.

[27] *De Consol. Philosophiae*, II, *metrum* 8; see Colville's paraphrase above, Part II.

[28] *Hymne in Honour of Beautie*, 57-60; and see Part II, p. 114.

[29] Cf. St. Thomas, *Summa Theol.*, I-II, QQ. 27-28, and also *Comment. in De Div. Nominibus Dionysii Areopagitae, cap.* IV, *lect.* viii.

[30] *De Trinitate, lib.* 8, *cap.* 10, 14, *P. L.*, XLII, 954, 960.

[31] *De Ascensione Mentis in Deum per Scalas Rerum Creaturarum, Gradus secundus, Opera Omnia* (Paris, 1873), VIII, 243. English trans. by T. B. Gent. (1616), reprinted, London, 1928. See p. 35.

15

The following " Platonism " is taken from the Spanish mystic Diego de Estella:

> If beauty has such power to captivate the desires, why O my heart, art thou not captivated by the infinite beauty of thy Creator? . . . If these works cause thee such admiration, which works cannot be impressed with the perfection which they possess in the divine pattern, on account of the dullness of the material whereon they have been elaborated, how is it that thou art not transfixed beyond thyself when contemplating the beauty and perfection which exist in the pattern from which they were derived? [32]

Spenser also sings of " that wondrous Paterne, wheresoere it bee, . . . Whose face and feature doth so much excell / All mortall sence, that none the same may tell." [33] But all this is part of the familiar Theocentric contemplation which Spenser elaborates in the *Hymne of Heavenly Beautie*. In view, therefore, of the complex ancestry of Spenser's first two *Hymnes*, one feels hesitant in assigning to them the terms Platonic or Neoplatonic without definite qualification. This fact is recognized by Mrs. Josephine Waters Bennett in her second study of the philosophical content of the *Fowre Hymnes*, wherein she would prefer to call " Ficinism," after Marsilio Ficino, the prevalent Christian Neoplatonism of Spenser's time. She, too, lays stress upon the Christian mysticism in the *Hymnes* chiefly by way of Ficino and Pico della Mirandola.[34] Writing as Spenser did in the vein of exalted human love in the first pair of *Hymnes*, it is easily conceivable how he centered his attention on the godly love of the mystics in the final *Hymnes*.

The Hymnes of Heavenly Love and Heavenly Beautie

The *Hymne of Heavenly Love* exemplifies the Christocentric type of contemplation just as the Theocentric type is present in the *Hymne of Heavenly Beautie*. Peculiarly appropriate is Spenser's employment of this type of contemplation to celebrate

---

[32] *Meditations of the Love of God*, trans. by H. W. Pereira (London, 1898), pp. 22-23.

[33] *Hymne in Honour of Beautie*, 36, 41-42.

[34] " Spenser's ' *Fowre Hymnes* ': Addenda," *Studies in Philology*, XXXII (1935), 131-157.

heavenly love, since this attribute of God is strikingly manifest in the story of divine dealings with mankind; and, moreover, the divine dispensation of love is specifically provocative of reciprocal love on the part of man. This is the teaching of the mystics, who are ultimately indebted to the sublime directions of St. Paul and the Johannine writings. Equally fitting is the use of the Theocentric type of contemplation in the *Hymne of Heavenly Beautie.* This type was highly adaptable for descriptions of the heavens, and it answered the familiar cry of the mystic: If God's handiwork is of such beauty, how much more beautiful must be the place and the Person wherein all this beauty has its source![35]

The *Hymne of Heavenly Love* may be considered according to the events which lead up to Christ's redemptive act, and are united by the causal agency of love. Thus we have first, the relation of love to the Trinity (22-49), and secondly, the place of love in the successive creative acts of angels and of man, and then the defection of the angels and the fall of man (50-119). But love prompted the Redemption, and accordingly Spenser leads directly to the all-important Christocentric contemplation (127-252), and the *Hymne* closes with the effects of the entire meditation: renunciation, detachment, and a note of rapture and ecstasy.

We are dealing in this *Hymne* not so much with philosophy as with theology. It is traditional theology, partly speculative; and one which particularly appealed to the mystics. The contemplation of Christ is interpreted by them as essentially a contemplation of love. This is especially true also of the first part of the *Hymne* which relates the procession of Persons in the Trinity, and the successive impulses of love which lead to the Incarnation of Christ and the Redemption.

> That high eternall powre, which now doth moue
> In all these things, mou'd in it selfe by loue.
> It lou'd it selfe, because it selfe was faire;
> (For faire is lou'd;) and of it selfe begot
> Like to it selfe his eldest sonne and heire,
> Eternall, pure, and voide of sinfull blot.[36]

---

[35] See Part I, pp. 45-55.   [36] *Hymne of Heavenly Love,* 27-32.

This poetic rendering of Christian theology is fully consonant with the traditional teaching of the mystics. " Divine love," wrote the Pseudo-Dionysius, " did not permit Him to be without offspring." [37] And St. Thomas explained that " it is the essential idea of love, that whoever loves wishes the good of the object loved. But God wishes his own good and the good of other beings; and in this respect he loves himself and other beings." [38] " Love cannot exist in solitude," concluded Diego de Estella.[39]

> With him he raignd, before all time prescribed,
> In endlesse glorie and immortall might,
> Together with that third from them deriued,
> Most wise, most holy, most almightie Spright.[40]

These lines and the passage above are fully explained, for instance, in the following from Henry Suso, which is a paraphrase of the Pseudo-Dionysius. They are descriptive of the operation of heavenly love in the Trinity.

In the Father there is an outflowing of the Godhead, and this outflowing or stream pours itself out naturally in the outrunning Word, who is the Son by nature. He also pours Himself out according to the loving bountifulness of the will into the Son, and the Son in turn pours Himself out according to the lovingness of the will into the Father, and this is called a reciprocal love, and is the Holy Ghost. . . . And since this love is in the will after an intellectual or spiritual fashion, like an inclination or love-bond present inwardly in the lover toward the object of his love, the third Person in the procession, who proceeds according to the loving manner of the will, fittingly receives the name of Spirit.[41]

The creation of the angels, their offices, and the defection through pride of a considerable number with subsequent con-

[37] *De Divinis Nominibus, cap.* IV, *lect.* 10.
[38] *Contra Gentiles, lib.* XCI, *ad.* 1.
[39] *Meditations on the Love of God*, p. 36.
[40] *Hymne of Heavenly Love*, 36-39.
[41] *Life of Henry Suso by Himself* (London, 1865), pp. 294, 296. See also John Davies of Hereford, above, p. 155.

demnation, make up a generous part of the meditations of the mystics,[42] who frequently conclude as does Spenser,

> And now of sinne to all ensample bee:
> How then can sinfull flesh it selfe assure,
> Sith purest Angels fell to be impure? [43]

The creation of man, his fall, and the doctrine of original sin are narrated in the manner made traditional since the *Cur Deus Homo* of St. Anselm.[44] Spenser's correct and concise rendering of the reason for the Incarnation indicates a more than ordinary familiarity with dogmatic Christianity.

> In flesh at first the guilt committed was,
> Therefore in flesh it must be satisfyde:
> Nor spirit, nor Angell, though they man surpas,
> Could make amends to God for mans misguyde,
> But onely man himselfe, who selfe did slyde.
> So taking flesh of sacred virgins wombe,
> For mans deare sake he did a man become.[45]

With a brief review of the Passion of Christ, the narrative part of the *Hymne* ends; and the more affective, mystical, and less strictly theological part of the *Hymne* begins. The typical contemplation of Christ beginning with line 155 is interspersed with appropriate ejaculations. This meditation, for such Spenser calls it,[46] has for its object Christ's love for man, and the reciprocal love of man for Christ and for his brethren.[47] No important detail of the gospel narrative concerning the historic Christ from the Nativity to the Passion is omitted; even the institution of the Eucharist is included. Indeed, no element foreign to the Christocentric type of contemplation finds place

[42] See Part I, p. 43, and note Ruysbroeck, *The Spiritual Marriage*, Bk. 1, cap. 2; also *Paradiso*, xxix, 46-63.

[43] *Hymne of Heavenly Love*, 96-98.

[44] *P. L.*, CLVIII, 359-432; see also *Meditatio* XI, *De Redemptione Humana* (*P. L.*, CLVIII, 762-763, 765, 766, 767). *Meditatio* XII, *De Humanitate Christi* (*ibid.*, 769).

[45] *Hymne of Heavenly Love*, 141-147.

[46] Through meditation of his endlesse merit (255).

[47] Cf. the Pseudo-Rolle, *Contemplations of the Dread and Love of God*, ed. by Frances M. Comper (London, 1916), cap. VII, pp. 54-56. But the idea is a commonplace in mystical contemplations.

in this *Hymne*. In accord with the directions of the mystics the consideration of Christ was the essential condition for the right ordering of love,[48] and for progress to perfection.[49] Mystical contemplation of Christ induces renunciation in the manner of a *Contemptus Mundi*,[50] and rapture of love and exalted vision. Renounce utterly all other loves, and deplore them; then give thyself fully and freely to Christ—that is the spiritual fruit of the entire meditation.

> All other loues, with which the world doth blinde
> Weake fancies, and stirre up affections base,
> Thou must renounce, and utterly displace,
> And giue thy selfe vnto him full and free,
> That full and freely gaue himselfe to thee.[51]

The second effect of the Christocentric contemplation, Spenser makes clear.

> Then shalt thou feele thy spirit so possest,
> And rauisht with deuouring great desire
> Of his deare selfe, that shall thy feeble brest
> Inflame with loue, and set thee all on fire. . . .
> Then shall thy rauisht soule inspired bee
> With heauenly thoughts, farre aboue humane skil.[52]

The closing lines of the *Hymne* are in complete accord with

---

[48] See Part I, pp. 40-45. For further confirmatory evidence: Suso's *Eternal Wisdom,* chapters XIV and XV: "On the Unspeakable advantage to be derived from meditating on the Divine Passion." The advice of Tauler is typical: "Thou must be transformed into the beauteous image of our Lord by a constant, earnest contemplation thereof, considering His holy weakness and humility, . . . the boundless charity, . . . His blessed poverty. . . . Then look attentively at thyself, how unlike thou art to this Image, and behold thy own vision" ("How we are to ascend by three stages to true peace and purity of heart," *Life and Sermons of John Tauler,* pp. 300-301).

[49] "Among all the devotions in the world," wrote Granada, "there is none more secure, none more profitable, or more universal for all kind of persons than the remembrance of the holy Passion of our Saviour Christ. There is none other exercise more fit and convenient to direct us to goe unto God" (*Of Prayer and Meditation,* Part II, p. 143).

[50] "Now if thou bee desirous to see a most perfect patterne of *The Contempt of the World,*" wrote Granada, "and all the honours, riches, pleasures, and delights that be therein—behold our Saviour uppon the Crosse" (*Of Prayer and Meditation,* Part II, p. 178).

[51] *Hymne of Heavenly Love,* 262-266.   [52] *Ibid.,* 267-270, 281-282.

terminations of this type of contemplation, and illustrate the rapture of the mystic experience. Granada, for instance, affirmed that this meditation " will lift uppe thy minde into such a great admiration and love of him, that thou wilt bee astonished, as Moses was in the Mount. . . . This was the great languishing and faintnesse of spirit which the Spouse felt in the Canticles." [53]

The *Hymne of Heavenly Beautie* opens in the same high strain which marks the close of the third *Hymne*. The soul that has been ravished with divine love through contemplation of Christ is now fixed on God in critical appreciation of divine beauty. The poet will now sing " Of that immortall beautie, there with thee " in order that the hearts of men,

> Transported with celestiall desyre
> Of those faire formes, may lift themselues vp hyer,
> And learne to loue with zealous humble dewty
> Th' eternall fountaine of that heauenly beauty.[54]

With this beauty as his theme, Spenser develops the regular Theocentric type of contemplation. The ascent from created to uncreated beauty, originally Platonic, was a favored method with the mystics who gave to it its philosophical and theological basis.[55]

St. Augustine was enamoured of divine beauty in its mani-

---

[53] *Of Prayer and Meditation,* Part II, p. 174. Note the same sentiments in another mystic: " I will go forth out of myself, loving thee without being in myself—inebriated with this holy love, and transported out of myself, because love surprises and creates ecstasy " (*Meditations on the Love of God,* p. 30). See the same treatment in the mystical poems of Nicholas Breton, above.

[54] *Hymne of Heavenly Beautie,* 18-21.

[55] See Part I, pp. 45-55. The complex background of the Theocentric type of contemplation, and its relation to beauty are seen in Granada's words: " A pagan philosopher amazed at the work of God once wrote, ' Look up at the sky and begin to philosophize.' That is to say, by that great variety and beauty which here you see, know and consider the wisdom and omnipotence of its Author. And the Prophet, too, could philosophize equally well upon this matter, and he exclaimed: ' I shall see, O Lord, Thy heavens which are the work of Thy hand, the moon and the stars which Thou hast founded ' " (*Introd. to Symbol of the Faith,* Part I, cap. 4). See Peers, *Spanish Mysticism* (New York, 1924), p. 94.

fold effects; [56] once he touched upon it in the rare experience of the mystic vision.[57] The medieval mystics considered contemplation of divine beauty and goodness subsisting in Nature and in the Divine Essence to be a grace-endowed privilege of souls already skilled in the meditation upon Christ. What Spenser has done in the last pair of *Hymnes* accords with their method. Vitally important is the unity of these two *Hymnes* by the bond of Christocentric-Theocentric contemplation. Rolle and Hilton, carrying over the continental tradition, especially advised employment of the two types of contemplation in conjunction.

" Also thou may hafe mynde of the manhede of oure Lorde," wrote Rolle, " in his byrthe or in his passion, or in any of his werkes, and fede thi thoghte with gastely ymagynacyon of it, for to stirre thyne affeccion to mare lufe of Hym. . . . Also mynd of the myghte of the wysdome and the gudnes of our Lorde in all his creaturs." [58]

The counsel of Hilton is significant: " For it is an opening of the spiritual eye into the humanity of Christ, and may be called the fleshly love of God, as S. Bernard saith. . . . And so after to the *Contemplation* of the God-head. For a man shall not come to the spiritual light in *Contemplation* of Christ's Godhead, unless first he be exercised in imagination and steadfast thinking of His humanity." [59] In another place he is no less explicit. " First of his glorious humanity, and afterwards of His blessed Divinity, for by knowing of creatures is known the Creator; and then beginneth the soul to perceive a little of the mysteries of the blessed Trinity." [60] One of Granada's books

---

[56] Cf. *Confessions*, X, 27.

[57] *Ibid.*, IX, 24. And see Part I, p. 28.

[58] *English Prose Treatises of Richard Rolle of Hampole,* " Good Thoughts for Meditation," *EETS,* orig. series, 20, pp. 38, 40.

[59] *The Scale of Perfection,* Bk. I, cap. II, p. 41.

[60] *Ibid.*, Bk. III, cap. XV, p. 258. The *Speculum S. Edmundi,* a popular source for the English mystics, explicitly enjoins the two-fold contemplation. The following excerpt is of Rolle's translation: " Now hase thou matire and manere for to thynke of goddis manhede. And eftirwarde sall thou wit how thou sall thynke one hym in his heghe godhede " (C. Horstmann, *Richard Rolle of Hampole* [London, 1895], I, 235-237). The MS. Vernon of the *Mirror of S. Edmond* gives these headings to chapters 17-18:

which enjoyed enormous popularity in England during Spenser's life makes specific mention of " both the one and the other manner of contemplation in the *same exercises*." [61] He also tells how the one type of contemplation will lead to the other.

It appeareth that this first manner of meditating (by way of taking compassion of the bitter paines of our Sauiour) is as it were a meane or a ladder unto the other. And for this very cause S. Bonaventure made great account of the manner of meditation upon the Passion, because it is sensibly seene that this manner of meditation openeth the way unto all the other maners of meditating.[62]

Bellarmine wrote a complete exposition of the Theocentric type of contemplation called *De Ascensione Mentis in Deum per Scalas Rerum Creaturarum*.[63] It presents the medieval spirit and method together with a certain external coloring and terminology which reflects the Platonizing influence of his time. This treatise would serve admirably in assisting one unacquainted with earlier works of Christian mysticism to interpret the *Hymne of Heavenly Beautie*.

This *Hymne* accords with the Theocentric type of contemplation in the manner of its ascent.

> Beginning then below, with th' easie vew
> Of this base world, subiect to fleshly eye,
> From thence to mount aloft, by order dew,
> To contemplation of th' immortall sky (22-25).

To arrive at this immortal heaven, the created world must be surveyed and surmounted. Spenser does not draw up a precise cosmogony, and his " dew order " is relative only.[64] Spenser first views the wide universe and admires the beauty of its living creatures, then observes in particular the four elements

Of Contemplacion of God in his Manhede; Of Contemplacion of God in his Godhede (*ibid.*, p. 241).

[61] *Of Prayer and Meditation,* Part II, cap. V, p. 89.

[62] *Ibid.,* Part II, cap. VI, p. 162.   [63] *Gradus* XIII.

[64] One would expect an arrangement whereby lines 36-49 would precede lines 29-35 i. e. the basic elements would precede the divers creatures of the " wyde universe." Spenser's order is that of *Timaeus,* 30; also Ovid, *Met.,* 1. 21 ff.

which make up the terrestrial world.[65] The starry heavens, the moon and the sun are next observed and the mind rises from the material to the spiritual heavens.

> For farr aboue these heauens which here we see,
> Be others farre exceeding these in light,
> Not bounded, not corrupt, as these same bee,
> But infinite in largenesse and in hight.[66]

Here Spenser distinguishes first the realm of celestial spheres. These " by degrees arize Vntill they come to their first Mouers bound," [67] which is the Primum Mobile according to the Ptolemaic cosmology familiar to Dante and the medieval mystics. The upward ascent continues to the heaven of " happy soules," who in enjoyment of felicity, behold the face of " the diuine eternall maiestie.[68] More beautiful than the abode of the blessed is the place where the eternal *ideas* or *forms* have their being together with the " pure Intelligences from God in-spyred." [69] These Intelligences are spiritual powers which were thought to move the celestial spheres through a divinely-be-stowed virtue, but most generally they are simply called angels. Dante explicitly calls the angels Intelligences,[70] and St. Thomas explains how angels were sometimes called by this name.[71] St. Bernard speaks of angels as " pure intelligences," and, indeed, the term was commonly applied to the angels since very early patristic times.[72] Spenser pauses in his ascent to praise the beauty of the angelic choirs. He, unlike Dante,[73] who follows

---

[65] This is a commonplace in medieval treatises.
[66] *Hymne of Heavenly Beautie*, 64-67.
[67] *Ibid.*, 71-72.   [69] *Ibid.*, 82-84.
[68] *Ibid.*, 78-81.   [70] *Paradiso*, XXVIII, 76-79.
[71] " Substantiae separatae, quas nos angelos dicimus, *intelligentiae* vocan-tur " (*Summa Theol.*, I, Q. 79, a. 10).
[72] See, for example, St. Augustine, *De Civitate Dei*, XXII, 1-2; Gregory Nazian., *Orationes*, XXXVIII, 9; John Damascene, *De Fide Orthodoxa*, II, 3. St. Bernard, speaking of the intellectual and spiritual heavens in contrast to the material heavens, said, " It also like the other, is stretched out like a curtain, not indeed, over extents of corporeal spaces, but in the spiritual affections of pure intelligences." He then considers the angels. (*Serm. on the Cant. of Canticles*, XXVI, " The Beauty of the Spouse," I, 307.)
[73] *Paradiso*, XXVIII, 97-132.

the Pseudo-Dionysian order mentions eight choirs with, however, no apparent arrangement.[74]

Leaving the spiritual heavens, the " utmost parts " of God,[75] Spenser now contemplates the attributes in the Divine Essence, which, quite properly, he calls the " essentiall parts " of the Deity.[76] Of these attributes at the outset he names eight,

> How much more those essentiall parts of his,
> His truth, his loue, his wisedome, and his blis,
> His grace, his doome, his mercy, and his might (109-111).

The attributes of Beauty and Goodness are writ large in Nature;[77] but one must ascend far higher to fashion those other attributes which in particular denote qualities predicated of creatures, existing supereminently in God. The first is Glory.

> Thence gathering plumes of perfect speculation,
> To impe the wings of thy high flying mynd,
> Mount vp aloft through heauenly contemplation,
> From this darke world, . . .
> On that bright Sunne of glorie fixe thine eyes (134-139).

A number of attributes are named with some figurative significIation of each. First, the " footestoole of his Majestie " (142), and the seat of his Mercy (148). Then follow Eternity (152), Righteousness (155), and Truth (159-174) from which proceeds the immortal light of God's Knowledge, whereby " all mortall actions here, And euen the thoughts of men, do plaine appeare " (172-173). Divine Justice, Glory, and Light receive especially attention.[78] The brightness of the Divine Essence which so appealed to Dante[79] also attracted Spenser. His

---

[74] Spenser's list is as follows: Powres, Potentates (= Principalities), Seates (Thrones), Dominations, ' Cherubins,' ' Seraphins,' Angels, Archangels. The Virtues alone are omitted. Recall, however, Spenser's mention of the " trinal triplicities " in *The Faerie Queene*, I, vii, 39, and in the *Hymne of Heavenly Love*, 64. For the place of the angels in Theocentric contemplation, see Part I, pp. 48-51.

[75] *Hymne of Heavenly Beautie*, 108.

[76] See Part I, pp. 51-55 for the attributes in Theocentric contemplation.

[77] *Hymne of Heavenly Beautie*, 127-132.

[78] Note lines 111, 150, 158, 182 relative to Justice; lines 139, 161, 176 are in praise of Glory.

[79] *Paradiso*, xxxiii, 82-176.

description of this Light which, amazing its beholder's sight, " enlumineth the darke and dampish aire," [80] is reminiscent of the " divine darkness " of the Pseudo-Dionysius.

Finally, crowning these admirable and " essentiall parts " of the Deity, Spenser speaks in glowing praise of the queen of all the divine attributes—Sapience or Wisdom, of which he had already made mention in the first catalogue of attributes.[81]

Spenser's entire treatment of the divine attributes and his emphasis on the light of the Deity can be more fully appreciated when compared immediately with the teaching of a great mystic —St. John of the Cross.

God in his one and simple essence is all the power and majesty of His attributes. He is wise, omnipotent, good, merciful, just, strong, loving; He is all the other attributes and perfections of which we have no knowledge here on earth. He is all this. When the soul is in union with Him, and He is pleased to admit this soul to a special knowledge of Himself, it sees all these perfections and majesty together in Him. And as each one of these attributes is the very being of God, who is the Father, the Son, and the Holy Ghost; and as each attribute is God himself, and as God is Infinite *light*, and infinite divine fire,—it follows that each attribute gives light and burns as God himself.[82]

Spenser personified the divine attribute of Sapience or Wisdom, terms interchangeable in his time,[83] as a female figure of great beauty and power subsisting in the bosom of the Deity.

> There in his bosome Sapience doth sit,
> The soueraine dearling of the Deity,
> Clad like a Queene in royall robes, most fit
> For so great powre and peerelesse maiesty (183-186).

In a superlative degree he endowed this figure with qualities already applied to the Divine Essence. The praise of Sapience makes up the apex of the contemplative ascent. The mind has risen by degrees until, in the impenetrable light of the final

[80] *Hymne of Heavenly Beautie,* 162-168.
[81] *Ibid.,* 111.
[82] *The Living Flame of Love,* Stanza III, v. 1; cf. A. Tanqueray, *The Spiritual Life* (Tournai, 1930), p. 659.
[83] Cf. Grace Warren Landrum, " Spenser's Use of the Bible and his Alleged Puritanism," *PMLA,* XLI (1926), p. 528.

Vision, adequate description always fails, and figures and personifications attempt to express the inexpressible. Vision of
the face of Sapience, a privilege vouchsafed only to the
worthy,[84] overcomes the soul with sweet contentment, rapture,
transport, and ecstasy.

> . . . it doth bereaue
> Their soule of sense, through infinite delight,
> And them transport from flesh into the spright.
>
> In which they see such admirable things,
> As carries them into an extasy (257-261).

This is the typical end of the mystic quest, and its reward.
Spenser also described it in terms of music,[85] and the *Hymne*
closes with a note of repentance, complete renunciation, and
rest.[86] The blissful conclusion of the vision is the answer to
that longing which Spenser expressed in the last stanza of the
Mutabilitie cantos, even as the " Sabbath of the soul " in mystical language [87] betokens the fruition of the mystical experience:

> But thence-forth all shall rest eternally
> With Him that is the God of Sabbaoth hight:
> O that great Sabbaoth God, graunt me that Sabaoth's sight.[88]

The three ways or stages of Christian mysticism which correspond to spiritual growth and development without, however, sharply defined boundaries are readily discernible in the
Fowre Hymnes.[89] The first two *Hymnes* emphasize the purificatory element which is a prerequisite to a right exercise of
heavenly love and to a full enjoyment of heavenly beauty. The
" Neoplatonic " steps of love in the first two poems do not
identify the universalized human love with heavenly and divine
love—that is left to the last pair of *Hymnes*. The *Hymne of
Heavenly Love* furnishes a parallel to the stages of purification
and illumination. The element of purification, prominent in the

---

[84] *Hymne of Heavenly Beautie*, 239-245; 253-255.
[85] Cf. Rolle's *Incendium Amoris*, cap. 34, pp. 241-244.
[86] *Hymne of Heavenly Beautie*, 295-301.
[87] See Part I, p. 60.   [88] *The Faerie Queene*, VII, viii, 2.
[89] Cf. Greenlaw, " Spenser's Influence on Paradise Lost," 350; also *Modern
Language Notes*, XLV (1930), 326.

first pair of *Hymnes*, is implicit in the opening stanzas of the
third *Hymne*; and reappears throughout this *Hymne* to fuse
with that definite illumination which proceeds from the meditation on Christ.[90]   The specific note of the Illuminative way,
however, is emphasized in the gradual turning away from
earthly things,[91] in the illumination of spirit consequent upon
meditation,[92] and the hope of a still higher elevation for the
" ravisht soule." The *Hymne of Heavenly Beautie* celebrates
the ascent from material and spiritual creation to intimate communion with the Creator.   This Theocentric type of contemplation is favored by those who are no longer beginners, but are
proficient, the adepts already in the Unitive way.   The vision
of the Godhead seen through a " divine darkness " in the
attributes, and especially in Sapience, are productive of such
ecstasy and transport as mark the Unitive way.

The Nature of Sapience

Sapience in the last *Hymne* has aroused much critical comment.[93]   The interpretation based on spiritual and mystical
usage is that Sapience, personified as a female figure, is an
attribute of God. Spenser took Sapience from out his catalogue of attributes,[94] and, retaining the traditional personification, clothed it with such dignity and splendor as is befitting
this important attribute of the Deity. Of Sapience are predicated powers proper only to God: highest sovereignty, creator
and ruler of heaven, earth and all creatures; whose fullness
fills the world, and whose beauty " darkes the earth with
shadows of her sight." [95]   And, moreover, Sapience or Wis-

[90] Professor Padelford wrote that " the essential theme of the third hymn
is the illumination that comes from contemplation of the life and passion of
Christ, and from the efforts of the Christian to model his life thereon"
(" Spenser's *Fowre Hymnes*: A Resurvey," 232).

[91] *Hymne of Heavenly Love*, 274.   [92] *Ibid.*, 280.

[93] Mrs. Bennett (*Studies in Philology*, XXVIII [1931], 43-46), discusses
the character of Sapience and (note 34) gives a summary of scholarly inter-
pretations. See especially Charles G. Osgood, " Spenser's Sapience," *Studies
in Philology*, XIV (1917), 167-177.

[94] *Hymne of Heavenly Beautie*, 111.

[95] *Ibid.*, 229.

dom is placed last among the divine attributes which are a final and essential part of Theocentric contemplation.

This treatment of Sapience and other divine attributes is not an isolated case in Spenser's poems. In *The Teares of the Muses,* the poet lets Clio speak of those who " despise the brood of blessed Sapience." [96] She says at the close of the sixth stanza (89-90) :

> For God himselfe for wisedome most is praised,
> And men to God thereby are nighest raised.

Melpomene also adds :

> She solaceth with rules of Sapience
> The gentle minds, in midst of worldlie smarts.[97]

In the words of Urania, Spenser gives us not only the mystic movement of the fourth *Hymne* in miniature, but also a small catalogue of the divine attributes :

> From hence wee mount aloft vnto the skie,
> And looke into the Christall firmament,
> There we behold the heauens great *Hierarchie,*
> The Starres pure light, the Spheres swift mouement,
> The Spirites and Intelligences fayre,
> And Angels waighting on th' Almighties chayre.

> And there, with humble minde and high insight,
> Th' eternall Makers maiestie wee viewe,
> His loue, his truth, his glorie, and his might,
> And mercie more than mortall men can vew.
> O soueraigne Lord, O soueraigne happinesse
> To see thee, and thy mercie measurelesse.[98]

Wisdom or Sapientia conceived as a divine attribute, as has been pointed out, is basic in the Theocentric type of contemplation. John Tauler, in a brief exhortation to employ both

---

[96] *The Teares of the Muses,* 72.   [97] *Ibid.,* 135-136.
[98] *Ibid.,* 505-516. Dr. Lotspeich has noted that here Spenser, probably following Du Bartas, makes Urania the patroness of mystical contemplation. (H. G. Lotspeich, " Spenser's Urania " *Modern Language Notes,* L (1935), 141-146.) The same view is offered by Rosamond Tuve, " Spenser and the ' Zodiak of Life,' " *Journal of Eng. and Germ. Phil.,* XXXIV (1935), 16-17.

types of contemplation, significantly mentioned Wisdom in its proper place:

In thy hours of meditation set before thy mind whatever thou shalt find most helpful to thee, whether it be the life of Christ, or His sufferings, or the eternal and essential Godhead, the Holy Trinity, or the Eternal Wisdom or the Divine Power, etc.[99]

Rolle, not unlike Spenser, wrote of those who are " illuminated by the increated Sapience, and feel the heat of the uncircumscribed light in whose beauty they are enraptured." [100] To go further and interpret Spenser's Sapience as one of the Persons of the Trinity is not warranted by either word or phrase in the *Hymne*. There is a strong tradition in theological and homiletic literature which associated Wisdom with Christ, and one much less strong wherein Wisdom is the Holy Spirit, but both conceptions derive from the same patristic sources which drew up the theology of the attributes of God without distinction of the divine Persons. Thus St. Augustine, who taught that Wisdom is Christ the Word or the Divine Logos, also insisted that Wisdom is a divine attribute: " The Father is Wisdom, the Son is Wisdom, the Holy Spirit is Wisdom, and together not three Wisdoms, but one Wisdom." [101] And, furthermore, it is Wisdom or Sapience as a divine attribute which is proper to the Theocentric type of contemplation, and as a divine attribute, Wisdom or Sapience is chiefly found in both mystical and non-mystical literature.[102]

Professor Osgood has pointed out that Spenser's Sapience is drawn chiefly from the Hebrew personification of Wisdom found in the Old Testament " Apocrypha " and in the Books of Proverbs and Job.[103] In the face of evidence adduced by

[99] *Op. cit.*, p. 346. See also Lessius, *The Names of God*, pp. 136-138, cited above, Part I, p. 53.

[100] *Incendium Amoris*, cap. 37, p. 255. See also *Good Thoughts for Meditation*, EETS, orig. series 20, pp. 38-40; *The Cloud of Unknowing*, ed. by Justin McCann (London, 1924), pp. 94, 194.

[101] *De Trinitate, lib.* VII, *cap.* 3.

[102] " In general, Wisdom is considered an attribute of God," is the conclusion of a study by Sister Mary Frances Smith, *Wisdom and Personification of Wisdom Occurring in Middle English Literature before 1500* (Catholic University Press, Washington, 1935), p. 164.

[103] " Spenser's Sapience," p. 167 ff.

Professor Osgood, Biblical influence in forming and coloring Sapience is unquestioned, and to it is due that vivid portraiture wherein at times it seems Spenser would separate Sapience and God—so stark is the personification![104] But Spenser would have found ample justification for his personified Sapience in mystical literature. The Sapiential books of the Old Testament were familiar to the mystics; and the female gender of Sapience in Latin, Greek, and Hebrew may have rendered this particular personification more authentic.[105] St. Bernard, for example, spoke of Wisdom as " the valiant woman [who] hath put out her hand to the distaff, and her fingers have taken hold of the spindle." [106] Henry Suso received his mystical revelation from Eternal Wisdom who appeared to him as a woman of wondrous beauty, and the virtual sameness in descriptions of Spenser's Sapience and Suso's Wisdom is interesting.

The eternal Wisdom is represented in Holy Scripture under a lovely guise, as a gracious loving mistress, who displays her charms with the intent to please every one; discoursing the while tenderly, in female form, of the desire she has to win all hearts, and saying how deceitful all other mistresses are, and how truly loving and constant she is. . . . She showed herself to him in this wise. She floated high above him in a choir of clouds; she shone like the morning star, and her radiance was dazzling like the rising sun; her crown was eternity; her vesture bliss; her words sweetness; her embrace the fullness of every delight; she was far, yet near; high, yet lowly; she was present, yet hidden; she forbade not to converse with her, yet no one can comprehend her. She reaches the depths of the abyss; she spreads herself from end to end mightily, and disposes all things sweetly. . . . Whence come all tenderness, beauty, joyousness and loveableness? Comes it not all from the outbursting fountainhead of the pure Godhead? [107]

The conception of God as the Bridegroom of the soul was

---

[104] *Hymne of Heavenly Beautie*, 201, 207, 235, 241, 251. " I was with Him forming all things " (Prov. VIII, 30).

[105] *Sapientia, σοφία*; חָכְמָה. So also such expressions which refer to wisdom as, " I am the mother of knowledge " (Ecclus. i, 24), and, " Say to Wisdom, thou art my sister " (Prov. vii, 4).

[106] *Serm. on the Cant. of Canticles*, XV, " *On the Names of God*," I, 141.

[107] *The Life of Henry Suso by Himself*, trans. by T. F. Knox (London, 1865), pp. 13, 17-18.

16

a familiar one to the mystics after St. Bernard, and in such instances, says one authority, " He takes the feminine character of Mercy or Wisdom," [108] and St. John of the Cross explained that after the dark night of the soul, " there is union with the bride which is the wisdom of God," [109] and St. Bonaventure wrote that " Divine Wisdom is the daughter and spouse and friend of God, and sister and co-heir with Him." [110]

Other instances of this kind present themselves from medieval literature. Lady Wisdom is Prioress in the *Abbey of the Holy Ghost*,[111] and Lady Sapience appears in De Guileville's *Pilgrimage of the Life of Man*.[112] Dame Sapience is guide and preceptress in the *Court of Sapience*,[113] and the woman Wisdom is found in Hawes' *Example of Virtue* and in his *Passtyme of Pleasure*.[114]

In the religious drama, Hrotswitha's " Sapientia " is mother of the three virgin martyrs in the play of that name; [115] and Lady Sapience appears in the late Morality called *The Marriage of Wit and Wisdom*.[116] An orison familiar to most Elizabethans asks of God for " wisdome which is euer about thy seate," that He may send her from the throne of His majesty, " that she may be with me and labour with me; for she knoweth and understandeth all things; and she shall conduct me right soberly in thy works, and preserve me in her power." [117] There is, then, a long and well-known usage of Wisdom or Sapience both as a divine attribute and as a per-

---

[108] A. Paulain, *Des Graces D'Oraison*, English trans. by L. Smith (London, 1910), f. n. p. 289.

[109] *The Ascent of Mount Carmel*, Bk. II, cap. II.

[110] *Intinerarium Mentis in Deum*, cap. IV, 15.

[111] C. Horstmann, *Richard Rolle of Hampole*, I, 326. " Wisdom " is also prioress in the *Charter of the Abbey of the Holy Ghost, ibid.*, p. 362.

[112] *Early English Text Society*, extra series, 78, ll. 5621 ff.

[113] Edited by Robert Spindler (Leipzig, 1927).

[114] For many other illustrations, see Sister Mary Frances Smith, *Wisdom and Personification of Wisdom* etc., pp. 145 ff.

[115] *Hrotswithae Opera Omnia, P. L.*, CXXXVII, 1045-1062.

[116] *Five Anonymous Plays*, ed. John S. Farmer, Early English Dramatic Series.

[117] *Liturgies and Occasional Forms of Prayer set forth in the Reign of Queen Elizabeth*, edited for the Parker Society by W. K. Clay (Cambridge, 1847), pp. 249-250.

sonified figure.[118] These two conceptions which are mutually consistent and traditionally united give the key to the nature of Spenser's Sapience in the *Hymne of Heavenly Beautie*.

The Theology of the ' Hymnes '

Certain " Platonic " expressions and modes of thought in the last two *Hymnes* find explanation not only in Platonism or in Renaissance Neoplatonism, but also in Christian theology. The Trinity passage of the third *Hymne* relates how the " High Eternall Powre "

> . . . mov'd in it selfe by love,
> It lov'd it selfe, because it selfe was faire (28-29).

Speculative and mystical theology conceived of God as loving Himself because of the beauty which is identical with His goodness; [119] and this love, essentially resident in the *Deity*,[120] is active not only in the procession of the second and third Persons of the Trinity, but also *ad extra* in the creation of all things.[121] Equally correct is Spenser's relation of the eternal generation of the second Person of the Trinity, who, being equal to the Father, " like to it selfe," is certainly not the Neoplatonic Logos or greater angel. He is " with equall honour crownd," and " with him raignd " before all time in glory and

---

[118] There is no need to assume with Professors Fletcher and Saurat that Sapience derives from non-Christian Gnostic or Cabbalistic sources in which a sex-relationship is understood between God and Schekina. Cf. Fletcher, *op. cit.*, Denis Saurat, " La ' Sapience' de Spenser et la ' Schekina' de la Cabale," *Revue de Litterature Comparée*, VI (1926), 5 ff.

[119] Although this is in the *Timaeus*, 29-30, St. Thomas gives the traditional teaching of the identity of goodness and beauty, and cites the Pseudo-Dionysius as authority. " Beauty and goodness are identical in all things fundamentally; for they are based upon the same thing, namely the form, and consequently goodness is praised as beauty " (*Summa Theol.*, I, Q. 5, a. 4).

[120] " In divinis non est amor ex amore: quia ibi est unus tantum amor perfectus " (*ibid.*, Q. 27, a. 5).

[121] " God's love is the principle of all things," wrote St. Thomas, " for as St. Denis [the Pseudo-Dionysius] says, ' God's love did not allow him to be unproductive ' " (*Contra Gentiles, lib.* I, *cap.* XCI). Cf. also *Summa Theol.*, I, Q. 20, a. 2. See also above, p. 212.

power (35-37). The first and second Persons have equal prerogatives,

> Together with that third from them deriued,
> Most wise, most holy, most almightie Spright!   (38-39).

This is Spenser's account of the *spiration* of " that third " Person.[122]   The effects of God's " fruitfull love " (50-51) whereby the angels and man came into being is consonant with the traditional theology.[123]   This two-fold creation of angels and of men is due principally to that love in God whereby all things came into existence.   Since love is the first movement of the will, and the divine will is the cause of creation, it, therefore, remained for theologians to assert the efficient causality of divine love in the creation *ad extra* of the angelic spirits and the human race.[124]

A Platonic ideology is apparent in certain passages of the last *Hymne*.

> Rapt with the rage of mine own rauisht thought,
> Through contemplation of those goodly sights,
> And glorious *images* in heauen wrought.[125]

Again, Spenser would have the hearts of men " transplanted with celestiall desyre of those faire *formes*," [126] and even the dwelling of the blessed does not compare in beauty with the place

[122] For the theology of the Trinity, see the Athanasian Creed.   This teaching was basically incorporated into the Reform theology without change. St. Thomas discusses the erroneous views of the Platonists regarding the Trinity in *Summa Theol.*, I, *Q*. 32, *a*. 1.

[123] Miss Winstanley observes that Spenser took it from scholastic theology. (*op. cit.*, p. 64.)

[124] Cf. *Summa Theol.*, I, *Q*. 20, *a*. 1.   In view of Spenser's reproduction of the traditional theological teaching relative to the angels, Professor Renwick errs in denominating Spenser's treatment as " heresy."   (*Daphnaïda and Other Poems* (London, 1929), pp. 220, 222).   Mrs. Bennett noted that Spenser uses the word " beget " in reference to the forming of the angels (*op. cit.*, p. 134), but St. Thomas, for instance, uses the word " produce " in like case.   (*Summa Theol.*, I, *Q*. 61, *a*. 2).   But this is refining Spenser's theology unnecessarily.

[125] *Hymne of Heavenly Beautie*, 1-3.   (Italics mine.)

[126] *Ibid.*, 18-19.

... where those Idees on hie
Enraunged be, which Plato so admyred.[127]

Here Spenser attempts to localize the divine beauty of the spiritual heavens existing in Ideas and forms, or reflected in earthly images. He uses these terms with the meaning they had in Platonic and Christian thought. Ideas, according to St. Augustine, are the master forms which are contained in the divine intelligence.[128] St. Thomas explained that the Greek word 'Ιδέα is in Latin *forma*. " Hence," he says, " by Ideas are understood the forms of things, existing apart from the things themselves." [129] For St. Bonaventure, the very source of our knowledge is the divine Ideas; [130] and Bellarmine could say that God is the first Cause and Exemplar who made all things according to forms or Ideas which He has in himself.[131] Hence, the fair forms, Ideas, and images which Spenser contemplated in heaven are the ectypes of earthly beauty, the prototypes of divine beauty, and objects of mystical rapture. Such Platonism lies at the very heart of Christian theology.[132]

The view that the theology of the last pair of *Hymnes* is in accord with that of Calvin's *Institutes* is accepted by a number of Spenser scholars.[133] Professor Padelford has modified his former view in the light of Christian mysticism in the *Hymnes*. " Calvin's theology," he wrote, " was based upon the theology of St. Augustine and of the Christian mystics." [134] The influence of St. Augustine upon Calvin is unquestioned, but it is of a purely doctrinal nature. Calvin was not a mystic; and one

[127] *Ibid.*, 82-83. Note in the third *Hymne*, the illumination coincident with the contemplation of Christ will bring a sight of " Th' Idee of his pure glorie present still / Before thy face " (284-285).

[128] *De Diversis Quaestionibus*, XLVI, *De Ideis*, 83, *P. L.*, XL, 29.

[129] *Summa Theol.*, I, *Q.* 15, *a.* 1.

[130] *Itinerarium Mentis in Deum*, cap. II, 9-12.

[131] *De Ascensione Mentis in Deum, Gradus* 10, p. 240.

[132] See the definitive chapter in the *Contra Gentiles* (*lib.* I, *cap.* LIV), where St. Thomas refers to Plato and to the Platonic teaching of St. Augustine and the Pseudo-Dionysius.

[133] Chief among these are J. B. Fletcher, *op. cit.*, F. M. Padelford, *Journal of English and Germanic Philology*, XIII (1914), 418 ff. and *Modern Philology*, XII, 1 ff.

[134] " Spenser's *Fowre Hymnes:* A Resurvey," 232.

looks vainly in the *Institutes* for the soaring spirit of contemplation which Spenser's *Hymnes* have in common with St. Augustine.[135] Where the *Hymnes* of Spenser accord with the theology of the *Institutes,* they likewise conform to the theology of the Anglican Church and to that of the medieval mystics. Indeed, Calvin's teaching is not in agreement with Spenser's lines on the Eucharist.

> And last the food of life, which now we haue,
> Euen himselfe in his deare sacrament,
> To feede our hungry soules vnto vs lent. (194-196).

Calvin taught that this sacrament is a *seal* of faith in Christ's presence in the soul, conformable to the life-giving efficacy of bread and wine, and is merely a symbol of our real participation of Christ through faith.[136] " I repeat it again," wrote Calvin, " since the sacred supper is nothing but a visible attestation of the promise, that Christ is ' the bread of life which cometh from heaven,' it requires the use of visible and material bread to represent that which is spiritual." [137]

Spenser affirms in the last *Hymne* that Sapience will disclose her lovely face to those only who are worthy, " those whom shee Vouchsafeth to her presence to receave." [138]   This is hardly the doctrine of election. Spenser may easily have had in mind the teaching of St. Paul, St. Augustine, or others who felt that heaven and the supreme vision is a gift of grace, as well as a reward to the few who are faithful to the discipline of the higher spiritual life. Thus Rolle wrote of the Elect of God, and of the chosen ones in terms which are much stronger than Spenser's.[139] It is not necessary to assume that in the third and fourth *Hymnes* Spenser reflects Calvin's two-fold distinction of the revelation of God in his works and in his treatment

[135] Note, for example, Calvin's " Meditation of the Future Life " wherein conditions of the present life are emphasized to complete exclusion of contemplation of the blessed in heaven or of God which characterizes mystical treatment of this subject. (*Institutes of the Christian Religion,* trans. by John Allen [Philadelphia, 1909], I, pp. 639-645.)

[136] *Institutes,* Bk. IV, cap. XVII, 4, p. 528.

[137] *Ibid.,* cap. xvii, 14, p. 538.

[138] *Hymne of Heavenly Beautie,* 253-254; 239-241.

[139] *Incendium Amoris,* cap. 26: " De diversis electorum donis."

of mankind, or in other words, " between God's works of the first and the second class." [140] The human manner of arriving at knowledge of God apart from divine revelation, which Calvin explains, is a problem fundamental in Theodicy irrespective of particular creed. His treatment is in the traditional manner, based upon the Platonic and Pauline arguments which the mystics developed in the Theocentric type of contemplation. The approach is strictly theological and mystical, and where it is definitely " Calvinistic," Spenser does not bear him out. Thus, Calvin asserts the possibility of knowing God through his handiwork, but because of human weakness, this knowledge must actually be sought not in the structure of the world, but in the Scriptures. " We need another and better assistance," wrote Calvin, " properly to direct us to the Creator of the world. Therefore he hath not unnecessarily added the light of his word." [141] The theology of the *Fowre Hymnes* of Spenser, in fine, is an essential point they have in common with Christian mystical literature; they are singularly free from direct ecclesiastical bias. Religious and doctrinal they are, but in the free spirit of the mystics.

Résumé

The *Fowre Hymnes* present a remarkable symmetry. The first two celebrate pure, idealized human love and beauty; the last pair treat of heavenly Love and Beauty as essentially resident in the Source of their earthly counterparts. Christian mysticism, not Neoplatonism or Calvinism, is the underlying philosophy of the last two *Hymnes*. They embody respectively the Christocentric and the Theocentric types of contemplation, and one can see in them, particularly in the last two *Hymnes*, the three ways or stages of the mystical life. The theme of the third *Hymne* is Love, as it is the prime factor in the generation of the Son, and is exemplified by that Son in earning man's love. Briefly, the theme of the last hymn is Beauty. Beauty which radiates from the trinal source—" Unity amid Variety "—and as one of God's attributes is identical with that Sapience which brings the divine diapason to an end.

[140] Cf. H. S. V. Jones, *A Spenser Handbook* (New York, 1930), p. 368.
[141] *Ibid.*, Bk. I, cap. vi, 1.

CONCLUSION

ELIZABETHAN MYSTICISM

The study of Elizabethan mysticism presents a new and rarely-noted picture of the period. If to the writings of Christian mysticism we add the outpourings of devotional hymnody and the prose works of every description from manuals of devotion to the *Plaine Man's Way to Heaven*, one is forced to disagree with an all too prevalent concept of the Elizabethan age. Any description of its literature which does not take into account the sober and deliberate searchings of soul for peace in prayer and for the consolations of contemplation is one-sided and only partly true.

Professor Chambers notes an aspect of the Elizabethan period not generally recognized when he recalls the old, traditional notion of Elizabethanism as sensuous, comprehensive, extravagant, disorderly, thirsty for beauty, abounding in the zest for life. Then he adds significantly " there is much truth here, but it is not the whole truth." [1] He goes on to speak of the other side of the picture: of the classical, ordered writings of such men as Daniel, of the sober, sensible philosophy of Spenser and Raleigh, and the patient, scientific patriotism of the geographers and historians. The general tenor of this age does doubtless manifest youth and fervent, inspired action, compared to the more mature and more complex sophistication of the age which followed. But it is a youth which has much of the seriousness befitting older years; a gravity occasioned by spiritual uncertainty and fraternal strife over religious questions, by bewildering cross-currents of economic prosperity and distress, and by Elizabeth's own policy of dilatoriness, of shiftiness and of compromise. Professor Osgood gives a penetrating glance at this neglected side of Elizabeth's time. " Elizabethan society," he says, " was crude and unstable. The medieval aristocracy was gone; parvenus arose by sudden

[1] E. K. Chambers, " The Disenchantment of the Elizabethans," in *Sir Thomas Wyatt and Some Collected Studies* (London, 1933), p. 183.

232

wealth, politics, and bold strokes of adventure; speculation and vulgar extravagance prevailed; sudden ruin was common." And thus one can see the reason for " the literary fashion of ' complaints,' the popularity of ' Fortune,' and ' Mutability ' as themes of Elizabethan song and story." [2]

There was much genuine reflection and thought-laden verse and prose in this period which balances the fresh exuberance of lightsome sonnet and zest-inspiring ode. There are the serious lines of Sidney with that heavy vein of melancholy which goes back on one side to the *Mirror for Magistrates* and on the other side joins with the *Contemptus Mundi* writings of the English mystics. In this vein is a vast amount of Elizabethan literature—much of it among the best of this prolific age, which includes the homely and at times cynical moralizing of Shakespeare and the calm reflections of the ' sage and serious ' Spenser. We may therefore make much of the vague Platonism and the love-inspired Petrarchism of the period; and we may exalt the humanism and the puritanism and the Calvinism, but the age is all more medieval than the Elizabethans themselves realized or even cared to admit. And the high plane of spiritual fervor which is indicated by the writings of devotion and of Christian mysticism places the Elizabethan on a par with or even above the age of Tennyson and Browning which Professor Corson accounts highest in the rise and fall of religious literature in England.

There is then a close relation between the " serious " literature of this age and the literature of the mystics of the same period. Christian mysticism gave fullest expression and a natural outlet for the pent-up feelings of disillusion and of spiritual unrest, and it furnished a ready-made and consoling philosophy of peace and rapturous communion with God. Elizabethan mysticism with its foundations in medieval spirituality and in ancient philosophy was for the few who accepted it (and in no age are they many) the answer to the aspirations of those who were satisfied with nothing short of the " vision splendid."

[2] Charles G. Osgood, *The Voice of England* (New York and London, 1935), p. 146.
[3] Hiram Corson, " The Spiritual Ebb and Flow in English Poetry " in *An Introduction to the Study of Robert Browning's Poetry* (Boston, 1896), p. 31.

APPENDIX

MYSTICAL WORKS IN ENGLISH

Printed at London, 1500-1600.[1]

ALCOCK, JOHN:

The Mons Perfectionis, or The Hill of Perfection, printed by Wynkyn de Worde, 1497, 1501.[2]

SAINT AUGUSTINE:[3]

De essentia divinitatis, a supposititious work. *Certein places gathered out of S. Austin's boke intituled, De essentia diuinitatis*, printed by H. Bodius, 1548.

Twelve Sermons. Translated by Thomas Paynol, n. d. (before 1550).

Certaine select prayers gathered out of S. Augustine's meditations. Printed 1574, 1575, 1585, 1586. This is part of the *Manuale*, a supposititious work.

The glasse of vaine-glory. Trans. by W. P[rid], 1585, 1587, 1600.

Godly Meditations made in the forme of prayers, n. d. Printed by J. Daye.

Manuale seu Libellus de Contemplatione Christi, printed as *S. Augustine's Manuel* by J. Daye, 1577.[4]

S. Augustine's Manuel. Trans. by Thomas Rogers, 1581, 1591, 1600.

An introduction to the loue of God. Accompted among the workes of S. Augustine. Trans. by Edmund Freke, Bishop of Rochester. Printed by T. Purfort, 1574 (B. M.).

An introduction to the loue of God. Trans. by R. Fletcher, 1574, 1581.

A pretious booke of heauenlie meditations. Trans. by Thos. Rogers, 1581, 1600.

A right Christian treatise entituled S. Augustine's praiers. Trans. by Thos. Rogers, 1581, 1591, 1600.

BARNES, BARNABE:

A Divine Centurie of Spirituall Sonnetts, 1595.

---

[1] This list of mystical writings is not exhaustive; and a few titles extend beyond the year 1600.

[2] F. A. Gasquet, " The Bibliography of some Devotional Books printed by the earliest English Printers." *Transactions of the Bibliog. Society* (London, 1904), VII, 181.

[3] *Short Title Catalogue of Books Printed in England, Scotland and Ireland, and of English Books Printed Abroad*, 1475-1640, ed. by Pollard and Redgrave (London, 1926).

[4] *Supplement to the Short Title Catalogue* (1933).

SAINT BERNARD: [5]

A compendious & moch fruytefull treatyse of wele liuing. Trans. by Thos. Paynell, 1545 (?).

An epistle of Sainte Bernarde, called the golden epistle. Printed by T. Godfray, 1530 (?), 1535 (?). (The British Museum copy adds: "After the sayd epistle, followeth four revelations of Saint Bergit. Hereafter followeth the LXV chapter of the fyrst boke of Schola Perfectionis.") Other editions printed by de Worde, 1530, 1531; by R. Wyer, 1531.

Medytacions of saynt Bernarde. Tr. by a student of Cambridge. (A supposititious work). Printed by de Worde, 1496, 1499, 1525.

BRETON, NICHOLAS:

A Solempne and repentant Prayer, for a former life misspent, 1577, in *A Floorish upon Fancie.*

The Pilgrimage of Paradise, 1592.

The Countesse of Penbrookes Loue, 1592.

A Solemne Passion of the Sovles Loue, 1595, 1598, 1623.

Mary Magdalene's Loue, 1595.

Auspicante Iehova: Marie's Exercise, 1597.

The Soules Heavenly Exercise, set down in diverse godly meditations, 1601.

The Rauisht Soule, 1601.

The Blessed Weeper, 1601.

The Longing of a Blessed Heart which loathing the World doth long to be with Christ, 1601.

The Soule's Harmony, 1602.

Divine Considerations, 1608.

SAINT CATHERINE OF SIENNA:

The Lyfe of saint Katherin of Senis, by Raymond de Vineis. Printed by de Worde, 1493; another edition printed by John Hart, 1551, 1569 (?).

The Orcharde of Syon, . . . the reuelacyons of Seynt Kathryne of Senis. Trans. by D. James, printed by de Worde, 1519.

CLOUD OF UNKNOWING, THE:

Reprinted in 1582, probably abroad.[6]

COLET, JOHN: [7]

A ryght frutefull monycion, 1534, 1563.

The contemplation of sinners. Printed by de Worde, 1499; another edition, *A Dyall of dayly contemplacion*, 1578.

---

[5] *Short Title Catalogue.*

[6] *The Cloud of Unknowing*, ed. by Justin McCann (London, 1924), p. 291.

[7] *Short Title Catalogue.*

Godly contemplations for the unlearned, Louvain (?), 1568 (?)
Paraphrase of the Pseudo-Dionysius.[8]

COLVILLE, GEORGE:

Boethius' Consolations of Philosophy. Trans. and paraphrased by
George Colville, printed by John Cawood, 1556, 1561.

DAVIES OF HEREFORD, JOHN:

Mirum in Modum, 1602.
The Holy Roode, 1609.
The Muses Sacrifice, 1612.

DIEGO DE ESTELLA:

The contempte of the worlde and the vanitie thereof. Trans. by
G. C. Douay, 1584.
*Methode unto Mortification, called heretofore the contempt of the
world and the vanity thereof.* Trans. by Thos. Rogers, 1588.

DIONYSIUS THE CARTHUSIAN:[9]

The Mirroure of golde for the synfull soule. Trans. by Margaret,
Countess of Richmond, from *Speculum aureum.* Printed by de
Worde, 1522, 1526; another edition by Pynson, no date.

LUIS DE GRANADA:[10]

Of Prayer and Meditation. Trans. by Richard Hopkins, 1582, 1583,
1592, 1601; Edinburgh, 1600.
The Sinners Guyde. Trans. by Francis Meres, 1598.
Granados Devotions. Trans. by Francis Meres, 1598.
A Memorial of a Christian Life. Trans. by Richard Hopkins, 1586,
1599.
*A Spirituel Doctrine containing a Rule of Live Wel, with diuers
praiers and meditations.* Trans. by Richard Gibbons, 1599.[11]
Granadas Spirituall and heauenlie exercises. J. Roberts for J.
Browne, 1598. Another edition, 1600.
A Most fragrant Flower; or devoute exposition of the Lords Prayer.
Trans. by J. G., 1598.
The Flowers of Lodowicke of Granado, Trans. by Thomas Lodge,
1601.
The Paradise of Prayers gathered out of the works of L. of Granada,
Trans. by T[homas] L[odge], 1601.[12]

---

[8] See above, Part II, p. 76.   [9] *Short Title Catalogue.*
[10] William J. Harris, *The First Printed Translations into English of the
Great Foreign Classics* (London, 1909), p. 92.
[11] *Short Title Catalogue.*
[12] The *Short Title Catalogue* lists twenty-four editions and reprints of
Granada's writings in English. See also, M. Hagedorn, *Reformation und die
Spanische Andachtsliteratur,* Leipzig, 1934.

HILTON, WALTER:

Scala Perfectionis—The Scale of Perfection. Printed by de Worde, 1494, 1519, 1525, 1563; by Julian Notary, 1507; by Pynson, 1517.[13]
Letter to a devoute man in temporal estate. Printed by Pynson, 1506. Later reprinted with *The Scale of Perfection.*[14]
The Song of Angels. Printed by Pepwell, 1521.[15]

HUME, ALEXANDER:

A Treatise on the Felicitie of the Life to Come, 1594. *Hymnes or Sacred Songs,* 1599.

HOWARD, PHILIP, EARLE OF ARUNDEL:

The Four-Fould Meditation of the foure last things, 1606.
An Epistle of Jesus Christ to the Faithful Soul, trans. from Lanspergius, 1595 (?), 1596, 1610.
A Hymne of the Life and Passion of our Saviour Christ, trans. from Lanspergius, 1595.
A Hymne wherein the praises of all Creatures are offered up unto the Creatour, trans. from Lanspergius, 1595.

IMITATION OF CHRIST, THE:

A Devout and Gostely Treatise in The Imytacyon and Folowinge of Cryste (1415-1424) *compiled in Latin by J. Jerson [sic].* Trans. by Wyllam Atkinson. Printed by Pynson, 1502, 1503, 1517; by de Worde, 1502, 150? [15a]

KEMPE, MARGERY:

A shorte treatyse of contemplacyon, 1501, printed by Pepwell, 1521.
The Booke of Margery Kempe, edited by W. Buller-Bowdon (London, 1936). This is a newly discovered text of the complete book of Margery Kempe. Modernized version. Original text being prepared for *E. E. T. S.*

LODGE, THOMAS:

The Diuel coniured, 1596.
Prosopopeia, 1596.
Flowers of Lodowicke of Granado, 1601.
The Paradise of Prayers, 1601.

---

[13] *Short Title Catalogue;* Gasquet, p. 182.
[14] Edmund Gardner, *The Cell of Self-Knowledge* (London, 1921), p. xxii.
[15] J. E. Wells, *Manual of the Writings in Middle English* (New Haven, 1916), p. 769.
[15a] *Short Title Catalogue.* The *Short Title Catalogue* contains 47 entries of the *Imitation of Christ* ascribed variously to Gerson, à Kempis, or St. Bernard, with the greatest number appearing in the late decades of the century.

LOK, HENRY:

Sundrie Christian Passions, Contained in Two hundred Sonnets, 1596, 1597.

Ecclesiastes: abridged and dilated in English poesie; whereunto are annexed sundrie sonnets of christen passions. 2 parts, 1597, entered in Stat. Register, 1596.

MARGUERITE OF NAVARRE—QUEEN ELIZABETH:

A Godly medytacion of the Christen Soule, concerning a Loue towards God and Hys Chryste. Trans. by the Lady (later Queen) Elizabeth, 1548; another edition by H. Denham, 1568 (?), entered in Stat. Register, 1567-1568; another edition, n. d.[16]

MARKHAM, GERVASE:

The Teares of the Beloved, 1600.
Marie Magdalene's Teares, 1601.

MARY MAGDALEN:

The Lamentacyion of Mary Magdalein. Trans. from Origen, *Hom.* IX (a supposititious work) in *Opera*, III, edition of 1512, by John Lydgate. Printed in Chaucer's *Works*, 1561.
A Homilie of Mary Magdalene, Declaring her Fervent Loue and Zele towards Christ. Trans. 1575.[17]

MIRROUR OF A MANS LYFE, THE:

The Mirrour of a Mans lyfe, trans. of *De Contemptu Mundi*, of Pope Innocent III, by H[enry] K[erton], 1576, 1580, 1586. Dedicated to Anne Herbert, Countess of Pembroke.[18]

MIRROUR OF THE BLESSED LYFE:

Mirrour of the Blessed Lyfe of Jesus Christ, paraphrase of the Pseudo-Bonaventure, *Meditationes Vitae Christi*, printed by de Worde, 1517, 1523.

MORE, SAINT THOMAS:

The Four Last Things. Printed 1557.
A Dialogue of Comfort against Tribulation. Printed in *Complete Works* by Rastell, 1557. Earlier edition in *Works* by R. Tottel, 1553.

PARSONS, ROBERT:

The Christian Directory, or Booke of Resolution, 1582 (Rouen), 1587,

---

[16] *Short Title Catalogue.*
[17] Gasquet, p. 182.
[18] Mary Augusta Scott, *Elizabethan Translations from Italian* (New York. 1916), p. 260.

1598; Edmund Bunny's edition, 1584, with numerous reprintings from 1584-1600.[19]

Seconde Parte of the booke of Christian exercises, R. P., 1591.[20]

PILGRIMAGE OF THE SOUL, THE:

The Pilgrimage of the Soul. Trans. from Guillaume de Guilleville, printed by Caxton, 1483; reprinted by Pynson as *Peregrinatio Humani Generis.*

RICHARD ROLLE OF HAMPOLE:

Contemplacyons of the dread and loue of God. (A supposititious work.) Printed by de Worde, 1506, 1510.[21]

The Remedy agenst the troubles of temptacyons. Printed by de Worde, 1508, 1519. Includes part of *The Form of Perfect Living.*[22]

De Emendatione Vitae, printed by Hopyl at Paris for William Bretton, with *Speculum Spiritualium*, 1510.

RICHARD OF ST. VICTOR:

Benjamin Minor. Printed by Pepwell, 1521.

SOUTHWELL, ROBERT:

Mary Magdalene's Funerall Teares, 1591, 1594, 1602.
The Triumphs over Death, 1595, 1596.
St. Peter's Complaint, 1595 (twice), 1596, 1597, 1599, 1602.
Maeoniae, 1595 (twice), 1596, 1598.
Myrtae, 1595.

SPENSER, EDMUND:

" The House of Holiness " in Canto X, Book I, *Faerie Queene*, 1590, 1596.
The Fowre Hymnes, 1596.

SUSO, HENRY:

The seven points of true love and everlasting wisdom, or the Orologium Sapientiae. Printed by Caxton, 1490; another edition, *Hore beate* [sic] *Mariae*, 1503.[23]

WALPOLE, HENRY:

A Prisoner's Song in *The Song of Mary the Mother of Christ*, 1601.[24]

---

[19] *Short Title Catalogue.*

[20] *Supplement to Short Title Catalogue.*

[21] Gasquet, p. 182; Hope Emily Allen, *Writings ascribed to Richard Rolle*, etc. (London, 1927), p. 9.

[22] Gasquet, p. 182; C. Horstmann, *Richard Rolle of Hampole* (London, 1896), I, 106.

[23] Gasquet, p. 182; Allen, p. 10.   [24] *Short Title Catalogue.*

INDEX

17